MARITIME ISSUES REVIEW

Volume I

WRITTEN BY
JIN YONGMING

TRANSLATED BY
CHEN LING

图书在版编目（CIP）数据

海洋问题时评. 第一辑 = Maritime Issues Review（Volume 1）: 英文 / 金永明著; 陈玲译. —北京: 中央编译出版社, 2017.12

ISBN 978-7-5117-2510-3

Ⅰ. ①海… Ⅱ. ①金… ②陈… Ⅲ. ①海洋法—文集—英文 Ⅳ. ①D993.5-53

中国版本图书馆 CIP 数据核字（2017）第 310520 号

海洋问题时评. 第一辑

出 版 人: 葛海彦
出版统筹: 贾宇琰
责任编辑: 薛迎春
责任印制: 刘 慧
出版发行: 中央编译出版社
地 址: 北京西城区车公庄大街乙 5 号鸿儒大厦 B 座（100044）
电 话: （010）52612345（总编室） （010）52612335（编辑室）
（010）52612316（发行部） （010）52612317（网络销售）
（010）52612346（馆配部） （010）55626985（读者服务部）
传 真: （010）66515838
经 销: 全国新华书店
印 刷: 北京印刷一厂
开 本: 787 毫米 ×1092 毫米 1/16
字 数: 296 千字
印 张: 26.5
版 次: 2017 年 12 月第 1 版
印 次: 2017 年 12 月第 1 次印刷
定 价: 128.00 元

网 址: www.cctphome.com 邮 箱: cctp@cctphome. com
新浪微博: @ 中央编译出版社 微 信: 中央编译出版社（ID: cctphome）
淘宝店铺: 中央编译出版社直销店（http: //shop108367160.taobao.com） （010）55626985

本社常年法律顾问: 北京市吴栾赵阎律师事务所律师 闫军 梁勤
凡有印装质量问题，本社负责调换。电话: （010）55626985

CONTENTS

Preface / i
Foreword / vii

Theory of the Law of the Sea and China

On History and Development Trend of the Law of the Sea / 3
Institutional Defects of the Law of the Sea to Be Corrected Gradually / 12
Limitations of Laws of the Sea / 17
How to Draw the Baseline of the Territorial Sea / 22
How to Conduct Delimitation When the Exclusive Economic Zone and the Continental Shelf Overlap / 28
The Relation between Marine Scientific Research and Military Survey Activities / 34
How to Deal with Military Exercises in Exclusive Economic Zone / 40
Cracking down on Somalia Piracy from the Perspective of International Law / 46
Escort by China Navy in Urgent Need of Legal System

Development / 52
Arbitration System not Applicable to Ocean Disputes with China / 56
Whether Okinotorishima Is An Island or A Rock / 60
Broadening the Horizon and Developing China's Ocean Undertakings / 66
Basic Characteristics of the United Nations Convention on the Law of the Sea / 73

East China Sea Reviews

Path Chosen by China to Promote Development in East China Sea / 81
Japan Must Honor Law of Sea / 86
Keeping Calm at Sea Essential / 91
China Shall Make Japan Admit a Dispute on Ownership over Diaoyu Islands / 96
China to Make Detailed Preparation for Negotiation on the Sea with Japan / 102
China Shall Strengthen Comprehensive Management of Diaoyu Island and Its Affiliated Islands / 106
Dispute Denial Will Not Work / 113
Formation and Development of Japanese Ocean Strategy / 117
Japan-US Alliance on Sea Power Suggesting Joint Efforts to Develop New Sea Power / 123
Origins and Trends of Disputes over Diaoyu Islands / 130
Japan Should End the Farce / 140

China Should Be Well Prepared that The Issue of Diaoyu Islands Will Last for a Long Time / 144
China and Japan Shall Accelerate Their Paces in Negotiation on Maritime issues / 153
Necessities for China and Japan to Reiterate the Principles of China-Japan Treaty of Peace and Friendship / 160
Defuse Dangerous Tensions between China and Japan / 167
Several Thoughts and Suggestions on Improving Sino-Japan Relations / 172
China Should Improve Law Enforcement System for Sea and Air Security of East China Sea / 179
Work to Make a Sea Change / 184
On Connotation of Japanese So-called "Inherent Territory" / 188
China Should Re-define Sino-Japan Relations / 194

South China Sea Review

China Should Deal with South China Sea Issues Tier by Tier /203
For Order in South China Sea / 208
Peaceful Resolution of South China Sea Issues in Accordance with International Law / 212
How to Resolve the South China Sea Issue / 219
May Better Sense Prevail in Sea Disputes / 224
Is It Groundless for China's Proposition Based on U-shaped Line of South China Sea? / 229

Practical Steps to Resolve South China Sea Issues / 239
Reflection on "Setting Aside Disputes and Joint Exploitation" / 246
Legal Obstacles in Settling Territorial Disputes over Nansha Islands and Reefs / 254
China Must Safeguard Island / 273
Analysis of Huangyan Island Incident from the Perspective of International Law / 277
No Negative Example Set by the Huangyan Island Incident / 284
Manila all at Sea Over Islands / 292
It's Unreasonable for Philippine to Apply for Arbitration on South China Sea Dispute / 296
Views on Philippine's Gunshot at Taiwanese Fishing Boat from the Perspective of International Law / 302
How to Build a Sea of Peace and Amity / 307
Manila Barking up the Wrong Tree / 311
Hanoi Must Stop Muddying the Waters / 316
Drilling is Legal and Legitimate / 320
Resolve South China Sea Issue First / 324

China and Ocean Issues

Review on Scientific Expedition in the Antarctica after the Return of Xuelong / 331
The Century of the Sea Needs Harmonious Sea / 336
Essence and Legal Construction of China's Development of Ocean

Economy / 340

The Inevitable Path for China to Resolve Maritime Issues Tier by Tier / 348

China Should Enact and Implement Basic Law of the Sea as soon as Possible / 353

Enacting the Basic Law: An Active Choice for Dealing with Maritime Issues / 359

Connotation of China's Construction of Ocean Power / 366

Maritime State to Maritime Power / 373

China Should Avoid "Linkage among Three Seas" / 377

Top-down Design of China's Maritime Power Strategy / 383

Index for Extended Reading / 397

Afterword / 402

Profile of the Author / 405

Profile of the Translator / 406

Profile of Ad Mare / 407

Preface

Mr. Jin Yongming has long been dedicated to the study of international law of the sea and achieved a lot. This time, he compiles his research results on many major maritime issues faced by China, especially East China Sea issues and South China Sea issues, combining situation of ocean issues, and publishes them for the readers in the form of *Maritime Issues Review*. Congratulations!

The sea is the real resources of human life.

The United Nations Charter and its basic principles of international law are the core of existing international legal order and the cornerstone of orderly development of international relations. The United Nations Convention on the Law of the Sea (hereinafter referred to as Convention) and its ocean legal system are the kernel and footstone of legal system of the sea, becoming the international compulsory legal norms. The Third UN Conference on the Law of the Sea puts forward the principle of Common Heritage of Mankind, but it is not applied for determining the ownership and sovereignty of territories. In the Preamble of the Convention, it is clearly stated that with due regard for the sovereignty of all States, a legal order for the seas and oceans which will facilitate international communication, and will promote the peaceful uses of the seas and oceans, the equitable and efficient utilization of their resources, the conservation of their living resources, and the study, protection and preservation of the marine environment, bearing in mind that the achievement of these goals will contribute to the realization of a just and equitable international economic order which takes into account the interests and needs of mankind as a whole. Meanwhile, the Convention also clearly puts forward that any unsettled dispute concerning sovereignty or other rights over continental or insular land territory shall be excluded from any compulsory procedures. In a new century, peaceful settlement of disputes is still a basic principle and negotiation is the preferential choice and best way of settling disputes. The Security Council of United Nations, when it considers necessary, shall urge parties involved to settle their dispute by this means. It should be pointed out that the legal basis of international in history is Roman law which governed equal parties. International judicial institution has only consensual jurisdiction and its judgment lacks enforcement. Just like International Court of Justice, International Tribunal for the Law of the Sea renders definite judgment which shall be followed by parties involved in the dispute. However, such judgment shall be not binding on parties for issues other than such specific dispute. The international law is not a case law so any case is not binding on any third party, is not a law or can not change current laws and rules of international law before it evolves to be a customary law.

The development of international society, especially the development of scientific technology prompts the law of the sea to evolve continually. Communist Manifesto points out that the discovery of America and navigation bypassing the Africa created a new world for emerging bourgeoisie. (*Collected Works of Marx and Engels*, Volume 2, Beijing, People's Publishing House, 2009 Edition, p.32). Thus, the scopes of ocean exchange between countries and the utilization of the sea are expanding; therefore the scope of the law of the sea is inevitably expanding. All world powers are ocean powers, which is a final conclusion by history. Spain used to seize countless treasures by taking advantage of its unbeatable fleet; Britain opened doors of all countries in the world through its powerful warships and cannons; nowadays the fleet with Star-Spangled Banner will go to any place related to American interest all over the world at any time. Beyond all doubt, each ambitious nation shall not and will not remain indifferent when seeing this historic track. China is an ocean power and clearly states in Government Working Paper of 2014 that China shall insist on coordination of the land and the sea to implement the ocean strategy all over the country, develop ocean economy, preserve ocean environment, firmly protect China's ocean rights and vigorously build an ocean power.

Diaoyu Islands in East China Sea is an inherent territory of China; Dongsha Islands, Xisha Islands, Zhongsha Islands and Nansha Islands are an integral part of Chinese sacred territory since ancient times. China holds definite historical and legal foundations for this. These islands were once occupied by Japanese invaders but invasion can not lead to sovereignty nor become the basis of law-violator's legal rights. American president Roosevelt said that these principles are very simple. They include returning stolen properties to the original owner when he signed the Cairo Declaration in 1943. Article 8 of the Potsdam Proclamation clearly points out that the terms of the Cairo Declaration shall be carried out. Moreover, the Cairo Declaration clearly stipulates that all the territories Japan has stolen from the Chinese, such as Manchuria, Formosa, and the Pescadores, shall be restored to the Republic of China. China firmly opposes and suppresses that Japan invades China's sovereignty over Diaoyu Islands in any form. China's sovereignty over islands in South China Sea and sovereign rights and jurisdiction over South China are formed in the long course of historical development. Chinese government restored islands in South China Sea from Japanese invader according to the Cairo Declaration and the Potsdam Proclamation and drew the dotted lines. Other littoral countries around the South China Sea did not put forward any doubt for this before the 70s of 20th century. The Convention which has become effective since 1994 recognizes historic rights in the sea. The United States and Japan, respectively as one of victorious nations and one of the defeated nations in the World War II should know this history well.

However, there are a great deal of volatilities in East China Sea and South China Sea and the situation is serious and complex. Encouraged by the US's strategy of Asian rebalancing, Japan and some countries are eager to try and attempt to create chaos and suppress China. China has clear and persistent stance that it will unswervingly protect the integrity of national sovereignty and territory and unshakably defend fruits of victory of the world anti-fascist war. China will make no compromise on two matters of principle: history and territory. We hope that the US and Japanese leaders could understand these basic principles and respect human conscience and the base line of international justice. Ocean problems in recent years were triggered due to provocation of some nations. China will not give up the long-standing stance of peaceful settlement of disputes, but facing such provocation, China must make powerful response to not only protect its own sovereign rights but also maintain the peaceful and stable order in the whole region.

International law plays an increasingly important role in promotion of world peace and development. Every country values the international law more and more to protect its own rights and interests. This is a trend of international society which is worthy of attention. We shall follow and maintain rules of international law and also, together with people all over the world, continue to make efforts to improve and develop international law, push the international law to head for facilitating establishment of a new peaceful, stable, fair and reasonable international political and economic order. How to reasonably handle and deal with maritime issues is a major issue faced by Chinese government and people and also a significant research task for scholars. It is undoubtedly an important path selected to research maritime issues from the perspective of the law of the sea. Many international law and ocean law scholars and practitioners home and abroad have made comprehensive and thorough research into maritime issues and disputes and have achieved fruitful results. A number of insightful papers and books have been published. It is gratifying.

Maritime Issues Review, published by Mr. Jin Yongming, is a fruit of such effort. Mr. Jin Yongming must be a man with the above-mentioned endeavor. He, from the perspective of the law of the sea, combines the situation of maritime issues to conduct a profound study in simple terms on many major maritime issues faced by China, especially East China Sea issues and South China Sea issues, in the hope of making some academic contribution to China's construction of an ocean power including cognizing and understanding maritime issues as well as developing China's ocean undertakings, and also playing a certain role as a scholar by providing materials and references for further publicity and explanation of the essence of maritime issues. It is worthy of praise and recognition.

I am looking forward to more excellent academic achievements. The aforesaid serves as a preface.

Zhou Zhonghai
Professor, PhD Supervisor the School of
International Law of China University of Political Science and Law
July 2014
Jinqiu Garden, Zhichun Road, Beijing

Foreword

China is and will be facing threats and challenges from maritime issues for long at present and for some time to come. In other words, China has entered a period of outbreak of maritime issues, a key period of dealing with maritime issues and an important period of researching maritime issues. How to reasonably handle and deal with maritime issues is a major issue faced by Chinese government and people and also a significant research task for scholars. To research maritime issues from the perspective of the law of the sea is undoubtedly an important path selection. Therefore, *Maritime Issues Review* (Volume I), from the perspective of international law, combines the situation of maritime issues to explain a profound study in simple language on many major maritime issues faced by China, especially East China Sea issues and South China Sea issues, with the aim to make a small academic contribution to China's construction of an ocean power including getting knowledge of and understanding maritime issues as well as developing China's ocean undertakings and also play a small role as a scholar by providing materials and references for further publicity and interpretation of the essence of maritime issues.

Theory of the Law of the Sea and China

On History and Development Trend of the Law of the Sea

China is and will be facing a lot of maritime issues at present and in the future. It is one of effective ways to resolve various maritime issues according to principles and systems of the law of the sea. Therefore it is necessary to expound the development history of the law of the sea and connotation of relevant systems for the purpose of further recognizing and understanding the essence of the law of the sea to reasonably resolve maritime issues.

I. Sources and Historical Development of the Law of the Sea

It is well known that the life on the earth is originated from the sea and more than 90% of the present living things live in the sea which occupies 70% of the surface area of the earth. The sea connects the world through personnel exchange and trade, so it becomes national and regional boundaries and will still play an important role in human history. The customary law related to the sea has long history and can be dated back to ancient Greek times. In Roman times, according to Jus gentium, the sea was open to all men. Private occupation and segmentation were prohibited. This is so-called Freedom of the sea. After entering the Middle Ages, European countries began to claim dominium on coastal waters, thus anti-freedom of the sea powers emerged. At the Age of Exploration in 1500, the sea empires, Spain and Portugal, divided the world into the land and the sea and imposed control on them. The Dutch jurist of international law Grotius, who is regarded as the Father of international law and produced *Mare Liberum* in 1609, strongly opposes ownership or control over the sea which shall be all men's property and advocates the principle of freedom of the sea. He only admits national jurisdiction in exceptional situations such as coastal states' ownership over bays and straits according to customary laws and coastal state's certain jurisdiction over offshore littoral. For this, in order to justify the Britain's control over the sea, Seldon from the Britain (1584—1654) put forward the view of Ownership over the Sea and published *Mare Clausum* in 1618.

In international society after the Age of Exploration, the sea was generally divided into two parts: Narrow Territorial Sea covered by state power and Wide High Seas belonging to no one but for free use (the Principle of Freedom of High Seas). Because the territorial sea is directly related to the safety and fishing resources of coastal countries and enjoys fairly important status, it was generally 3 nautical miles in 18th century and began to increase to 4 nautical miles at the second half of the 19th

Century and then developed to be 12 nautical miles. At that time, treaties stating rights and duties of belligerent countries and neutral countries on the sea and the original customary international laws became the sources of the law of the sea.

After 1900s, with enlargement of the trade and development of ocean fishing industry, the utilization and demand of the sea is increasingly enlarging. Especially in terms of fishery rights, right to navigation in straits and the status of a warship, countries have different stances and propositions, a single relevant legal system can not deal with these issues. Therefore, in 1930, in order to codify customary laws related to the sea, a conference on compiling international laws was held in the host of the League of Nations in the Hague. On such conference participated by over 50 states, no relevant treaty was signed due to opposite opinions on the breadth of the territorial sea. But this conference started the process of enacting the law of the sea by international community.

Later, an important turning point for paying attention to the law of the sea was that the American president Truman published the Continental Proclamation (Truman Proclamation on Policy of the United States with Respect to the Natural Resources of the Subsoil and Sea Bed of the Continental Shelf) in September, 1945 after the World War II. This Proclamation points out that the Government of the United States regards the natural resources of the subsoil and sea bed of the continental shelf beneath the high seas but contiguous to the coasts of the United

States as appertaining to the United States, subject to its jurisdiction and control. After the release of such proclamation, most countries did the same successively to claim the coastal state's jurisdiction over contiguous sea waters, therefore the United Nations held the First UN Conference on the Law of the Sea (1958). After discussion and deliberation, Four Geneva Conventions on the Law of the Sea including Convention on the Territorial Sea and the Contiguous Zone and Convention on the High Seas were signed. However, this conference did not stipulated the scope or breadth of the high seas, so the United Nations held the Second UN Conference on the Law of the Sea in 1960 but also failed to reach an agreement on the breadth of the high seas due to serious opposition of opinions by states and a pressure of time. After the 1960s, the emerging countries in Africa and the Middle-South America began to claim rights on the territorial sea and the exclusive economic zone which extend within 200 nautical miles from the coast. Against such background, especially with the advancement of scientific technology, specifically the development of countries' technology of exploring seabed resources of the continental shelf, there is a trend that traditional continental shelf is expanded limitlessly and occupied by technology-developed countries. Therefore, the Third UN Conference on the Law of the Sea was held in 1973 in order to conclude a convention on the law of the sea for comprehensive management of the sea. After ten years' discussion and deliberation, the international society passed United Nations Convention on the Law of the Sea in 1982.

II. System and Developing Prospect of United Nations Convention on the Law of the Sea

United Nations Convention on the Law of the Sea is regarded as the charter of the sea by comprehensively formulating systems on various types of waters. It is comprised of the main text and nine annexes. There are over 500 articles including implementation agreements or enforcement agreements concluded afterwards. We can learn the inclusiveness of the content and the complexity of the issues. Especially United Nations Convention on the Law of the Sea gives detained regulations on legal status of various types of waters, rights and duties of coastal states and non-coastal states and also gives clear regulations on systems of preserving marine environment and disputes settlement. United Nations Convention on the Law of the Sea sets forth that the farthest extent of the territorial sea is 12 nautical miles and establishes new systems on exclusive economic zone and the international sea bed. Meanwhile, it creates the International Tribunal for the Law of the Sea to solve marine disputes, International Sea-bed Authority to manage international sea-bed activities and the Commission on the limits of the Continental Shelf to examine the continental shelf beyond 200 nautical miles.

There was another 12 years from the passing of United Nations Convention on the Law of the Sea by the international society with 10 years' effort to its effectiveness in 1994. The main reason for so long time during which the Convention was not effective is that most developed countries were not satisfied with the relevant rules on the international sea bed system based on Common Heritage of Mankind and held passive attitudes towards its ratification, resulting in delay of the effectiveness of United Nations Convention on the Law of the Sea. In order to accelerate its effectiveness, especially to make it as a general system and rule, two rounds of 15 times of informal discussion had been held under the presiding and promotion of the UN Secretary-General since 1990. Finally, Agreement relating to the Implementation of Part XI (International Seabed Area) of the UNCLOS was passed in July 1994. Such implementation agreement considers issues and eliminates obstacles concerned by most developed countries, therefore accelerated the accession of main development countries to United Nations Convention on the Law of the Sea and the pace of generalization of UNCLOS. So far, there are 162 states (including EU) acceding to United Nations Convention on the Law of the Sea and becoming states parties of UNCLOS, thus United Nations Convention on the Law of the Sea has developed as a generalized treaty.

The International Tribunal for the Law of the Sea, established in 1996 according to United Nations Convention on the Law of the Sea, is an international judicial authority especially for solving problems concerning the interpretation and application of United Nations Convention on the Law of the Sea. Its permanent office is in Hamburg, Germany. The tribunal is comprised of 21 judges who are elected by giving consideration to the geographic principle. Every three years 7 judges will be elected in States Parties' Conference of UNCLOS. For a marine dispute between countries or/and regions, if parties involved can not resolve it through negotiation, any party may file a case to any agency among the International Tribunal for the Law of the Sea, thc International Court of Justice, an arbitral tribunal or a special orbital tribunal. The other party, if only it is a state party of UNCLOS and such a dispute is not relevant to demarcation, territorial sovereignty or military activities, shall be under jurisdiction of the above-mentioned judicial organs in principle.

Although the International Tribunal for the Law of the Sea can not solve all marine problems or it is not an omnipotent judicial organ, it enjoys certain jurisdiction over marine disputes resolution. For example, after the arising of a dispute and before the awarding of judgment by s judicial organ, the International Tribunal for the Law of the Sea has the power to order a binding temporary measure for the purpose of stopping enlargement of damage caused by such a dispute among relevant countries and preserving parties' rights and preventing marine environment from severe damage. This tribunal may also promptly issue an order to release a ship and its crew arrested and detained due to violation of laws of a coastal state.

In 2009, the International Tribunal for the Law of the Sea accepted such a key case as sea waters demarcation between Bangladesh and Myanmar for the first time which is still during the trial. Because the

United Nations Convention on the Law of the Sea contains so many articles and most articles are products of compromise and concession, there are a lot of different opinions in its application. But it is certain that with the increase of important cases accepted by the International Tribunal for the Law of the Sea, after the precedents are accumulated, it will make some contribution to establishment and development of relevant systems of the United Nations Convention on the Law of the Sea.

The 21st Century is referred to as an Ocean Century. At present, except for traditional marine issues, international society faces other issues such as crime of piracy, pollution of ocean environment, unlawful fishing and abuse of marine resources, competition for marine energy and resources. That is to say, there are various and complex issues related to the sea and many fields unknown to the human beings. In order to settle these issues, it needs the international society to act as a whole, especially the international society shall comply with systems and rules of the United Nations Convention on the Law of the Sea including through dialogue and communication, amending relevant clauses to reduce different opinions in understanding and application of the United Nations Convention on the Law of the Sea, creating conditions for giving further play to such judicial organs as the International Tribunal for the Law of the Sea in order to unify the interpretation of and improve the meaning of systems and rules of the United Nations Convention on the Law of the Sea, maintain marine order and create benefits for all the mankind. That is to say, the international society shall make efforts to observe, interpret and apply principles and systems of the United Nations Convention on the Law of the Sea including through dialogue and cooperation and other means to peacefully settle various marine issues and disputes and obtain energy, resources and other interests necessary for human society development from the ocean and its resources. Therefore, on one hand, China shall make further study on relevant principles and systems of the United Nations Convention on the Law of the Sea in order to provide theoretical guaranty for settlement of marine disputes faced by China, on the other hand, it is more important for China to continually improve its marine policies and legal systems, especially China shall formulate national marine development strategy including vigorously developing ocean economy to settle marine issues and disputes in a coordinated way and develop marine undertakings in China.

This article was originally published on Page 4 of *China Ocean News* on Oct. 14, 2011

Institutional Defects of the Law of the Sea to Be Corrected Gradually

The United Nations Convention on the Law of the Sea is a product of compromise and concession. The original aim is to let most countries accept its systems to increase its generalization. However, the weaknesses of its vague statement have been shown in the national practices. Such institutional defects shall be corrected and complimented in the future amendment to the Convention.

This year is the 15th anniversary of the effectiveness of the United Nations Convention on the Law of the Sea (hereinafter referred to as the Convention). In the present international society with issues such as increasing population, increasing demand for resources and energy, serious security and environment problems, the importance of the sea is emerging. Because main countries in the world formulate and implement their respective principles on marine conducts according to systems and requirements of the Convention, it is necessary to study the Convention.

The Convention was passed on the Third UN Conference on the Law of the Sea (from Dec. 1973 to Dec. 1982). On the signing date (Dec.10, 1982), there are represents from 117 states signing the Convention among 167 state delegations taking part in the conference from time to time. Therefore, this conference was a diplomatic one with most participants, largest scale and longest duration in the history of international relations and also a conference producing a convention with the most articles and signatory states in the history of compiling of international law. Thus, the Convention enjoys the most extensive representation.

This Convention which is referred to as the Charter of the Sea has the following three important achievements:

Firstly, it establishes farthest extent of the breadth of the territorial sea. Article 3 of the Convention reads that every State has the right to establish the breadth of its territorial sea up to a limit not exceeding 12 nautical miles, measured from baselines determined in accordance with this Convention, so it solves the lasting problem of the breadth of the territorial sea between the ocean powers and coastal states which could not be solved in the First and Second UN Conferences on the Law of the Sea.

Secondly, it gives detailed regula1tion on the scope of waters and the jurisdiction of coastal states according to different status of waters. Namely, the Convention divides the sea waters into internal waters, the territorial sea, the contiguous zone, the exclusive economic zone, continental shelf, high seas and international sea bed, etc., gives them different legal status and specify coastal states' jurisdiction over the sea waters, thus establishes corresponding systems for each state to develop and utilize the ocean and its resources, especially provides legal warranty for each state to reasonably develop and utilize the above-mentioned sew waters and the resources through amending continental shelf system (standard and scope), establishing exclusive economic zone and international seabed systems. It is more worthwhile to mention that the Convention sets up agencies for determining the limit of the continental shelf beyond 200 nautical miles and managing the international seabed system — the Commission on the Limits of the Continental Shelf and International Seabed Authority.

Thirdly, it establishes a dispute settlement system. Namely, the Convention does not only set forth the means of dispute settlement, but also establish the procedure and agency for dispute settlement — the International Tribunal for the Law of the Sea, thus overcoming the weakness of the Four Geneva Conventions on the Law of the Sea produced by the First UN Conference on the Law of the Sea that the mechanism for dispute settlement was not included in the main text but only in the auxiliary protocol. Of course, the International Tribunal for the Law of the Sea also enlarges the scope of the claimant, namely, which includes any entity other than a state party meeting a certain conditions, for example, self-governing consortium, non-autonomous region, international organization, International Seabed Authority, the Enterprise, state-owned enterprise, natural person or legal person may bring a lawsuit to the International Tribunal for the Law of the Sea.

In order to encourage as many countries as possible to accede to or rectify the Convention thus making it as the generalized convention of the law of the sea, according to requirements of some countries especially the ocean powers, the international society amended and improved the Convention by adopting Implementation Agreement of 1994 and Implementation Agreement of 1995. The former aims at urging some developed countries to accede to or rectify the Convention as soon as possible and the latter aims at improving cooperation among countries in order to make flag states, port states and coastal states more effectively enforce measures formulating for conservation and management of straddling fish.

The defects existing in the Convention include that the definition of the Continental Shelf, issues concerning a warship's navigation through the territorial sea of other state, delimitation of the sea waters between States with opposite or adjacent coasts, international sea-bed development system and so on give too many preferences to some developed countries and also it fails to answer a question whether relevant systems of the Convention apply to the development of polar resources. Because the Convention is a product of compromise and concession, some articles are vague and have possibilities to make different interpretation, the aim of which was to make most countries accept its system in order to increase its generalization.

These defects have been shown in the national practices including causing different interpretation even disputes thus increasing the possibility of confrontation and conflict among relevant countries, which influences the coastal states' marine interests and rights and security interest and further endangers the international and regional peace and safety. Therefore, these institutional defects shall be amended and corrected in the future amendment to the Convention.

For example, regarding the delimitation of sea waters between states with opposite or adjacent coasts, there are different opinions between the principle of Median Line and the Principle of Equality in international society. However, from the perspective of international cases and national practices, the Principle of Equality has been developed as a rule of customary law. As for the military activities in the exclusive economic zone, there is opposition between the Liberty School and Consent School. Considering that other states' military activity will influence or endanger a coastal state's peace and safety, therefore, the coastal state has the power to formulate relevant rules and adopt the principle of advance consent. Concerning the regime of island, there are different interpretation and theories on Article 121 of the Convention. Therefore, when amending the Convention, such aforesaid factor and the latest development trend shall be taken into account in order to make rules on these issues clear and avoid difference and opposition.

This article was originally published on Page A12 of *Dongfang Daily* on Nov. 23, 2009

Limitations of Laws of the Sea

The series US-Republic of Korea (ROK) military exercises has, for justified reasons, caused widespread concern in China. The scale and non-peaceful purpose of the joint drill, conducted perilously close to China' maritime border, make it different from normal military exercises.

International disputes should be settled through peaceful dialogues within the framework of international laws and conventions, not by saber rattling. But the media in China should not fan nationalist sentiments over the drill without providing background information on the laws of the sea. Some vague reports may mislead the public that the joint drill was conducted in China's territorial waters, which is impossible.

The waters on the landward side of the baselines of the territorial sea of China constitute its internal waters. The breadth of the territorial sea of China is 12 nautical miles, measured from the baselines of the territorial sea, which is determined by the UN Convention on the Law of the Sea (called Convention hereafter). A country's sovereignty extends to the air space over the territorial sea, as well as its bed and subsoil.

And the waters of archipelagic countries extend to an adjacent belt of sea, described as the territorial sea.

The laws of the sea don't include any concepts or terminologies of military drills, which incidentally need a large area of a sea to conduct and forces all other maritime activities to be suspended.

The Convention on the High Seas (1958) guarantees freedom of navigation, fishing, laying submarine cables and pipelines, and flying over the high seas to all countries, coastal or landlocked. These freedoms, and others which are recognized by the general principles of international law, should be exercised by all states with reasonable regard to the interests of other states in their exercise of the freedom of the high seas. Plus, the high seas should be reserved for peaceful purposes.

Though holding military drills has long been regarded as a traditional freedom on the high seas, the international community is yet to agree on a clear specification. And many countries use this freedom to flex their military muscles on the high seas.

So, we should focus on military drills in exclusive economic zones. An exclusive economic zone is an area beyond and adjacent to the territorial sea. A country's exclusive economic zone cannot extend beyond 200 nautical miles from the baseline from which the territorial sea is drawn.

In its exclusive economic zone, a country has the sovereign right to explore and exploit, and conserve and manage the natural resources, whether living or non-living, of the waters superjacent to the seabed and of the seabed and its subsoil, and with regard to other activities for economic exploration and exploitation of the zone, such as the production of energy from the water, currents and winds.

The international community has not agreed on how a military exercise in exclusive economic zones should be viewed. Some strong sea powers adamantly cite Article 58 of the Convention to say they can hold military drills without seeking permission from other coastal countries.

Some other countries argue a military drill should be judged on the basis of its purpose and nature. Drills that include firing torpedoes and navy artilleries are banned. The legally accepted exercise model is interpreted only as maritime activities involving warships. As for exercises with weapons and explosive materials, the organizers have to negotiate with coastal countries beforehand. The international community has not agreed on the legitimacy of military drills or missile trials that hamper other countries' use of a large area of a sea.

The third group of countries supposes that the Convention is not clear on the exclusive rights of surrounding coastal countries to permit another country to conduct military exercises involving weapons near their waters. The difference in understanding of the problem of naval military drills has long been a controversial issue.

In this sense, the peaceful use of the sea should be a universal code. A proper analysis of military exercises in exclusive economic zones should be based on a drill's intentions and the principles of exclusive economic zones. Coastal countries have legal obligations and rights over the natural resources in their exclusive economic zones. Military drills held by a country (or countries) in a special zone should not interfere with another (coastal) country's rights.

Some of the big sea powers dodged a detailed discussion on maritime military activities at the 3rd UN Conference on the Law of Sea, silencing some developing countries' voices to exercise their rights in their exclusive economic zones. That's why the Convention is apparently defective. Still, Article 59 of the Convention can serve as a guiding principle to settle disputes in exclusive economic zones.

If a conflict of interest arises between a coastal country and any other country or countries, it should be settled on the basis of equity. The settlement should take into account the respective importance of the interests of the parties involved and that of the international community.

Thus, China can protest against the military drill in the territorial sea and exclusive economic zone of the ROK because it posed a potential threat to China's national security.

When it comes to the military drill in China's exclusive economic zone, the government should voice its concern and demand that the other parties respect its national security and legitimate rights in its exclusive economic zones. A country holding a military drill is obliged to inform the other countries around the coast about the area, scale and nature of its drill in advance.

The dispute over military drills between China and the US can be settled by strengthening mutual trust. If the two countries can build a maritime security negotiation mechanism or reach an agreement in dealing with maritime emergencies, not only can disputes be avoided, but also Sino-US ties will be consolidated.

As far as military drills in China's exclusive economic zones are concerned, Beijing can also start strong protest campaigns for the drafting of a common law to plug the loopholes in the Convention. According to Article 313 of the Convention, China can propose an amendment related to military drills. And not being a contracting party to the Convention, the US will face more pressure and may be pushed on the back foot.

This article was originally published on Page 9
of *China Daily* on Aug. 24, 2010

How to Draw the Baseline of the Territorial Sea

As we all know, the United Nations Convention on the Law of the Sea divides the sea waters into internal waters, the territorial sea, the contiguous zone, archipelagic waters, exclusive economic zone, continental shelf, high seas and international sea bed. The limit or scope of the aforesaid sea waters is determined from the starting point of the baseline of the territorial sea. In other words, the baseline of the territorial sea is a line joining each base point based on which the scope of sea waters of a coastal state is determined.

Then, how is the baseline of the territorial sea determined? Generally speaking, there are three methods of determining the baseline of the territorial sea: Normal baseline, Straight baselines and Hybrid baseline.

According to Article 5 of the Convention, the normal baseline for measuring the breadth of the territorial sea is the low-water line along the coast as marked on large-scale charts officially recognized by the coastal State.

Paragraph 1 of Article 7 of the Convention sets forth that in localities where the coastline is deeply indented and cut into, or if there is a fringe of islands along the coast in its immediate vicinity, the method of straight baselines joining appropriate points may be employed in drawing the baseline from which the breadth of the territorial sea is measured.

Of course, in order to avoid too large area of sea waters after adopting straight baselines by the coastal state, the Convention imposes limitation on drawing straight baselines which maily includes as follows: firstly, the drawing of straight baselines must not depart to any appreciable extent from the general direction of the coast, and the sea areas lying within the lines must be sufficiently closely linked to the land domain to be subject to the regime of internal waters. Secondly, the system of straight baselines may not be applied by a State in such a manner as to cut off the territorial sea of another State from the high seas or an exclusive economic zone.

For the third method of combined baselines, Article 14 of the Convention sets forth that the coastal State may determine baselines in turn by any of the methods of normal baselines and straight baselines to suit different conditions.

After the baseline of the territorial sea is determined, the breadth of the territorial sea, the outer limit of the territorial sea and the scope of internal waters can be determined. Article 3 of the Convention stipulates that the breadth of the territorial sea of a State is up to a limit not exceeding 12 nautical miles (1 nautical mile=1852 meters), measured from baselines determined in accordance with this Convention. Article 4 reads that the outer limit of the territorial sea is the line every point of which is at a distance from the nearest point of the baseline equal to the breadth of the territorial sea. Paragraph 1 of Article 8 sets forth that waters on the landward side of the baseline of the territorial sea form part of the internal waters of the State.

Considering the situation that the distance between opposite coasts of two states is less than 24 nautical miles, there is an issue of delimitation of the territorial sea between such states. The Convention establishes the principle of median line for the delimitation of the territorial sea. Namely, Article 15 of the Convention sets forth where the coasts of two States are opposite or adjacent to each other, neither of the two States is entitled, failing agreement between them to the contrary, to extend its territorial sea beyond the median line every point of which is equidistant from the nearest points on the baselines from which the breadth of the territorial seas of each of the two States is measured.

In addition, Article 16 of the Convention sets forth that the baselines for measuring the breadth of the territorial sea determined or the limits derived therefrom, and the lines of delimitation drawn shall be shown on charts of a scale or scales adequate for ascertaining their position. Meanwhile, the coastal State shall give due publicity to such charts or lists of geographical co-ordinates and shall deposit a copy of each such chart or list with the Secretary-General of the United Nations.

It can be seen that in order to determine the scope of the territorial sea of the coastal state, the baseline must be marked on a chart. Therefore, the domestic law is needed for proof and in order to determine the scope of the territorial sea. On Feb. 17, 2009, the Parliament of Philippines adopted a bill on the baseline of the territorial sea which included China's Huangyan Island and part of islands and rocks of Nansha Islands as the territory of the Philippines and tried to determine the sea areas based on that.

For this, Ministry of Foreign Affairs of China pointed out that Huangyan Island and Nansha Islands are always a part of Chinese territory and China has indisputable sovereignty over these islands and their adjacent sea areas. Any claim of territorial sovereignty over Huangyan Island and Nansha Islands made by any other state is illegal and void.

Regarding the territorial sea of China, Declaration of the China on the Territorial Sea was promulgated on Sept. 4, 1958, namely the breadth of the territorial sea of China is 12 nautical miles and it applies to all territory of China including the mainland and its coastal islands, Taiwan and its adjacent islands, Pescadores, Dongsha Islands, Xisha Islands, Zhongsha Islands, Nansha Islands as well as other islands belonging to China. At the same time, China announced that the territorial sea of the Mainland and its coastal islands of China takes straight lines joining each base point of the shore of the mainland and outer islands of the coast and the waters extending 12 nautical miles from the baselines are the territorial sea of China.

It can be seen that China adopts the method of straight baselines to determine its territorial sea and the breadth is 12 nautical miles. These facts are confirmed by Law of China on the Territorial Sea and Contiguous Zone (published and brought into force on Feb. 25, 1992). For example, Article 3 sets forth that the breadth of the territorial sea of China is 12 nautical miles measured from the baseline of the territorial sea; the baseline of the territorial sea of China is delimited by the method of straight baselines which is composed by straight lines joining adjacent base points; the outer limit of the territorial sea of China is a line every point of which is at a distance from the nearest point of the baseline of the territorial sea is equal to 12 nautical miles.

The top priority at present is that China shall announce other part of the baseline of the territorial sea to improve the territorial sea system. Because China has not published other part of the baseline of the territorial sea since China published Declaration of Chinese Government on the Baseline of the Territorial Sea on May 15, 1996 and announced part of baseline of the territorial sea of the mainland and Xisha Islands. Meanwhile, the aforesaid declaration sets forth that Chinese government will announce other part of the baseline of the territorial sea of China which provides legal basis for China to announce other part of the baseline of the territorial sea of China. The announcement of other part of the baseline of the territorial sea by China, especially the baseline of the territorial sea of Nansha Islands, is significant for China to determine the scope of sea waters under jurisdiction of China, maintain China's marine interests and rights, enhance law enforcement of cruise.

This article was originally published on Page A14
of *Dongfang Daily* on May 4, 2009

How to Conduct Delimitation When the Exclusive Economic Zone and the Continental Shelf Overlap

From the perspective of international justice and national practices, the principle of equity on sea waters delimitation has become customary law. If the application of median line may produce equity, it can be applied. If the result is not fair, it can not be applied. Meanwhile, such median line must be recognized and agreed on by relevant states, otherwise it can not be sued as the starting line of delimitation.

In regard to Exclusive Economic Zone, Article 55 and Article 57 of the United Nations Convention on the Law of the Sea stipulate that the exclusive economic zone is an area beyond and adjacent to the territorial sea which shall not extend beyond 200 nautical miles from the baselines from which the breadth of the territorial sea is measured.

Concerning the Continental Shelf, Paragraph 1 of Article 76 sets forth that the continental shelf of a coastal State comprises the seabed and subsoil of the submarine areas that extend beyond its territorial sea throughout the natural prolongation of its land territory to the outer edge of the continental margin, or to a distance of 200 nautical miles from the baselines from which the breadth of the territorial sea is measured where the outer edge of the continental margin does not extend up to that distance.

It is clear that within 200 nautical miles, the submarine areas of the Exclusive Economic Zone and those of the Continental Shelf overlap. Meanwhile, when the breadth of the sea waters is less then 400 nautical miles, there is an issue of delimitation of Exclusive Economic Zone and the Continental Shelf between states with opposite or adjacent coasts.

As for the delimitation of Exclusive Economic Zone and the Continental Shelf, the Convention has the same regulations which are set forth in Article 74 and Article 83. For example, Article 83 of the Convention stipulates that the delimitation of the continental shelf between States with opposite or adjacent coasts shall be effected by agreement on the basis of international law, as referred to in Article 38 of the Statute of the International Court of Justice, in order to achieve an equitable solution. If no agreement can be reached within a reasonable period of time, the States concerned shall resort to the procedures of dispute settlement. Pending agreement as provided above, the States concerned, in a spirit of understanding and co-operation, shall make every effort to enter into provisional arrangements of a practical nature and, during this transitional period, not to jeopardize or hamper the reaching of the final agreement. Such arrangements shall be without prejudice to the final delimitation.

From the abovementioned statement, it is obvious that when there is dispute over delimitation of sea waters between the states, firstly it shall be effected by agreement to ensure an equitable solution; secondly, if no agreement can be reached, the states shall make every effort to enter into provisional arrangements which meanwhile, shall not jeopardize or hamper the reaching of the final agreement. Thirdly, such regulation does not involve the principle of median line or the principle of equity but just sets forth that the delimitation result shall be equitable. Therefore, if the delimitation by the median line recognized by the states concerned may produce an equitable result, the median line can be applied, otherwise it shall not be applied.

Regarding the relationship between the Exclusive Economic Zone and the Continental Shelf, there are two types of opinions in the international society. The first one is Absorption Theory, namely the system of Exclusive Economic Zone has absorbed the system of the Continental Shelf. The second one is that Parallel Theory or Independence Theory, that is to say, the Exclusive Economic Zone are different and independent systems.

The Author prefers to the latter opinions because of the following reasons. Firstly, the objectives of their establishment are different, namely the system of Exclusive Economic Zone regulates biological resources related to economic activities and the system of the Continental Shelf regulates the sea bed, ocean bed and its subsoil (natural resources). Secondly, the scopes are different. 200 nautical miles is the biggest scope of Exclusive Economic Zone but the smallest scope of the Continental Shelf. Thirdly, the right bases are different. The coastal state's rights over the Continental Shelf are inherent and there is no need to announce it. However, the coastal state's rights over the Exclusive Economic Zone need the state to make announcement and may be altered according to a treaty. Fourthly, the factors taken into account for delimitation are different. Factors related to economy are considered more for the delimitation of Exclusive Economic Zone while factors related to geography are considered more for the delimitation of the Continental Shelf.

China is a geographically disadvantaged ocean country and has to conduct sea waters delimitation with many countries including disputes over island sovereignty. At present, China only enters into Agreement on Delimitation in Beibu Bay with Vietnam and hasn't finished the delimitation of sea waters with other countries. Under the situation that there are disputes over islands sovereignty and disagreement in disputed sea waters, China holds the principle of Setting Aside Dispute and Seeking Joint Development, but there are still disputes. For example, on Mar. 5, 2009, the Premier of Malaysia landed on Swallow Reef of Nansha Islands to claim sovereignty over such reef and its adjacent sea areas attempting to enlarge the scope of governed sea waters. Therefore, at present, in the South China Sea, an important task is to produce detailed regulation of Declaration on the Conduct of Parties in the South

China Sea such as A Code of Conduct of Parties in the South China Sea to maintain the stability of the South China Sea.

As for the scope of Exclusive Economic Zone, Article 2 of the Law of China on Exclusive Economic Zone and the Continental Shelf (promulgated and implemented on June 26, 1998) reads that China's Exclusive Economic Zone is an area beyond and adjacent to the territorial sea which extends to 200 nautical miles from the baselines from which the breadth of the territorial sea is measured. As for the scope of the Continental Shelf, Article 2 of such law reads that the Continental Shelf comprises the seabed and subsoil of the submarine areas that extend beyond its territorial sea throughout the natural prolongation of its land territory to the outer edge of the continental margin, or to a distance of 200 nautical miles from the baselines from which the breadth of the territorial sea is measured where the outer edge of the continental margin does not extend up to that distance. Article 2 also stipulates that where Exclusive Economic Zone and the Continental Shelf claimed by China and the country with opposite or adjacent coast overlap, the delimitation shall be conducted on basis of international law according to the principle of equity.

From the perspective of international justice and national practices, the principle of equity on sea waters delimitation has become customary law. If the application of median line may produce equity, it can be applied. If the result is not fair, it can not be applied.

Meanwhile, such median line must be recognized and agreed on by relevant states, otherwise it can not be sued as the starting line of delimitation.

This article was originally published on Page A17 of *Dongfang Daily* on May 5, 2009

The Relation between Marine Scientific Research and Military Survey Activities

On May 1, 2009, the U.S. surveillance ship Victorious entered Chinese Exclusive Economic Zone in the Yellow Sea without China's permission, which is a violation of relevant international law as well as Chinese laws and regulations. Because the Convention fails to make clear regulation on military survey, foundation may only be sought from the perspective of marine scientific research. State parties may give a written notice to the UN Secretary-General asking for amendment to the Convention by adding regulation on military survey.

There have been several incidents that foreign warships and survey ships conducted survey in China's Exclusive Economic Zone seriously endangering China's national security since China Surveillance vessels began its regular safeguard cruise in the sea waters under China's jurisdiction on July 20, 2006. Because the United Nations Convention on the Law of the Sea does not have clear rules on military survey nor give a word to the term of military survey, we shall make analysis from the perspective of marine scientific research and seek relevant foundation.

The so-called marine scientific research means the scientific research carried out in accordance with this Convention exclusively for peaceful purposes and in order to increase scientific knowledge of the marine environment for the benefit of all mankind (Paragraph 2 and Paragraph 3 of Article 246 of the Convention). Article 238 of the Convention reads that all States have the right to conduct marine scientific research. Article 240 stipulates principles of marine scientific research: marine scientific research shall be conducted exclusively for peaceful purposes and in compliance with all relevant regulations including those for the protection and preservation of the marine environment.

Marine scientific research in the exclusive economic zone and on the continental shelf shall be conducted with the consent of the coastal State. Coastal States shall, in normal circumstances, grant their consent for marine scientific research projects by other States. However, Coastal States may in their discretion withhold their consent if that marine scientific research project: (a) is of direct significance for the exploration and exploitation of natural resources, whether living or non-living; (b) involves drilling into the continental shelf, the use of explosives or the introduction of harmful substances into the marine environment; (c) involves the construction, operation or use of artificial islands, installations and structures; (d) contains information regarding the nature and objectives of the project which is inaccurate or if the researching

State or competent international organization has outstanding obligations to the coastal State from a prior research project.

While concerning research or survey activities, Paragraph 2 of Article 19 of the Convention considers the carrying out of research or survey activities to be prejudicial to the peace, good order or security of the coastal State. Paragraph 1 of Article 21 reads that the coastal State may adopt laws and regulations relating to innocent passage through the territorial sea in respect of marine scientific research and hydrographic surveys.

It is evident that the scope of research or survey activity is bigger than that of marine scientific research and hydrographic surveys as the former includes other investigation and survey activity. Especially military survey activity the investigation result is usually not open to the pubic, so it seemingly ought to be distinguished from other marine scientific research. However, due to its prejudice to the peace and safety of coastal states, some countries adopt the principle of advance consent.

If other country conducts investigation activity in The exclusive economic zone without application for consent or the investigation activity is not being conducted in accordance with the application, the coastal State may require the suspension of the cessation of such activity (Article 253 of the Convention).

Because the Convention is vague in regulation of military survey activity, national practices are different. Specifically speaking, the US and Britain hold the opinion that military survey activity shall be free in principle and not be governed by the coastal State. While most countries, for example, Japan, India, China and so on, believe that military survey activity shall be conducted by sticking to the principle of consent from the coastal State, otherwise it is forbidden.

The problem is that the situation is more complex and the coastal State could employ very limited means to deal with the situation when ships of other country, especialy warships or ships with governmental entrustment conduct military survey activities without consent of the coastal State, because they enjoy the full immunity according to Article 95, Article 96, Paragraph 2 of Article 58 of the Convention.

Because the Convention does not explain what peaceful purposes are, it is generally believed that any military activity not in conflict with the United Nations Charter is permissible. If the coastal State discovers that a warship of other country is conducting survey or investigation activity in its exclusive economic zone, it can only take steps such as interference, tailing, requiring cessation or leave except for protesting through diplomatic means. If the other party chooses to ignore such step and continue its activity, there seems nothing the coastal State can do. Of course, the coastal State may dispatch a warship for threatening, but it may result in more intense situation.

In fact, there is an effective legal means: State Parties may give written notice to the UN Secretary-General asking for amendment to the Convention by adding regulations on military survey activity for the purpose of resolving disputes arising from different interpretation of States of military survey activity. Most countries insist on the stance that military survey activity shall be conducted with the consent of the coastal State, which make some ocean powers feel pressured, especially the USA hasn't rectify the Convention and could not give its opinion on the amendment mentioned in the aforesaid written notice. Such written declaration, with positive response from most state parties, may promote the amendment to the Convention and then resolve this difficult problem.

The laws and regulations of China on marine scientific research comprise Law on Exclusive Economic Zone and the Continental Shelf (promulgated and brought into force on June 26, 1998) and Regulations on Management of Foreign-related Marine Scientific Research (promulgated on June 18, 1998 and brought into force on Oct. 1, 1996). For example, Article 9 of Law on Exclusive Economic Zone and the Continental Shelf sets forth that any international organization, foreign organization or individual must obtain approval from competent authority of China and comply with Chinese laws and regulations for conducting marine scientific research in China's exclusive economic zone and the Continental Shelf. Article 4 of Regulations on Management of Foreign-related Marine Scientific Research reads that the marine scientific research activity conducted by the foreign party exclusively or jointly with Chinese party must be approved by national marine administration or the State Council through the report of national marine administration and in compliance with relevant laws and regulations of China.

The marine administration in the aforesaid articles refers to State

Oceanic Administration of People's Republic of China, but such articles do not give a definition of military survey activity. In fact, China adopts the extensive concept of marine scientific research activity (including military activity) and exercises the system of advance permission. Therefore, China shall amend relevant articles of the aforesaid laws and regulations to make the competent authority and military survey activity clear.

This article was originally published on Page A19 of *Dongfang Daily* on May 7, 2009

How to Deal with Military Exercises in Exclusive Economic Zone

The joint military exercises recently made by the USA and the South Korea which is just 170 kilometers away from Shandong Peninsula, China, seriously influenced and endangered maritime security of China.

Generally speaking, as for military exercises in the territorial sea and exclusive economic zone of South Korea, China can only protest against those endangering China's national defence security; regarding the issue of military exercises in the exclusive economic zone of China, China shall put forward its concerns to the states conducting military exercises and express the hope that they respect China's rights and interests in the exclusive economic zone including national defense security and resolve relevant issues through bilateral dialogue and negotiation. Before military exercises, the states conducting such exercises are under the obligation to notify relevant states of information such as the date and region through diplomatic channel. The joint military exercises made by the USA and South Korea in recent time are more than general military exercises in terms of scale and frequency. They aimed at specific target and had non-peaceful intention, thus attracting a lot of attention. Especially such military exercises were held in the region very close to sea waters under the jurisdiction of China, so its damage to China was more profound. In other words, threat or use of force is against the settlement of disputes and may only cause more serious problems and more difficulties.

There is no such a concept or term as military exercises in the law of the sea. The military exercises in the high seas are regarded as a kind of traditional freedom in the high seas. Of course, there are different opinions on military exercises in the high seas and no relevant clear regulations in the international society, however, in fact there are most countries continuing to conduct military exercises in the high seas and such exercises have become a kind of customs. Therefore, we shall pay more attention to the issue of military exercises in the exclusive economic zone.

There are three opinions on the issue of military exercises in the exclusive economic zone in the international society without unified view.

The first opinion reads that Article 58 of the United Nations Convention on the Law of the Sea admits in principle that foreign States may conduct military exercises in other States' exclusive economic zone without the consent of the coastal State. This is the so-called Theory of Free Conduct and main ocean powers hold this opinion.

The second opinion reads that whether the military exercises shall be permitted depends on its nature. This is the so-called Theory of Distinguishing Conduct. Exercises such as those in accompany with torpedo firing and shipboard shooting are forbidden; military exercises which are interpreted as activities following the warship are one of the international legal uses of the exclusive economic zone; exercises such as those with the use of weapons and explosives shall be held with advanced negotiation with the coastal State; it is not clear whether the military exercises and missile test interfering with other States' use of extensive sea waters in a period of time are legal or not.

The third opinion reads that there is no clear regulation on activities such as exercises with weapons in the Convention, namely the Convention does not determine whether it is a right of the coastal State or of the State conducting such exercises. This is the so-called Theory of Undetermined Conduct.

It is obvious that there are different understandings on the issue of military exercises and therefore there are different even opposite national practices.

There was no discussion on the issue of military exercises during the enactment of the Convention, therefore study can only be conducted from the perspective of peaceful use of the sea. The clauses concerning peaceful use of the sea are Paragraph 2 of Article 58, Article 88 and Article 301, but they do not define the peaceful purposes nor give a clear definition. Therefore, the issue of military exercises in the exclusive economic zone shall be analyzed specifically according to their own characteristics and natures, especially in combination with the legislative aims of the exclusive economic zone and relevant systems to seek a solution.

The exclusive economic zone is a special kind of sea waters between the territorial sea and the high seas and enjoys special legal status which is reflected in the jurisdiction of the State over the zone. For example, in the exclusive economic zone, the coastal State has sovereign rights for the purpose of exploring and exploiting, conserving and managing the natural resources of the waters superjacent to the seabed and of the seabed and its subsoil, and with regard to other activities for the economic exploitation and exploration of the zone, such as the production of energy from the water, currents and winds; meanwhile, the coastal State has jurisdiction with regard to the protection and preservation of the marine environment. Therefore, regarding the issue of other State's military exercises in our exclusive economic zone, we shall conduct specific analysis of the effect and nature of such military exercises activity.

It can be inferred from the aforesaid text that the system of exclusive economic zone contains the thought of most reasonable use of resources including entitlement of the coastal State to the sovereign right over resources and imposition of obligation of the coastal State to conservation and management of resources in a proper manner. Therefore, we can determine whether the due regard to the rights and obligations of the coastal states is given through analyzing whether military exercises activity brings about influences on the conservation and management of resources and marine environment.

It should be noted that most issues related to military activities in the high seas and exclusive economic zone are of political nature. Most of them belong to military secret, so military powers and marine powers made their efforts to avoid a clear regulation on the issue of military activities in the Third UN Conference on the Law of the Sea, which hampered some developing countries' efforts to seek maximized rights and interests in the exclusive economic zone, thus relevant articles in the Convention have obvious defects and there arise different interpretations and national practices.

The good news is that the issue concerning rights and obligations in the exclusive economic zone not allocated or even conflicted may be settled in compliance with Article 59 of the Convention on basis of equity and with reference to all relevant situations, in consideration of the significance of interests involved to each party and the whole international society. This article is instructive for issues concerning military exercises with a characteric of high technology in new era.

Meanwhile, because a dispute concerning military activities (military exercises) may be exempt from the compulsory procedures of the Convention by means of written declaration, China and the USA shall especially build mutual trust through maritime safety consultation mechanism including signing treaties such as Agreement on Marine

Accident Prevention. During consultation, China shall specify its stance of not intending to challenge the USA and recognizing the USA's role and status in the Asia, but China hopes that the USA could understand and respect its reasonable concerns and China seeks understanding and cooperation. The purpose is to stabilize the Sino-American relationship and avoid conflicts and confrontation. If these can not be achieved, China may use other means such as economic means at the right moment to make the USA understand that harmony brings about win-win and fighting results in mutual loss and then adjust relevant American tactics.

In a word, we only have limited means to deal with the issue of military exercises conducted by other countries in China's exclusive economic zone. Except for bilateral discussion, China may gradually accumulate national practices through continually expressing strong protest and declaration to make such practices become hard law or customary law. In addition, as a state party, China may, according to Article 313, propose amendment through simplified procedure to amend the system related to military exercises, thus placing the non-party USA in an embarrassing situation, imposing pressure on the USA and making such system related to military exercises become customary law as soon as possible.

This article was originally published on Page A14 of *Dongfang Daily* on Nov. 29, 2010

Cracking down on Somalia Piracy from the Perspective of International Law

There have been constant wars or chaos in Somalia and active pirate activities in its coastal regions since 1991. During Jan. 2008 to the mid-November, Chinese ships went through Aden Gulf and Somali waters frequently and 20% of them were attacked by pirates. This time, the escort which is conducted in compliance with relevant resolutions of UN Security Council and relevant international law has significance in maintaining a smooth international sea lane and the safety of Aden Gulf and Somali waters.

After ten days and ten nights' navigation, the naval fleet of China Navy going to the Aden Gulf and Somali waters to exercise this escort task successfully arrived at the task section in the early morning of the local time of Aden Gulf and began to conduct escort. According to introduction by a spokesman of Ministry of Transport, there have been 15 Chinese business ships applying for escort between Jan. 6 to Jan. 10.

Since 1991, there have been wars and conflicts continuously in Somalia and active pirate activities in its coastal regions. Waters off the

Somalia is regarded as one of the most dangerous waters in the world by International Maritime Bureau. According to statistics of International Maritime Organization, there were 120 cases of piracy in which more than 30 ships were robbed and over 600 seamen were kidnapped in 2008. Till now there are still 10 ships in the hands of the pirates. Chinese ships also go through Aden Gulf and Somali waters frequently. During Jan. 2008 to Nov. 2008, there were averagely 3 to 4 Chinese business ships passing-by. It is reported that 20% of them were attacked by pirates with 7 hijacking events. Chinese ships and seaman are confronted with serious safety threats.

So far, NATO, EU, Russia, India and South Korea have already sent and have been ready to send warships to Aden Gulf north of Somalia to combat pirates and maintain safety.

International Laws Specify that Each County May Combat Piracy

What is the definition of the Pirate in international society? And what are regulations on punishing and controlling piracy? We can learn them from the international law, especially relevant articles in Convention of the High Seas (formulated in 1958 and brought into force in 1962) and the United Nations Convention on the Law of the Sea (formulated in 1982 and brought into force in 1994).

Traditionally, Piracy means the illegal act of violence and

depredation conducted by a private ship on another ship in the high seas for private ends. However, the Convention in the High Seas adopted in the First UN Conference on the Law of the Sea expanded its definition which was endorsed by the United Nations Convention on the Law of the Sea adopted by the Third UN Conference on the Law of the Sea. Namely, any illegal acts of violence or detention, or any act of depredation, committed for private ends by the crew or the passengers of a private ship or a private aircraft are regarded as piracy. Article 14 of Convention of the High Seas and Article 100 of the United Nations Convention on the Law of the Sea specify that All States shall co-operate to the fullest possible extent in the repression of piracy on the high seas or in any other place outside the jurisdiction of any State. According to Article 15 of Convention of the High Seas and Article 101 of the United Nations Convention on the Law of the Sea, Piracy consists of any of the following acts: (1) any illegal acts of violence or detention, or any act of depredation, committed for private ends by the crew or the passengers of a private ship or a private aircraft, and directed: firstly on the high seas, against another ship or aircraft, oragainst persons or property on board such ship or aircraft; secondly against a ship, aircraft, persons or property in a place outside the jurisdiction of any State; (2) any act of voluntary participation in the operation of a ship or of an aircraft with knowledge of facts making it a pirate ship or aircraft; (3) any act of inciting or of intentionally facilitating an act described in the first and second subparagraph. According to Article 19 of Convention of the High Seas and Article 105 of the United Nations Convention on the Law of the Sea, on the high seas, or in any other place outside the jurisdiction of any State, every State may seize a pirate ship or aircraft, or a ship or aircraft taken by piracy and under the control of pirates, and arrest the persons and seize the property on board. The courts of the State which carried out the seizure may decide upon the penalties to be imposed, and may also determine the action to be taken with regard to the ships, aircraft or property, subject to the rights of third parties acting in good faith. According to Article 21 of Convention of the High Seas and Article 107 of the United Nations Convention on the Law of the Sea, a seizure on account of piracy may be carried out only by warships or military aircraft, or other ships or aircraft clearly marked and identifiable as being on government service and authorized to that effect.

Chinese Warships' Escort in Somali Waters Comply with Expectation of International Society

It is clear that each State has the power to combat piracy on the high seas or in any other place outside the jurisdiction of any State because pirates have been regarded as enemy of mankind. However, it should be noted that the so-called piracy shall meet the following two requirements: firstly, it must be an illegal act of violence, detention or depredation against another ship or aircraft by means of damaging navigation safety in the high seas; secondly, it must be any illegal acts of violence or detention, or any act of depredation, committed for private ends by a private ship or a private aircraft. If the decision is wrong and detention of (boarding on) a ship or an aircraft is conducted, the relevant state shall be liable for any caused loss or damage. For example, according to Article 20 and Article 22 of Convention of the High Seas and Article 106 and Article 110 of the United Nations Convention on the Law of the Sea, where the detention of (boarding on) a ship or aircraft on suspicion of piracy has been effected without adequate grounds, the State making the detention (boarding) shall be liable to the State the nationality of which is possessed by the ship or aircraft for any loss or damage caused by the detention (boarding).

Therefore, although international law, especially the law of the sea clearly specify that each State may combat and punish piracy through warships or military aircraft, or other ships or aircraft authorized to that effect, each State will not generally take rash action unless there is a resolution adopted by the United Nations Security Council due to unforeseeability and invisibility of piracy and extensity of sea waters especially the high seas. The four resolutions on combating piracy in Aden Gulf and Somali sea waters adopted by the United Nations Security Council in recent time offer clear legal guaranty for cooperative actions of States.

Eradicating Somali piracy needs a method addressing symptoms and root cause with the key that the United Nations strengthens its security and humanitarian aids in Somalia including dispatching the

UN peace-keeping force to practically improve its domestic order and meet refugees' demand for materials for avoiding the deterioration of situation. According to a resolution of the Security Council, as invited by the Somali government, after giving reference to practices of other States, Chinese government makes a decision to send its warships to Aden Gulf and Somali sea waters to carry out escort and combat piracy, which complies with the expectation of the international society and the international law and builds an image of great power that China is willing to undertake international obligation and wins extensive praise as an important steps by China to participate in international multilateral cooperation.

This article was originally published in Page 5
of *Wenhui Daily* on Jan. 7, 2009

Escort by China Navy in Urgent Need of Legal System Development

On Dec. 26, 2011, it is the third anniversary that China Navy dispatched escort fleet to Somali and Aden Gulf sea waters to carry out escort and combat piracy. During these three years, China Navy totally dispatched 10 batches of fleet including 25 ships and 8400 soldiers to carry out escort task for 403 batches of ships including 4383 Chinese and foreign ones and ensured 100% safety of the escorted ships and crews.

It is significant for China Navy to go to Somalia and Aden Gulf to combat piracy, maintain the safety of business ships and crews, maintain the safety of ships transporting humanitarian materials by international organizations such as the World Food Program and provide humanitarian salvage for foreign business ships, which also contributes to maintain regional and international peace and safety.

The escort operation of China Navy has the following characteristics:

In the first place, China Navy's flexibility and response capacity in over ocean area are further promoted. The anti-piracy action carried out in Somalia and Aden Gulf sea waters by warships of China Navy for the first time not only exercised China Navy's ability to carry out tasks in distant seas, but also played an important part in protecting China's overseas strategic interests, fulfilling international humanitarian obligations and ensuring safety of important transportation materials.

In the second place, the escort carried out by China Navy is deeply praised and encouraged. China achieved 100% of success in the action of 10 batches of escort fleets and created a new escort model including accompanying escort, regional escort, on-the-ship escort which greatly improved the efficiency of navy escort. For instance, on Sept. 4, 2010, Kunlun Shan Warship safely escorted 27 Chinese and foreign business ships and earned praises from other countries. In this escort operation, by taking advantage of large tonnage, strong mobility and endurance of LCAC (Landing Craft Air Cushion) and high-speed patrol boat carried by amphibious dock ship, China used loading dock boat which cooperated with a helicopter in issuing warning to enlarge the sea waters under control, so the escort capacity increased greatly which not only created new mode of escort but also improved escort efficiency.

In the third place, escort by China Navy shows a normalizing trend. As mentioned above, during the three years, there were 10 batches of escort fleets from China Navy taking part in escort. They strictly exercised a regularly shifted escort system which has been normalized. It is generally thought that as long as piracy exists in Somalia and Aden Gulf sea waters, especially as authorized by the UN Security Council and requested or approved by the coastal State, China will still continue to dispatch Navel vessels to carry out escort operation to maintain the safety of transportation materials and people of China and many other countries and protect the common interests of international society.

In the fourth place, the communication with navies of other countries is enhanced. Because States and international organizations such as the USA, Russia, Japan, EU also dispatched fleets to take part in anti-piracy escort operation in Somalia and Aden Gulf sea waters, China Navy, through taking part in escort operation in Somali and Aden Gulf sea waters, strengthened its exchange and communication with navies of other countries in terms of information coordination, waterway allocation and emergency treatment and so on, enhanced mutual trust and understanding including escort fleet of China Navy visiting other countries after finishing its escort task. Actions carried out by China's escort ships when they made supply and trim in Aden Yemen, Salalah, Jeddah, Saudi Arabia, Seychelles, Djibouti and other places enhanced their mutual friendship.

Although China Navy's escort in Aden Gulf and Somali sea waters is a decision made according to a resolution of the Security Council, as invited by the Somali government, after giving reference to practices of other States, to send its warships to Aden Gulf and Somali sea waters to carry out escort and combat piracy, after three years, China nowadays faces the issue of accelerating its pace of improving relevant domestic legal system. Because the international law including resolutions of the

UN Security Council can not be directly applicable in China. It generally needs to be converted into domestic laws or China needs to enact a domestic law that clearly specifies international law may be directly applicable. Therefore, China needs to enact a law repressing piracy or add an article in the Criminal Law on anti-piracy. It is especially necessary to specify the organization entitled to anti-piracy, the offence of piracy and punishment and other issues in relevant domestic laws.

This article was originally published in Page A16 of *Dongfang Daily* on Dec. 27, 2012

Arbitration System not Applicable to Ocean Disputes with China

The United Nations Convention on the Law of the Sea offers a set of detailed and flexible mechanism for marine dispute settlement. It does not only specify means of dispute settlement, but also establish procedures and organizations for dispute settlement, namely the International Tribunal for the Law of the Sea, thus correcting the defect that Four Geneva Conventions on the Law of the Sea failed to specify dispute settlement mechanism but only their auxiliary protocol specify that. That is to say, the Convention successfully sets forth dispute settlement mechanism in Part XV (Settlement of Disputes).

According to relevant articles in the Convention, a State is required to settle a dispute through peaceful means. The Convention respects a State's own choice of peaceful means in dispute settlement set forth in their agreements and endows states with rights to choose means of dispute settlement freely. For example, when signing, ratifying or acceding to this Convention or at any time thereafter, a State shall be free to choose, by means of a written declaration, one or more means for the settlement of disputes concerning the interpretation or application of this Convention, namely the International Tribunal for the Law of the Sea, the International Court of Justice, an arbitral tribunal and a special orbital tribunal. If the parties to a dispute have not accepted the same procedure for the settlement of the dispute, it may be submitted only to arbitration in accordance with Annex VII, unless the parties otherwise agree.

In other words, if relevant parties choose the same means for the settlement of the dispute, it may be submitted to that procedure; If relevant parties do not choose the same means for the settlement of the dispute, it may be submitted to arbitration, but whether arbitration is adopted for the settlement of the dispute depends on the approval of the other party; If one party wants to let the other party adopt a means it choose, the express approval of the other party must be obtained, otherwise the dispute may not be submitted to that means for the settlement.

Regarding the subject starting proceedings, Article 34 and Article 35 of the Statute of the International Court of Justice set forth that only states may be parties in cases before the Court. The Court shall be open to the states parties to the present Statute. It is obvious that the parties in cases before the International Court of Justice are limited to states. In the International Tribunal for the Law of the Sea, there are various subjects starting proceedings. They may be states parties and also entities other than States Parties only meeting certain requirements such as self-governing consortium, non-autonomous region, international organization, International Seabed Authority, the Enterprise, state-owned enterprise, natural person or legal person.

As for jurisdiction of the International Court of Justice, Article 36 of the Statute of the International Court of Justice sets forth that the jurisdiction of the Court comprises all cases which the parties refer to it and all matters specially provided for in the Charter of the United Nations or in treaties and conventions in force. As for governing issues of the International Tribunal for the Law of the Sea, Article 21 of Statute of International Tribunal for the Law of the Sea sets forth that the jurisdiction of the Tribunal comprises all disputes and all applications submitted to it in accordance with this Convention and all matters specifically provided for in any other agreement which confers jurisdiction on the Tribunal. It is clear that as for governing issues, the jurisdiction of the International Court of Justice comprises all cases, while the jurisdiction of the International Tribunal for the Law of the Sea comprises all disputes and all applications, so the jurisdiction of the International Court of Justice is larger than that of International Tribunal for the Law of the Sea.

In addition, a state party to the Convention may accept a compulsory jurisdiction of a court or a tribunal by means of a declaration according to Article 287. Meanwhile, a state party may declare in writing that it does not accept the compulsory jurisdiction of a court or a tribunal of its own choice with respect to one or more of categories of disputes. Such exceptional disputes include those relating to sea boundary delimitation, those involving historic bays or titles, those concerning military activities, and those concerning law enforcement activities in regard to the exercise of sovereign rights or jurisdiction, as well as those in respect of which the Security Council of the United Nations is exercising the functions assigned to it by the Charter of the United Nations. At the same time, a State Party which has made a declaration may at any time withdraw it.

Whereas there are many issues of sea boundary delimitation between China with other state, and China does not want to settle such disputes through international organizations as China holds a consistent stance that any dispute concerning major national interests shall not be settled by a third party, so China submitted a written declaration to the UN Secretary-General on Aug. 25, 2006 according to Article 298 of the Convention that Chinese government does not accept the jurisdiction of any international justice or arbitration tribunal provided for in section 2 of Section XV of the Convention with respect to disputes such as sea boundary delimitation, territorial disputes, military activities. It is evident that any marine dispute with China is not governed by arbitration system and shall be settled through consultation by parties involved.

This article was originally published on Page A14–15
of *Dongfang Daily* on May 13, 2009

Whether Okinotorishima Is An Island or A Rock

Japanese government holds the stance to separately deal with and understand Paragraph 1 and Paragraph 3 of Article 121 of the United Nations Convention on the Law of the Sea which is obviously against the opinion inferred from text interpretation and the original intention to specify Regime of Islands, and seriously contrary to fairness and impairs the freedom of the high seas.

Some countries have been keeping eyes on islands because if a rock or reef can become an island, a country involved may claim the exclusive economic zone and the continental shelf by taking such island as the base point to enlarge its sea waters greatly and thus earn greater marine interests. Therefore, the legal status of a rock or reef, namely, what the conditions are for them to be recognized as an island by the international society, becomes a key issue for a state involved to obtain the corresponding exclusive economic zone and the continental shelf.

The discussion on regime of islands by the international society began at international law codification conference held in Hague in

1930. The report on the high seas pointed out that all islands own their territorial sea. The so-called island in the report refers to a naturally formed area of land, surrounded by water, which is above water continuously at high tide or permanently. No relevant agreement or convention was signed during this conference.

Later, International Law Commission specified the above-mentioned definition of island in Article 10 of the draft regime of islands in preparation for the First UN Conference on the Law of the Sea of 1958 that an island refers to a naturally formed area of land, surrounded by water, which is above water permanently at high tide under normal circumstances. Paragraph 1 of such article sets forth that an island is a naturally formed land, surrounded by water, which is above water at high tide. Paragraph 2 sets forth that the territorial sea of an island is measured according to articles of this Convention. The amendments to regime of islands in the abovementioned articles were made mainly by taking into account of the stance of the USA.

Firstly, the USA held the opinion that an island must be a naturally formed land, but in the abovementioned draft, it includes an artificially formed land. The USA was afraid that states involved would claim the territorial sea on basis of an artificially formed land by illegal means to expand the territorial sea and thus impair the freedom of the high seas. Secondly, the USA believed that "under normal circumstances" and "permanently" in the aforesaid draft were contradicted each other and there were not specific activities, established in national practices, influencing the status of an island due to abnormal or seasonal tide activities, so the USA insisted that such element must be removed.

Meanwhile, the regulation on regime of islands in the Convention on the Territorial Sea and the Contiguous Zone has been absorbed in the regime of islands of the United Nations Convention on the Law of the Sea.

In the UN Ad Hoc Committee established in 1967 (changed to be the Committee on the Peaceful Uses of the Seabed and the Ocean Floor beyond the Limits of National Jurisdiction, a permanent organ in 1968) and the Third UN Conference on the Law of the Sea (from 1982 to 1973), there were also disputes over regime of islands which could be divided into the following two kinds of points of view.

The first one held that islands shall be classified according to a certain standard and each type of islands shall be endowed with different legal status. The reason was that if an island which could not sustain human habitation or economic life enjoyed owned extensive surrounding sea waters such as the exclusive economic zone extending to 200 nautical miles, it would seriously influence the free use of the sea and limit the scope of international seabed area based on Common Heritage of Mankind. Therefore, some states argued that islands and rocks (reefs) shall be distinguished according to various standards such as shape, size, and population.

The second one held that no specific standards shall be applied to islands and all islands shall enjoy the same status. After deliberation and coordination, the result was that they reached a compromise on the definition of the island (Article 121) of the Convention adopted in the Third UN Conference on the Law of the Sea.

Paragraph 1 of Article 121 of the Convention on the regime of islands specifies that an island is a naturally formed area of land, surrounded by water, which is above water at high tide. Paragraph 2 sets forth that except as provided for in paragraph 3, the territorial sea, the contiguous zone, the exclusive economic zone and the continental shelf of an island are determined in accordance with the provisions of this Convention applicable to other land territory. Paragraph 3 reads that rocks which cannot sustain human habitation or economic life of their own shall have no exclusive economic zone or continental shelf.

From the aforesaid text, we can see that the international society indirectly adopted the point of view of the school of the same status but not thoroughly because of the regulation in Paragraph 3 of Article 121 of the Convention.

From the aforesaid regulations, we can see that paragraph 1 to paragraph 3 are about regime of islands, so a rock set forth in Paragraph 3 shall be a type of an island set forth in Paragraph 1, that is to say, Article 121 of the Convention is wholly about regime of islands and rocks in Paragraph 3 are only exceptional islands thus being called rocks, so rocks in Paragraph 3 shall also satisfy the requirements of Paragraph 1.

Of course, there are different opinions on the text interpretation of the aforesaid Article 121 of the Convention. For example, when answering a question about the rock of Okinotorishima on a meeting of Construction Committee of House of Representatives held on Apr. 16, 1999, a representative of Japanese government pointed out that Okinotorishima satisfied the requirements on islands of Paragraph 1 of Article 121 of the Convention, so it was an island not a rock. He pointed out at the same time that paragraph 3 of Article 121 was not a regulation on islands but a regulation on rocks. Furthermore, there was no definition of a rock in the Convention, even from the perspective of national practices, this paragraph could not serve as a foundation that a specific terrain could not own the exclusive economic zone and the continental shelf. Japanese government still holds the aforesaid opinions. It is clear that Japanese government holds the stance to separately deal with and understand Paragraph 1 and Paragraph 3 of Article 121 of the United Nations Convention on the Law of the Sea which is obviously against the opinion inferred from text interpretation and the original intention to specify Regime of Islands, and seriously contrary to fairness and impairs the freedom of the high seas.

Finally, it shall be especially emphasized that although there is no definition of the rock in the Convention, nor relevant national practices establish or form an uniform standard, it can not be denied that Article 121 shall be interpreted on the strict side, otherwise paragraph 3 can not serve as a limitation on paragraph 2, and then there is no meaning to add paragraph 3 in that article.

This article was originally published on Page A13 of *Dongfang Daily* on July 13, 2010

Broadening the Horizon and Developing China's Ocean Undertakings

Recently, China Dayang Yihao (Ocean No. 1) has finished the third global scientific research task after an about 300 days' journey and successfully returned home. So far, China has basically investigated relevant situation of resources in the international sea bed (especially the sea bed areas of the East Pacific, the Southwest Pacific, the Southwest India Ocean) after three times of global voyage (from Apr. 2, 2005 to Jan. 22, 2006, from Jan. 8, 2007 to Aug. 15, 2007 and from May 22, 2008 to Mar. 17, 2009) which play an important role in ensuring that China obtains strategic resources necessary for economic and social development from the international sea bed and maintain the marine interests.

I. Regime of Legal Status and Resources Development of International Sea Bed

Dayang Yihao conducted activities mainly within the scope of the international sea bed (hereinafter referred to as the Area) prescribed in the United Nations Convention on the Law of the Sea. As for the scope of the Area, Article 1 and Article 133 of the Convention specify that the Area means the sea bed and ocean floor and subsoil thereof, beyond the limits of national jurisdiction; resources in the Area means all solid, liquid or gaseous mineral resources in situ in the Area at or beneath the sea bed, including poly-metallic nodules. As for the legal status of the Area, Article 136 of the Convention reads that the Area and its resources are the common heritage of mankind.

The principle of the common heritage of mankind established for the status of the Area in the Convention was a result of fight in the Third UN Conference on the Law of the Sea (from 1973 to 1982) between the developing countries and the developed countries who advocated the principle of res nullius, the principle of property in common, the principle of the freedom of the high seas. The principle of the common heritage of mankind mainly has the following characteristics: firstly, common ownership, namely the international sea bed and its resources belong to the mankind as a whole and serve for the interest of mankind as a whole. Secondly, common management, namely all rights in the resources of the international sea bed are exercised by the International Sea-Bed Authority on behalf of mankind as a whole, which manages the Area for mankind as a whole. Thirdly, joint participation, namely all activities in the international sea bed are open to all states with the aim to let all states improve technology and obtain training opportunities to seek development through fair participation in activities in the Area. Fourthly, common benefits, namely interests from activities in the international sea bed shall be shared by all states and be enjoyed by mankind as a whole.

As for the issue of manner of exploitation of resources in international sea bed, Article 153 of the Convention sets forth the parallel exploitation system which was a product of fight against the single exploitation system, the international registration system and the international license system. The international society has had a complete legal system on exploitation of resources in the international sea bed.

II. Achievements of China in Regime of International Sea Bed

China takes an active part in international marine issues after the General Assembly of the United Nations adopted resolution No. 2758 in 1972 on restoration of China's legitimate seat in the United Nations. Especially in the regime of international sea bed, China consistently supports the work of United Nations Sea-Bed Committee and holds the opinion that the international sea bed shall be used for peaceful purposes and its resources principally are under the common ownership of people of all states and thus shall be managed and exploited by an appropriate international organ established by all states, according to effective international system jointly formulated by all states.

The practices and process of China in regime of international sea bed are mainly divided into three phases.

The first one is the preparatory phase (from 1978 to 1990). China's ocean undertaking (deep sea undertaking) began in 1978. In April, 1978, the research ship Xiangyanghong No. 5 obtained poly-metallic nodules from the geological sample at the depth of 4784 meters in the sea in the course of its comprehensive investigation in specific sea areas of Pacific. In 1981, Chinese government declared that China had possessed the qualification as a pioneer investor in international sea bed. According to a document approved by the State Council in 1984, namely, Direction on Strengthening the Work of Resources Investigation of Manganese Nodule in the Ocean, China promoted the exploration of resources in the international sea bed. In 1990, China Ocean Mineral Resources R & D Association (hereinafter referred to as China Ocean Association) was established with approval of the State Council. It is the management organ exclusively dealing with the resources in the international sea bed.

The second one is the harvesting phase (from 1991 to 1999). China submitted an application to the President of Preparatory Committee (international sea bed) on Aug. 21, 1990, namely the application as a pioneer investor on behalf of China Ocean Association according to Resolution No. 2 of the Convention. After deliberation, the Preparatory Committee decided to approve the application of China to explore poly-metallic nodules mining area in the sea bed of Northeast Pacific on Mar. 5, 1991 and allocate the applicant pioneer area of 150000 square kilometer.

The third one is the improving phase (from 2000 to 2008). On

May 22, 2001, the Secretary-General of China Ocean Association and the Secretary-General of International Seabed Authority signed an Exploration Contract in Beijing, which marked China's exclusive right of exploring poly-metallic nodules in mining area of 75000 square meters and preferential right of business mining of poly-metallic nodules in such area. In terms of capacity construction, in 2002, China had completed modernization of a scientific research ship Dayang Yihao (Ocean No. 1). The scientific research ship after modification can fulfill tasks of investigation and experiment of terrain, gravity and magnetic force, geology and tectonics, comprehensive marine environment, marine engineering and deep sea technology. In terms of international affairs and status, China was re-elected as a member of Team B of the Council in 2000 and elected as a member of Team A of the Council.

III. Challenges and Tasks Faced by China in Exploring Resources of International Sea Bed

Firstly, domestic research into co-rich crust and hydrothermal sulfide shall be reasonably arranged. China shall put forward its own proposition and have a reasonable arrangement to strengthen research by taking advantage of the existing research results and investigation achievements of previous voyages, after taking into account special features of the aforesaid resources, mining system, requirements of business mining reserves, demand in international metal market, level of difficulty in exploitation technology and other factors.

Secondly, efforts to make breakthrough in deep sea mining technology shall be enhanced. The ultimate objective of regime of international sea bed is to carry out business exploitation of resources in the Area and the deep sea mining technology is a key factor of realizing exploitation. When ensuring the possession volume of deep sea resources, China shall consider and research deep sea technology including establishing deep sea technology development objective, setting up deep sea technology system, reserving key deep sea technology, and conduct international cooperation in core fields to realize China's leapfrog development of deep sea technology.

Thirdly, efforts to strengthen scientific research into deep sea shall be continued. China shall utilize the ocean investigation capacity accumulated for a long time by China Ocean Association, coordinate personnel resources cooperate with domestic units with advantage to strengthen marine scientific research in the Area and establish database and thus improve China's status in deep sea scientific research.

Fourthly, investigation of and research into global sea bed metal market shall be strenghtened. China shall enhance investigation of and research into global sea bed metal market and formulate reasonable relevant industrial policies and provide opinions and suggestion on formulation of relevant resources exploitation rules and regulations for the International Seabed Authority.

Fifthly, capital investment on research into regime of international sea bed shall be increased. It needs a huge sum of money to carry out exploration and exploitation of resources in the international sea bed, there for China shall enlarge the scope of investors and mode of cooperation including utilizing non-governmental capital, joint venture, sole investment and formulate relevant policies and measures such as preferential policies on financing and taxes.

Sixthly, formulation of domestic regulations on exploration shall be reasonably planned. China may formulate domestic regulations on mining poly-metallic nodules in the international sea bed, according to requirements of Regulations on Prospecting and Exploration for Polymetallic Nodules in the Area formulated by the International Seabed Authority in July 2000, to offer legal guaranty for Chinese enterprises to exploit such resources.

This article was originally published in Page 10 of *Wenhui Daily* on Mar. 23, 2009

Basic Characteristics of the United Nations Convention on the Law of the Sea

Adopted in 1982 and brought into force in 1994, the United Nations Convention on the Law of the Sea comprises 320 articles in the main text and 9 annexes and is called the Charter of the Sea due to its abundance and concreteness. The Convention has become a treaty comprehensively regulating marine issues in the international society and is generally binding upon all reads.

The Convention mainly has the following six basic characteristics:

Firstly, the farthest extent of the breadth of the territorial sea is established. Article 3 of the Convention reads that every State has the right to establish the breadth of its territorial sea up to a limit not exceeding 12 nautical miles, measured from baselines determined in accordance with this Convention. That is to say, a state may determine its territorial sea to the farthest limit of 12 nautical miles.

Secondly, the scope of sea waters is specified according to different status of waters. the Convention divides the sea waters into internal waters, the territorial sea, the contiguous zone, archipelagic waters, the exclusive economic zone, continental shelf, high seas and international sea bed, etc. Different sea waters enjoy different legal status and the coastal states' jurisdictions over them are different. In short, the farther the sea waters is away from the baseline of the territorial sea of the land, the weaker or less jurisdiction the state enjoys.

Thirdly, the standard or scope of regime of the continental shelf is amended and regime of outer limit of the continental shelf is created. Article 1 of Convention on the Continental Shelf (1958) specifies that the continental shelf refers to the seabed and subsoil of the submarine areas adjacent to the coast but outside the area of the territorial sea, to a depth of 200 meters or, beyond that limit, to where the depth of the superjacent waters admits of the exploitation of the natural resources of the said areas. This is the so-called standard of a depth of 200 meters or admission of exploitation. Therefore, Paragraph 1 of Article 76 sets forth that the continental shelf of a coastal State comprises the seabed and subsoil of the submarine areas that extend beyond its territorial sea throughout the natural prolongation of its land territory to the outer edge of the continental margin, or to a distance of 200 nautical miles from the baselines from which the breadth of the territorial sea is measured where the outer edge of the continental margin does not extend up to that distance. It is clear that the Convention adopts the standard of natural prolongation or a distance of 200 nautical miles for determining the scope of the continental shelf, thus greatly expands the jurisdiction of the coastal states over the continental shelf.

Meanwhile, in order to limit the scope of the continental shelf of the coastal states in regime of the continental shelf, the Convention gives conditional regulations on the scope of the continental shelf, namely regime of outer limit of the continental shelf which refers to rules and procedures with which a state shall comply when determining its outer limit of the continental shelf. The limitations of outer limit of the continental shelf of the coastal shelf are mainly reflected in the following aspects: the first one is the limitation on the distance of the limit; the second one is the limitation on the procedure for determining the limit; the third one is the limitation on exploitation of non-living resources. The Convention has the above-mentioned regulations with a main aim to let the International Sea-bed Authority on behalf of mankind as a whole fairly allocate interests from exploitation of non-living resources on the continental shelf beyond 200 nautical miles to realize the principle of truly fair sharing of interests and seek benefits for mankind as a whole.

Fourthly, regime of international sea bed is established and a special organ is set up. The Convention establishes the regime of international sea bed based on Common Heritage of Mankind (hereafter referred to as the Area System). For example, Article 136 stipulates that the Area and its resources are the common heritage of mankind. The so-called Area, according to Item (a) of Paragraph 1 of Article 1 of the Convention, means the seabed and ocean floor and subsoil thereof, beyond the limits of national jurisdiction; while the so-called resources, according to Paragraph 1 of Article 133 of the Convention, means all solid, liquid or gaseous mineral resources in situ in the Area at or beneath the seabed, including poly-metallic nodules.

Of course, the principle of the common heritage of mankind established for the status of the Area in the Convention was a product of fight against the principle of res nullius, the principle of property in common, the principle of the freedom of the high seas and a result of extensive unity and cooperation of the third world especially the group of 77 in the Third UN Conference on the Law of the Sea.

In addition, it should be pointed out that the Convention sets up an organ to manage activities in the Area — the International Seabed Authority (hereinafter referred to as the Authority). For example, Paragraph 1 of Article 157, The Authority is the organization through which States Parties shall, in accordance with this Part, organize and control activities in the Area, particularly with a view to administering the resources of the Area. Meanwhile, the Convention sets forth the parallel exploitation system which was a product of fight against the single exploitation system, the international registration system and the international license system. The so-called parallel exploitation system means that, according to Paragraph 2 of Article 153 of the Convention, Activities in the Area shall be carried out by the Enterprise, and in association with the Authority by States Parties, or state enterprises or natural or juridical persons which possess the nationality of States Parties or are effectively controlled by them or their nationals, when sponsored by such States, or any group of the foregoing which meets the requirements provided in this Part and in Annex III.

Fifthly, dispute settlement system is created and the International Tribunal for the Law of the Sea is established. The United Nations Convention on the Law of the Sea offers a set of detailed and flexible mechanism for marine dispute settlement. It does not only specify means of dispute settlement, but also establish procedures and organizations for dispute settlement, namely the International Tribunal for the Law of the Sea, thus correcting the defect that Four Geneva Conventions on the Law of the Sea of 1958 failed to specify dispute settlement mechanism but only their auxiliary protocol specify that. That is to say, the Convention successfully sets forth dispute settlement mechanism in Part XV (Settlement of Disputes). According to relevant articles in the Convention, a State is required to settle a dispute through peaceful means. The Convention respects a State's own choice of peaceful means in dispute settlement set forth in their agreements and endows states with rights to choose means of dispute settlement freely. For example, when signing, ratifying or acceding to this Convention or at any time thereafter, a State shall be free to choose, by means of a written declaration, one or more means for the settlement of disputes concerning the interpretation or application of this Convention, namely the International Tribunal for the Law of the Sea, the International Court of Justice, an arbitral tribunal and a special orbital tribunal. If the parties to a dispute have not accepted the same procedure for the settlement of the dispute, it may be submitted only to arbitration in accordance with Annex VII, unless the parties otherwise agree. In other words, if relevant parties choose the same means for the settlement of the dispute, it may be submitted to that procedure; If relevant parties do not choose the same means for the settlement of the dispute, it may be submitted to arbitration, but whether arbitration is adopted for the settlement of the dispute depends on the approval of the other party; If one party wants to let the other party adopt a means it choose, the express approval of the other party must be obtained, otherwise the dispute may not be submitted to that means for the settlement.

Of course, the Convention does not only have the above-mentioned characteristics, but also have some flaws, for example, unclear ownership over the remaining rights in the exclusive economic zone, too vague regime of islands, lacking operability of the principle of delimitation of the exclusive economic zone and the continental shelf, so it needs amendment and improvement, but it still remains a code comprehensively regulating marine issues and all states must comply.

This article was originally published on Page 4
of *China Ocean News* on Aug. 29, 2012

East China Sea Reviews

Path Chosen by China to Promote Development in East China Sea

On Jan. 17, 2010, Japanese Foreign Minister Katsuya Okada, when meeting Chinese Foreign Minister Yang Jiechi pointed out that if China decided to carry out production in Chunxiao oil and gas field, Japanese government would regard it as a breach of an agreement on joint exploitation between both parties and take necessary measures. On Feb. 21, 2010, *Mainichi Shimbun of Japan* reported that if China conducted independent exploitation of oil and gas field in the East China Sea, Japan would submit this case to the International Tribunal of the Law of the Sea, which thus clarified the content of the so-called Necessary Measures emphasized by Japan.

However, according to Sino-Japanese Principled Consensus on the East China Sea Issues (hereinafter referred to as Principled Consensus), Japan may invest capital to participate in cooperative exploitation according to relevant laws of China, which is essentially different from Joint Exploitation.

After the emergence in the East China Sea was broke out in

May 2004, China and Japan are still unable to reach a compromise on delimitation in East China Sea, especially they have serious disagreement over the principles and methods applicable to delimitation of sea waters, sovereignty and its function of Diaoyu Islands. In order to build East China Sea as the sea of peace, cooperation and friendship, China and Japan, through careful consultation, unanimously agreed on cooperation during transitional period before delimitation without prejudice to legal stances of both sides, therefore, ministries of foreign affairs of both states promulgated the Principled Consensus on June 18, 2008.

In the document of Principled Consensus as a kind of political wish in nature, there are mainly two aspects of its content:

The first one is Sino-Japanese understanding on joint exploitation in East China Sea. The joint exploitation area is comprised of seven coordinates and occupies 2700 square kilometers. The requirement on the aforesaid joint exploitation area is that both parties shall choose a site with unanimous consent of both parties to carry out joint exploitation after joint exploration and on basis of the principle of mutual benefits. The premise is that both parties shall make efforts to respectively fulfill domestic procedures for implementing the aforesaid exploitation and reach a necessary bilateral agreement as soon as possible.

The second one is the understanding on Japanese legal person's participation in exploitation of Chunxiao oil and gas field in accordance with laws of China, namely Chinese enterprises are pleased that Japanese legal persons take part in exploitation of Chunxiao oil and gas field according to laws of China on foreign cooperation in exploitation of offshore petroleum resources. In other words, the exploitation activity of Chunxiao oil and gas field in Principled Consensus is a kind of cooperative exploitation with sovereignty belonging to China. Meanwhile, the aforesaid two aspects may be separately conducted without necessity to promote them together.

We can also learn from the aforesaid two aspects that there are both joint exploitation and cooperative exploitation in the Principled Consensus. The exploitation of Chuanxiao oil and gas field is a kind of cooperative exploitation. If a Japanese legal person does not apply for cooperative exploitation to a Chinese enterprise, the exploitation activity of Chuanxiao oil and gas field conducted by China may be continued. Therefore, Japanese foreign minister's remarks on this have no legal basis.

The key difference between the joint exploitation and the cooperative exploitation is whether there is dispute over sovereignty. The joint exploitation in traditional sense means one conducted on mineral deposit of disputed sea area and resources joining the mineral deposit near the sea boundary. However, the aforesaid joint exploitation area in designated areas is neither a disputed sea area nor an area joining the mineral deposit near the sea boundary, so the legal status of the joint exploitation area designated in the Principled Consensus is unclear.

The author considers that, in order to realize the political wish reached by heads of both states, China shall effectively promote the implementation of the Principled Consensus to change opponents' negative attitudes towards the Principled Consensus. Therefore, as for the issue of the Principled Consensus, the following aspects shall be noted:

Firstly, both states shall pave the way and cultivate a good environment suitable for promoting the implementation of the Principled Consensus. Especially the media shall accurately and comprehensively report relevant news and information to let nationals understand the necessity and importance of implementing the Principled Consensus in China and Japan.

Secondly, systems regulated in the Principled Consensus shall be observed earnestly. Although the Principled Consensus is a document without legal effect, both states must comply with and enforce it to increase mutual trust.

Thirdly, negotiation on implementing the Principled Consensus shall be actively carried out. This may be conducted through dual channels, i.e. the government channel and the non-government channel, including taking scholars' opinions and advice to formulate a specific plan of joint exploitation acceptable for both parties.

Fourthly, relevant domestic laws and bilateral systems shall be improved. In order to carry out joint exploitation in designated area of the Principled Consensus, which kind of laws or which state's laws are applicable need to be specified, therefore, China shall formulate a law like Law of Japan on Establishing Safe Waters for Marine Structures and make it apply to regime of joint exploitation in East China Sea. Meanwhile, in order to avoid a conflict in East China Sea between two sides, it is advised to implement and improve marine hotline contact mechanism to avoid unnecessary conflicts and accidents.

This article was originally published on Page 17
of *Dongfang Daily* on Feb. 25, 2010

Japan Must Honor Law of Sea

The 14 Chinese fishermen and their trawler, detained off Ishigaki harbor in Okinawa after a collision with Japan Coast Guard ships on Sept. 7, set off for home yesterday morning. But the Japanese authorities are still holding the Chinese captain of the trawler, Zhan Qixiong for allegedly "obstructing public duties". A Japanese court ruled on Friday that Zhan be detained for 10 days until Sept. 19.

The collision between the Chinese trawler and two Japan Coast Guard patrol vessels off the Diaoyu Islands in the East China Sea last Tuesday has developed into a diplomatic crisis between China and Japan. China has repeatedly demanded the release of the captain and its crew.

On Sunday morning, Japan Coast Guards towed the Chinese trawler into the sea near Ishigaki Island in Okinawa Prefecture to reenact the collision.

China is firmly opposed to any kind of investigation by Japanese authorities of the illegally-detained Chinese fishing trawler, Foreign Ministry Spokeswoman Jiang Yu said on Sunday. In a written statement,

Jiang said Japan's so-called evidence-collecting activities are illegal, invalid and conducted in vain, and China demands Japan stop activities that could escalate the situation.

On Sunday, Chinese State Councilor Dai Bingguo told Japanese ambassador to China Uichiro Niwa to make a "wise political resolution" and immediately release the Chinese fishermen and fishing boat.

On Friday, Foreign Minister Yang Jiechi had summoned Niwa and demanded Japan unconditionally release the boat and the crew, saying China's determination to defend its sovereignty over the Diaoyu Islands and the interests of the Chinese people was unswerving.

The Chinese government has sent a fishery law enforcement ship to the area, too, to safeguard Chinese fishermen and their assets.

Japan infringed upon China's sovereignty and territory integrity when Japanese patrol ships chased the Chinese fishing trawler and boarded it forcibly. But the Japanese Coast Guard did not stop at that. It even applied Japanese law in the waters off the Diaoyu Islands, which since ancient times have been Chinese territory. Japan had no right to press charges against the Chinese fishermen according to its domestic laws.

To strengthen its presence around the Diaoyu Islands, the Japanese Coast Guard has been sending patrol ships for some time now and has repeatedly chased Chinese fishing and survey vessels. But such action cannot alter the fact that Diaoyu Islands belong to China. And history vouches for that.

First, the Diaoyu Islands were named first by China. Names such as Diaoyu Island, and Chiweiyu and Huangweiyu islets have appeared in official Chinese documents since the Ming Dynasty (1368–1644). Even when the United States controlled these islands, their names did not change.

Second, the Diaoyu Islands have always been within the maritime defense boundary of China. Books written during the Ming Dynasty such as *Chou Hai Tu Bian* (Collection of Maritime Defense Charts) — edited by Hu Zongxian (1512–1565), then Defense Minister — *Wu Bei Zhi* (Record of Armed Forces) — edited by military scholar Mao Yuanyi (1594–1640) and *Wu Bei Mi Shu* (Secret Record of Armed Forces) — edited by another scholar Shi Yongtu in the later part of Ming Dynasty — clearly state that Diaoyu Islands are within China's maritime defense boundary.

Fu Sheng Liu Ji (Six Chapters of a Floating Life), a famous book written by Shen Fu during the Qing Dynasty (1644–1911), has records showing the Diaoyu Islands are part of Chinese territory. The book says Qing Emperor Jiaqing (1760–1820) granted a title to the ruler of Ryukyu Kingdom with detailed descriptions, which show the territory of Ryukyu Kingdom started from Gumi Mountain (renamed Kumejima after Japan annexed Ryukyu).

Third, during the Ming and Qing dynasties, every ruler of the Ryukyu Kingdom would accept missionaries from China who granted them titles. The documents clearly say the border separating China and the Ryukyu Kingdom was between Chiweiyu and Kumejima Island. In 1701, Cai Duo, an envoy from Ryukyu Kingdom, presented a book *Zhong Shan Shi Pu* to Qing Emperor Kangxi (1654–1722), which said the kingdom comprised 36 islands, not including Diaoyu Islands.

Last but not less important, Empress Dowager Cixi (1835–1908) issued an order in 1893, gifting the Diaoyu Island, and the Huangweiyu and Chiweiyu islets to an official, Sheng Xuanhuai. The document is still well preserved.

The Japanese cabinet decided to include Diaoyu Islands in its territory exactly on Jan 14, 1895, that is during the Sino-Japanese war (1894–1895), claiming them to be terra nullius (land belonging to no one). That step was audacious.

After World War II, according to the Cairo Declaration (1943) and the Potsdam Proclamation (1945), the Chinese government resumed its sovereignty over the Diaoyu Islands. But then the islands were "entrusted" to the US according to the San Francisco Peace Treaty (1951) between Japan and the US, and were "returned" to Japan in 1971. To put it simply, the San Francisco Peace Treaty is illegal, for it deals with the territory of a third party.

How could the US and Japan make a decision on Chinese territory? Besides, the US only granted Japan management over the Diaoyu Islands, not sovereignty.

The dispute has to be settled between China and Japan. But the Japanese government has always refused to sit at negotiations. The dispute over the Diaoyu Islands is one of the most pressing problems between China and Japan. It is impossible for China to ignore it. And only through negotiations and joint development can the two countries settle it amicably.

The Chinese government has taken the right path by sending a fishery law enforcement ship to patrol the waters off the Diaoyu Islands. It is up to the Japanese government to see reason, accept historical facts and prevent the incident from snowballing into a bigger dispute.

China hopes Japan would take the right decision by releasing the captain of the fishing trawler, apologizing for its action and giving fishermen proper compensation. Japan should ensure that such incidents are not repeated, for it is important for Sino-Japanese relations to develop healthily. And it is important that China use diplomatic channels to put pressure on Japan, and send fishing law enforcement ships, if needed, to safeguard Chinese fishermen.

This article was originally published on Page 9
of *China Daily* on Sept. 14, 2010

Keeping Calm at Sea Essential

China is facing a slew of maritime problems, and may continue to do so in the near future. In the South China Sea, it has disputes over maritime boundaries with several member states of the Association of Southeast Asian Nations (ASEAN). It also has different understandings and disputes over the free use of marine resources in the South China Sea's exclusive economic zone with some countries.

In the East China Sea, it faces resource development problems, demarcation disputes and conflicts over maritime safety with Japan.

In the high seas, it has to deal with marine safety issues such as piracy, environmental pollution caused by natural and man-made disasters, and problems caused by the setting of the outer continental shelf (OCS), which affect its national interests.

These issues have the potential to influence China's maritime, even national, security greatly. Therefore, it has to handle them with utmost care.

These issues have cropped up for three reasons. First, since surveys and delimitation of land boundaries between China and its neighboring countries are mostly done, maritime disputes have replaced land disputes.

Second, globalization means China has to develop and use the seas and marine resources with increasing frequency. That apart, the number of maritime interests that China needs to protect is growing, which in turn is giving rise to more disputes.

Third, China is a relatively disadvantaged country in terms of oceanography, because of which it has disputes with other countries over sea boundaries and island ownership.

But China's continuing reform and opening-up policy is expected to hasten its economic development further and help it secure its maritime boundaries to protect its sovereignty and national integrity. But this, to some extent, may cause misunderstandings among other countries about China's intentions and create further disputes.

To settle the disputes in the East China Sea, China should continue its talks with Japan, because an agreement on the delimitation of the sea would be the best solution for both countries.

The talks should focus on the dispute over the Diaoyu Islands and their adjacent islets and the corresponding institutional arrangement. China should emphasize its indisputable sovereignty over the Diaoyu Islands, make efforts to weaken Japan's control and management over the region and then seek joint exploitation of resources in and around the area.

As for resource development in the East China Sea, if Tokyo does not reach a compromise on the Diaoyu Islands, Beijing could set a relatively high bar for joint development in the Chunxiao fields.

To end the disputes over island ownership and demarcation of maritime boundaries with ASEAN member states, China needs to negotiate with the contenders under the principle and spirit of the Declaration on the Conduct of Parties in the South China Sea. The declaration says all parties should initiate friendly dialogue, promote the settlement of territorial and jurisdiction disputes through peaceful means and oppose the threat or use of force.

In addition, the parties involved have to exercise restraint by not making the dispute more complicated or let it harm regional peace and stability. They should build mutual trust, make efforts to discuss and promote cooperation, and hold dialogues to settle the disputes peacefully.

Generally speaking, the above propositions and principles do not comply with only the objectives of the Charter of the United Nations, the United Nations Convention on the Law of the Sea and other international laws, but also the current international developmental trends.

It is important to settle disputes through dialogues on the basis of equality and cooperation. For example, the countries with interests in the South China Sea could freeze their disputes to prevent them from deteriorating further.

On the disputes over freedom of navigation in the South China Sea's exclusive economic zone, China should reach an understanding with other countries through dialogue. China should declare that it welcomes the United States to continue playing an active role in the Asia-Pacific region as long as Washington does not impede upon the region's interests.

When it comes to sea-lane security on the high seas, China will continue playing an active role, especially in combating piracy in the Gulf of Aden and Somali waters.

It can replicate this action in other waters to fulfill its international commitments.

China will play its due role to deal with natural and manmade disasters in seas and oceans by participating in regional and international efforts. Its purpose is to protect not only its own interests, but also that of the international community.

As for the problems caused by the setting of the OCS, China should continue to pay close attention to the review process of the Commission on the Limits of the Continental Shelf. It must focus mainly on the potential influence of the review and further strengthen the exploration of its continental shelf in the East China Sea and South China Sea, propose its OCS demarcation as soon as possible and consider cooperating on the exploration of the continental shelf.

China should work out different solutions to the different marine problems it faces according to some principles and measures.

First, China should insist on peaceful settlement of disputes over island ownership and demarcation of waters.

Second, it must discuss new patterns for joint exploitation for resources and new mechanisms on maritime safety maintenance with the disputing parties.

Third, along with developing its sea power, it should strengthen mutual trust and understanding through exchanges and dialogues with other countries to avoid misunderstanding and miscalculation.

Fourth, it has to selectively participate in international marine affairs to enhance understanding and fulfill its due obligations.

And fifth, it should actively promote its stance on marine issues through websites and by hosting international symposiums to help other countries better understand its maritime policies.

Moreover, China has to study the law of the sea to better prepare for possible revision and to establish a framework and system for cooperation with other countries to protect its maritime rights and interests.

This article was originally published on Page 9
of *China Daily* on Oct. 12, 2010

China Shall Make Japan Admit a Dispute on Ownership over Diaoyu Islands

If Japan admits there is a dispute over Diaoyu Islands, Chinese government may request Japan to get rid of illegal guarding system in sea waters surrounding Diaoyu Islands and pave way for implementing the principle of Setting Aside Disputes and Joint Exploitation to realize the objective of sharing resources.

At the beginning of 2012, four congressmen of Kinawa, Ishigaki of Japan, ignoring the warning of Japan Coast Guard, illegally landed on Diaoyu Island which is an inherent territory of China. Although this island landing behavior was treated reasonably by Japanese government from the perspective of the whole situation, Sino-Japanese relations remained unchanged, marine factors being able to influence Sino-Japanese relations will continuously emerge or burst out, therefore China and Japan shall conduct practical negotiation on marine issues to seek specific solutions.

When China and Japan utilize high-level marine issue consultation mechanism to negotiate about marine issues including East China Sea issues, it is certainly impossible to avoid the meaning of East China Sea. Although both states do not clarify the meaning of East China Sea, it is generally believed that East China Sea issues include a dispute over island ownership, a dispute over delimitation of sea waters, a dispute over resources exploitation and conflicts of law enforcement in the sea. The core issue is the dispute over island ownership, namely the dispute over Diaoyu Islands.

Although China and Japan had launched the first round of Sino-Japanese negotiation on delimitation in the East China Sea since Aug. 1998, such negotiation was terminated after the eighth round in Dec. 2003 due to obstacles established by Japan for China's exploitation of Chunxiao oil and gas field in Aug. 2003. After the outburst of East China Sea issues in May 2004, China and Japan held the eleventh negotiation on East China Sea issues which was in a state of deadlock due to serious opposition and disagreement of both parties on sovereignty of disputed islands, principles and methods of delimitation of sea waters. Later, after several negotiations in private, especially for realizing the political wish of heads of both governments of making East China Sea the sea of peace, friendship and cooperation, ministries of foreign affairs of both states respectively promulgated Sino-Japanese Principled Consensus on the East China Sea Issues (hereinafter referred to as Principled Consensus) on June 18, 2008.

In other words, both states have obtained stepwise achievements regarding disputes over East China Sea. However, due to failure to reach an agreement by both states on essential issues (disputed islands, principle of delimitation, etc.), there are still disagreements and opposition. That is to say, in regard to East China Sea issues, Japan adopts a divide-and-conquer tactic, namely denying the existence of disputed islands, setting aside disputes over delimitation and trying its best to obtain substantive interests in resources exploitation.

If China and Japan can not reach an agreement through negotiation with exchange of notes between governments, China may propose to continue to negotiate for delimitation in East China Sea, namely resume the negotiation process for delimitation in East China Sea. In fact, the resumption of negotiation process for delimitation in East China Sea by China and Japan is in compliance with the content and principle of the Principled Consensus because it specifies that both parties unanimously agree on cooperation during transitional period before delimitation without prejudice to legal stances of both parties and agree to carry forward negotiation in the future. In other words, the Principled Consensus sets aside the dispute over the delimitation in the East China Sea but does not close the door for both parties to carry out negotiation. It must be pointed out that because the delimitation in the East China Sea is very complicated which concerns not only sovereignty over islands, the principle and method of delimitation, but also the relationship between the exclusive economic zone and the Continental Shelf, the agreement will generally not be reached soon if neither party makes suitable concession or compromise. It is predictable that negotiation on delimitation in the East China Sea still features the characteristics of lasting long and being hard.

If China and Japan make breakthrough to achieve a substantial result, namely both states reach an agreement on joint exploitation and cooperative cooperation through governmental negotiation with exchange of notes, it is a very good conduct to obtain resources in the East China Sea through agreement which is also a great present for the 40th anniversary of normalization of diplomatic relation between China and Japan. However, Chinese government must insist on its stance that the agreement on resources exploitation shall specify the legal status of Diaoyu Islands. If Japan continues to deny such dispute, it is very difficult to reach an exploitation agreement on resources exploitation.

Unfortunately, Japan has denied the existence of a dispute over Diaoyu Islands for a long time during the process of consultation or negotiation on marine issues between China and Japan, resulting in no progress in such consultation or negotiation. Then, is there a dispute over Diaoyu Islands? Although both states claim that Diaoyu Island is an inherent territory of their own state, an inherent territory is not a term of international law or a legal term, but a political term. In reality, whether there is a dispute between states needs to be studied from the perspective of international law. It can be learned from the judgment of the Mavrommatis Palestine Concessions awarded by the Permanent Court of International Justice that the so-called dispute is a disagreement on a point of law or fact, a conflict of legal views or of interests between two persons (or states). From the content of this judgment and stances of China and Japan on Diaoyu Islands, we can learn that there is a dispute on Diaoyu Islands between China and Japan. Meanwhile, it is well known that there is a dispute over Takeshima (Dokdo) between Japan and South Korea. Comparing it with the issue of Diaoyu Islands, Japan's status in Takeshima is the same as that of China in Diaoyu Islands. Ministry of Foreign Affairs of Japan holds the following stances on Takeshima: (1) in reference to historical facts and international law, Takeshima is obviously an inherent territory of Japan. (2) South Korea's occupation of Takeshima is illegal and baseless in international law, so any measure taken for Takeshima by South Korea on basis such illegal occupation is illegitimate. In addition, before Japan effectively controls Takeshima and establishes its sovereignty, South Korea failed to present specific evidences to prove factual control over Takeshima. Therefore, Chinese government may take the same attitude towards Japan as that of Japan towards South Korea. This is so called paying somebody back in his own coin. Thus Japan can not deny the existence of a dispute over Diaoyu Islands between China and Japan, otherwise, it constitutes a denial of a dispute over Takeshima between Japan and South Korea.

If Japan recognizes such a dispute over Diaoyu Islands, Chinese government may request Japan to get rid of illegal guarding system in sea waters surrounding Diaoyu Islands and pave way for implementing the principle of Setting Aside Disputes and Joint Exploitation to realize the objective of sharing resources. Thus, it is to be expected that Sino-

Japanese relation will definitely go into a new development phase and Sino-Japanese strategic relation with mutual benefits will be greatly enhanced and developed.

This article was originally published on Page A19 of *Dongfang Daily* on Jan. 19, 2012

China to Make Detailed Preparation for Negotiation on the Sea with Japan

There arise disputes over marine issues between China and Japan again. Both states shall utilize existing mechanisms and platforms including restarting negotiation on delimitation in East China Sea to appropriately handle disputes over marine issues between both states through equal dialogue and on basis of historical facts and laws.

However, if China and Japan restart negotiation on delimitation in the East China Sea, the following issues will be inevitably unavoidable, so we must deliberate them and make sufficient preparation.

The first thing is how to regard the relationship between the Sino-Japanese negotiation on delimitation in the East China Sea and the Sino-Japanese governmental negotiation with exchange of notes on Sino-Japanese Principled Consensus on the East China Sea Issues. The latter negotiation was ceased due to the incident that Japan Coast Guard illegally seized Chinese fishing boats and fishermen in waters adjacent to Diaoyu Island and its affiliated islands (hereinafter referred to as Diaoyu Islands) and has not been resumed so far. Under the circumstance of no progress in consultation which Japanese government requested to conduct with Chinese government on negotiation with exchange of notes, if Chinese government proposes resumption of negotiation on delimitation in the East China Sea, then Japanese government puts forward the issue that how Chinese government deals with governmental negotiation with exchange of notes, How should Chinese government respond? For this, Chinese government is in a situation that it must answer the question and give specific reasons and it can not repeat answers or reasons given before (such as different opinions in China, opposition existed or not good timing and so on). In addition, China shall also answer the question whether the negotiation on delimitation in the East China Sea is only limited to delimitation in the East China Sea or includes issues relating to disputes of sovereignty over Diaoyu Islands. Therefore, Chinese government needs to be well prepared for the aforesaid questions and has a clear attitude with sufficient preparation for these set topics.

The second thing is the necessity of starting the Sino-Japanese governmental negotiation by means of exchange of notes on Sino-Japanese Principled Consensus on the East China Sea Issues. Both China and Japan's efforts are made to conclude a bilateral agreement on joint exploitation as soon as possible and go through necessary domestic formalities for concluding agreement on Chunxiao oil and gas field. Therefore, in order to realize such objective, both parties are obliged to conduct consultation on governmental negotiation with exchange of notes.

The third thing is how to give consideration to Chinese enterprises' interests in exploitation of Chunxiao oil and gas field. Because both parties have opposite and different understanding on the Principled Consensus, even both parties continue to hold governmental negotiation with exchange of notes, it is very difficult to achieve substantive results on both cooperative exploitation and joint exploitation. If it is unable to carry forward the cooperative exploitation and joint exploitation at the same time, how will Chinese enterprises' interests in exploitation of Chunxiao oil and gas field, namely, the predictable losses of interests of the enterprise, losses of investment caused by the aging of equipment be protected and how will their damage be recovered? Therefore, may Chinese government request to include auxiliary conditions in negotiation with exchange of notes, namely, if both parties reach a consensus on cooperative exploitation or joint exploitation after negotiation and consultation for a period of time, they may include auxiliary conditions in such an agreement including that both parties agree to reach a consensus on joint exploitation or cooperation exploitation during the prescribed period as soon as possible and Chinese enterprises enjoy priority in exploiting resources in the agreed sea area.

Another tentative plan is that if both parties fail to reach an agreement through negotiation with exchange of notes, China may propose to continue the consultation on delimitation in the East China Sea, namely restart a negotiation on delimitation in the East China Sea. In fact, the resumption of a negotiation on delimitation in the East China Sea between China and Japan is in compliance with the content and sprit of the Principled Consensus. Because the delimitation in the East China Sea is very complicated which concerns a lot of issues, the agreement will generally not be reached soon if neither party makes suitable concession or compromise. It is predictable that negotiation on delimitation in the East China Sea still features the characteristics of lasting long and being hard.

If both states reach an agreement on joint exploitation and cooperative cooperation through governmental negotiation with exchange of notes, it is a very good conduct to obtain resources in the East China Sea through agreement which is also a great present for the 40th anniversary of normalization of diplomatic relation between China and Japan. However, Chinese government must insist on its stance that the agreement on resources exploitation shall specify the legal status of Diaoyu Islands. If Japan continues to deny such dispute, it is very difficult to reach an exploitation agreement on resources exploitation.

This article was originally published on Page A15
of *Dongfang Daily* on Feb. 9, 2012

China Shall Strengthen Comprehensive Management of Diaoyu Island and Its Affiliated Islands

Diaoyu Island and its affiliated islands have been China's inherent territory since ancient times, which may be proved in all historical, geographical and legal terms, and China enjoys sovereignty over Diaoyu Islands.

Firstly, the earliest record of the discovery, naming and use of Diaoyu Island and its affiliated islands can be found in the book *Voyage with a Tail Wind* wrote by envoys sent by the imperial court to oriental and western countries in the first year of Yongle of Ming Dynasty (1403). Imperial envoys of Ming and Qing Dynasties went to Diaoyu Islands for many times in order to survey shipping line and adjust needle mark and they regarded these islands as shipping marks leading to Ryukyu. This constitutes a kind of Inchoate Title in the international law.

Secondly, the boundary between the kingdom of the Ryukyu and China has been determined clearly since Ming Dynasty. As for the boundary, from the perspective of China, it is Chiwei Yu; from the perspective of Ryukyu, it is Gumi Mountain (Kume Island). The separating line of the sea waters between China and the kingdom of Ryukyu lies in Hei Shui Gou (namely Okinawa Trough) between Chiwei Yu and Gumi Mountain.

Thirdly, the earliest record of placing Diaoyu Yu, Huangwei Yu and Chi Yu under Chinese administration can be found in *An Illustrated Compendium on Maritime Security* (*Chou Hai Tu Bian*) published at the beginning of the 41st year of Jiajing of Ming Dynasty (1562). This book was compiled by Zheng Ruozeng under the auspices of Hu Zongxian, the supreme commander of the southeast coastal anti-Japanese military headquarter China. It is of the nature of an official document and mark clearly in the map that Diaoyu Islands belong to Fujian and under the jurisdiction of the coastal defense of the Fujian.

Finally, from the geological perspective, Diaoyu Islands, prolonged southeast from Chinese mainland, is a hump of the Continental Shelf of the East China Sea; from the perspective of tectonic structure, Diaoyu Islands belong to volcanic belt of Datun mountain in North Taiwan and Ryukyu Islands belong to volcanic belt of Kirisima. Meanwhile, there is the Okinawa Trough at a depth of 2700 meters between Ryukyu Islands and the Continental Shelf of China Sea.

On the contrary, Japanese did not notice the existence of Diaoyu Islands untill in about 1885 through westerns' sea chart (mainly the *Sailing Directions* of Britain). British navy learned the name of Diaoyu Islands through Fujianese and Taiwanese, Japanese noticed Diaoyu

Islands through British.

After the World War II, the United States held trusteeship over Ryukyu according to Treaty of San Francisco signed in 1951 and incorporated Diaoyu Islands into the interzone line of Ryukyu Islands and returned Diaoyu Islands together with Ryukyu Islands to Japan in 1972, which led to the current situation that Diaoyu Islands are under illegal de facto control by Japan and arose a forty years' dispute of territorial sovereignty over Diaoyu Islands between China and Japan.

According to Ordinance No. 68 on the territory of Ryukyu promulgated by the US Headquarter imposing trusteeship over Ryukyu pursuant to the Treaty of San Francisco, the US incorporated all islands between latitude 24° N–28° N and longititude 122° E–133° E into the territory of Ryukyu. Diaoyu Island, Huangwei Yu, Chiwei Yu and five surrounding small islands are fallen within the scope. Such instruction is the so-called foundation of the international law based on which Japanese government claims that Diaoyu Islands are its inherent territory and the crux of Sino-Japanese of disputes over Diaoyu Islands.

However, the method adopted by the US to determine the boundary of territory of Ryukyu according to archipelagic baselines delimitation method, namely determining longitude and latitude first and then cutting by geometric straight line to make the boundaries and the Meridian and Parallel coincide, violates the restrictive condition of delimitation by archipelagic baselines—islands, waters and other natural landforms in essence constitute an entity of geology, economy and politics, or are regarded as conditions for such an entity in history. However, Diaoyu Islands do not have the above-mentioned conditions, that is to say, Diaoyu Islands and Ryukyu Islands are not united in geology or integrated in politics. Diaoyu Islands has never been under the jurisdiction and control of the old imperial court of Ryukyu, thirty-six islands under the administration of which have never included Diaoyu Islands. On the contrary, there are a lot of historical literature which proves that Diaoyu Islands are under the effective control and jurisdiction of Ming and Qing dynasties of China and are not terra nullius. It is evident that the boundary of territory of Ryukyu determined unilaterally by the US is not in compliance with systems of the international law and a breach of regulation on Japanese territory unanimously agreed upon by four states. The US is obliged to recover Diaoyu Island and its affiliated islands from Japan.

The conduct that Japan has always relied on the US including the US's favoring Japan and the practice that Japan denies a dispute over Diaoyu Islands and refuses to negotiate with China are the main reason for the protracted issues of Diaoyu Islands. Well, is there a dispute over Diaoyu Islands?

Firstly, what a dispute in the international law is. We can learn from the judgment of the Mavrommatis Palestine Concessions awarded by the Permanent Court of International Justice that the so-called dispute is the disagreement on a point of law or fact, a conflict of legal views or of interests between two persons (or states). By comparison with this view, there is a dispute on Diaoyu Islands between China and Japan.

Secondly, is there a consensus on Setting Aside Dispute? Although the term of Setting Aside Dispute did not appear in documents such as the China-Japan Joint Statement and the China-Japan Treaty of Peace and Friendship, answers made by Deng Xiaoping in Japan National Press Club showed the fact that such agreements do not involve Diaoyudao Islands during the two countries' negotiation of normalizing Sino-Japanese diplomatic relations and signing Sino-Japanese Treaty of Peace and Friendship. In other words, leaders of China and Japan agreed to setting aside disputes over Diaoyudao Islands, otherwise, Japanese government could give different responses after Deng Xiaoping gave his answers in Japan National Press Club. However, they did not express any different or opposite opinions, which showed that Japanese government give tacit consent to Setting Aside Disputes. Afterwards, Japanese government handled the issue of Diaoyu Islands according to the guideline of Setting Aside Disputes. After Democratic Party seized the power in 2009, Japanese government changed the tacit understanding between China and Japan and tried to deal with various issues mainly through the leader's political authority, so Japan adopted a stance to try to deal with Diaoyu Island incident with domestic laws in the collision incident of Sept. 7, 2010. The tough attitude of Japanese government results in serious opposition and disagreement in diplomatic relations between China and Japan. Afterwards, the differences regarding The issue of Diaoyu Islands are increasingly obvious and the management over it is enhanced.

The Sino-Japanese marine issues, especially the issue of Diaoyu Islands, are keys to opposition and tension in Sino-Japanese relations, so they must be suitable handled, especially it is necessary for Japanese government to respect history, facts and international law, conduct equal consultation and negotiation with Chinese government. However, from Japan's conducts concerning Diaoyu Island such as landing and naming, we can not see any wish of Japan to conduct amicable consultation. Therefore, China shall, on basis of announcing the standard name, further strengthen comprehensive management of Diaoyu Islands including announcing the coordinate of longitude and latitude, announcing the baseline of the territorial sea, determining administrative unit, strengthening investigation activities of the surrounding resources and environment, establishing public facilities such as navigator, meteorological station, ensuring the fishing right of fishermen from Chinese mainland and Taiwan, collecting evidences regarding The issue of Diaoyu Islands, strengthening research into system and cases of international justice, publishing papers and books concerning the issue of Diaoyu Islands and publishing the white paper on policies regarding the issue of Diaoyu Islands.

In short, Japan adopts a divide-and-conquer tactic to address marine issues between China and Japan, for example, denying the existence of a dispute over the issue of Diaoyu Islands, setting aside disputes over delimitation and trying its best to obtain substantive interests in resources exploitation. Therefore, China shall adopt comprehensive strategy to resolve Sino-Japanese marine issues, especially need organize human resources to further strengthen comprehensive study on the issue of Diaoyu Islands.

This article was originally published on Page A16 of *Dongfang Daily* on Apr. 20, 2012

Dispute Denial Will Not Work

It was absurd for Tokyo's controversial governor Shintaro Ishihara to say that his city prefecture is negotiating with the "owner" of the Diaoyu Islands, with the aim of "buying them by the end of this year".

Ishihara said in a speech in Washington on Tuesday that he had begun negotiations to "purchase" three islets of the Diaoyu Islands that are "owned by a Japanese family".

This is ludicrous, as all the islands belong to China.

China has indisputable sovereignty over the Diaoyu Islands. The Diaoyu Islands were named first by China and have always been within the maritime defense boundary of China since the Ming Dynasty (1368–1644). The islands were illegally occupied by Japan after Sino-Japan War (1894–1895).

After World War II, the Chinese government resumed its sovereignty over the Diaoyu Islands, but the islands were "entrusted" to the US in 1951, which in turn "returned" them to Japan in 1971. However, both these moves were illegal as they involved territory that wasn't theirs, and China never acknowledged these moves.

Japan has for a long time adopted the strategy of denying there is a dispute over the islands in order to exploit the islands' resources. The denial of a dispute over the Diaoyu Islands by Japan has prevented negotiations from progressing.

Though Diaoyu Islands are China's indisputable territory, China takes a pragmatic approach and hopes to solve the problem through talks with Japan.

However, this year some Japanese politicians repeated provocative words even though this year marks 40th anniversary of the normalization of China-Japan diplomatic ties.

In fact, what happened four decades ago exactly proved their denial wrong.

Four decades ago, when then Japanese prime minister Kakuei Tanaka met former Chinese premier Zhou Enlai on Sept. 27, 1972, they agreed to avoid talking about the islands in order to pave the way for the normalization of bilateral ties that year. In 1978, then Chinese vice-premier Deng Xiaoping proposed to "shelve the dispute and explore jointly", which led to the signing of the China-Japan Treaty of Peace and Friendship in 1978. All these showed Japan agreed that the two countries had a dispute over the Diaoyu Islands.

In 2008, diplomats from the two countries did a good job in reaching an agreement in principle on the East China Sea issue. That marked a beginning of efforts to find a way to resolve the disputes between them. But disparities and contradictions still exist because no consensus has been reached in the dispute over the islands and the maritime boundary.

In fact, Japan even denies there is a dispute. Yet according to a judgment by the Permanent Court of International Justice, a dispute is “a disagreement on a point of law or fact, a conflict of legal views or of interests”. This definition has since been applied and clarified on a number of occasions. So from the point of international law, there exists a dispute between China and Japan over the Diaoyu Islands.

Japan should accept that there is a dispute and withdraw its vigilance mechanism in and around the Diaoyu Islands, so that joint historical and legal research can be undertaken to solve the dispute.

The most important thing China can do at the moment is to break Japan’s argument that it has no dispute with China over the Diaoyu Islands. Only then will it be able to promote joint exploitation in and around the Diaoyu Islands.

What’s more, the Chinese government should show its sovereignty over the Diaoyu Islands by strengthening its management of the islands. It should announce standardized names for the islands, and make public their locations.

The mainland and Taiwan need to set up a joint authority to make surveys of the islands’ resources and environment, and they need to establish a GPS station and observatories. They should also enhance cooperation to protect Chinese fishermen and their rights to fish around the islands.

These will pave way for China to restart the process of drawing a boundary in the East China Sea.

This article was originally published on Page 9 of *China Daily* on Apr. 20, 2012

Formation and Development of Japanese Ocean Strategy

Japan is one of countries which value the sea most and the economic life of Japan greatly depends on the sea and its resources. For example, 99.7% of foreign trade of Japan lies in the sea and 40% of national food protein comes from the sea. Meanwhile, the country area of Japan is small so its defense and security are limited to and relied upon the sea. Especially after stepping into the 21st century, the strategies adopted by the international community to deal with marine issues, namely measures of formulating marine strategy and policy and improving legal system of the sea, prompt the formation and development of Japanese Ocean Strategy.

It is generally believed that the representative document of Japanese ocean strategy is the Sea and Japan: Suggestion on Ocean Policies in the 21st Century (hereinafter referred to as Suggestion on Ocean Policies) submitted by Ocean Policy Research Foundation to Japanese government on Nov. 18, 2005. The main suggestion included formulating outlines of marine policies, improving systems promoting the development of the basic law of the sea, expanding national jurisdiction to reach the land of the sea and strengthening international cooperation. Therefore, Japan formulated An Outline of Ocean Policies — Seeking a New National Strategy on the Sea on Dec. 7, 2006 and adopted the Basic Law of the Sea in Apr. 2007 (implemented from July 20, 2007) according to the suggestion set forth in Suggestion on Ocean Policies. The Headquarter of Comprehensive Ocean Policies established according to the Basic Law of the Sea is a special organ generally and comprehensively handling ocean issues.

It is more worth noting that the Basic Law of the Sea pointed out that Japan shall put emphasis on dealing with the following twelve ocean issues: forging exploration and exploitation of marine resources, protecting marine environment, promoting resources exploitation activities in the exclusive economic zone, ensuring competitiveness in ocean transportation, ensuring ocean safety, fostering marine investigation, developing marine technology, vitalizing marine industry and strengthening international competitiveness, implementing coastal comprehensive management, effectively utilizing and protecting islands off the land, enhancing international contact and fostering international cooperation, increasing nationals' understanding of the sea and cultivating more talents. Afterwards, Japanese cabinet passed the Basic Plan of the Sea on Mar. 8, 2008, specifically pointing out detailed policies and measures in regard to the aforesaid marine issues. The Basic Plan of the Sea is an action guideline giving instruction to Japanese marine affairs, so we must pay a lot of attention to it. From policies and measures on marine affairs introduced by Japan recently, this has been proved. Especially since its establishment in July 2007, the Headquarter of Comprehensive Ocean Policies has achieved a certain fruits and it is said to have enriched and developed the ocean strategy of Japan. Such fruits are mainly reflected in the following four aspects:

The first one is the exploration and exploitation of marine resources. The Headquarter of Comprehensive Ocean Policies passed Plan on Exploitation of Marine Resources and Mineral Resources in Mar. 2009.

The second one is the marine investigation. The Headquarter of Comprehensive Ocean Policies suggested that the government shall complete the investigation of and application for the continental shelf as soon as possible. Therefore, the Japanese government submitted application for delimitation of outer continental shelf of Japan to Commission on the Limits of the Continental Shelf on Nov. 12, 2008 after completing the investigation of the continental shelf. The biggest problem in this delimitation application is that Japan claims the exclusive economic zone and the continental shelf by taking Okinotorishima as the base point.

The third one is the ocean safety, especially combating piracy and protecting lane safety in Somali and Aden Gulf sea waters. Whereas piracy in Somali and Aden Gulf sea waters seriously influenced international navigation safety and Japanese business ships going through such sea waters amounted to 2000 in a year, Japanese cabinet decided to dispatch warships of Maritime Self-Defense Force to Somali sea waters to carry out ocean security operations on Mar. 13, 2009 and submitted Law on Anti-piracy to the Parliament. In reality, Japan's introduction of Law on Anti-piracy was rooted in the suggestion on anti-piracy in sea waters adjacent to Somalia, request of enacting Law on Suppression of Piracy and suggestion on dispatching warships to sea waters adjacent to Somalia to conduct escort activities submitted by Ocean Policy Research Foundation to the Headquarter of Comprehensive Ocean Policies and its request on Nov. 18, 2008 and Jan. 18, 2009. Afterwards, the Law on Anti-piracy submitted by Japanese cabinet was passed in the second voting of the House of Representatives on June 19, 2009 and the Law on Punishing and Dealing with Pirates on basis of the aforesaid law came into force on July 24, 2009.

The fourth one is the effective utilization and protection of islands off the land. The Headquarter of Comprehensive Ocean Policies passed the Basic Guidelines of Preservation and Management of Islands for Management of the Sea on Dec. 1, 2009 according to the suggestion of Ocean Policy Research Foundation. Afterwards, Japanese Transport Minister submitted to the Parliament draft legislation drawn up according to the aforesaid guidelines. The lower house and upper house of Japanese Parliament respectively passed Law on Preservation of Low Tide Line and Reorganization of Base Facilities on Apr. 18, 2010 and May 26, 2010 to protect the low tide line and relevant facilities of islands off the land. In the future, we shall pay attention to detailed plans targeting at preservation of low tide line of islands and improvement of relevant facilities.

In addition, other relevant documents proposed by Ocean Policy Research Foundation also have a certain effect on pushing Japan to formulate relevant policies and measures in ocean fields, so we must continue to pay attention to them. For example, Ocean Policy Research Foundation proposed Suggestion on Promoting Popularity of Sea Education in Primary Schools in Feb. 2008 and the suggestion on Blueprint of Sea Education in the 21st Century-Plan on Lessons and Units related to Sea Education (for Primary Schools) in Mar. 2009. The specific suggestion in the Suggestion on Promoting Popularity of Sea Education in Primary Schools includes specifying the content of sea education, improving studying environment for popularizing sea education, enriching and external support system for expanding sea education, cultivating talents of undertaking sea education and proactively promoting research into sea education. In Aug. 2009, Ocean Policy Research Foundation formulated Suggestion on Ocean Industry of Japan Surviving in the Asia-Starting from Japan in 2050 (hereinafter referred to as Suggestion on Ocean Industry of Japan) to give the following suggestion to Japanese government: Japan shall further enlarge ocean transport market in the Asian region and proactively cultivate talents in ocean transport; manufacture super energy-saving ships and comprehensively adopt ships with zero emission; develop industries attracting young people; improve the system of exploitation of marine resources and utilizing marine space from a new perspective; build the Asia into a comprehensive marine center.

It is clear that Japan's objective of formulating the Basic Law of the Sea to establish the Headquarter of Comprehensive Ocean Policies (including relevant laws submitted by organs without comprehensive management of marine issues) has been primarily achieved. After the formation of Japanese ocean strategy, its connotation is enriched and developed mainly through formulating marine policies and legislation and other means. Of course, the development of Japanese ocean strategy is not limited to domestic scope but also lies in bilateral efforts. For example, Japan published Suggestion on Japan-US Alliance in Sea Power on Apr. 7, 2009 with the aim to promote a close cooperation of marine affairs between two states to maintain marine order, protect marine safety, accelerate marine exploitation, handle and resolve new marine issues.

Finally, from the perspective of formation and development of Japanese ocean strategy, the role of Ocean Policy Research Foundation as a consultative organ deserves our attention. China's academic research institutions shall learn from it. Meanwhile, it is worthy of our attention to see the great promotion in developing national marine undertakings through the formulation, implementation and development of national ocean strategy including establishing an organ comprehensively managing ocean affairs.

This article was originally published on Page 4
of *China Ocean News* on June 25, 2010

Japan-US Alliance on Sea Power Suggesting Joint Efforts to Develop New Sea Power

In June 2009, Ocean Policy Research Foundation submitted to Japanese Defense Minister the suggestion named Japan-US Alliance on Sea Power for the Stable and Prosperous Sea formulated according to Japan-US dialogue conference on sea power, which showed that Japan not only based its ocean strategy on its own domestic efforts but also tried to develop the ocean strategy through bilateral relations especially Japan-US alliance and accelerated the realization of its objective of ocean strategy through implementing Japan-US Alliance on Sea Power.

I. Background of Introducing Japan-US Alliance on Sea Power

In recent years, Ocean Policy Research Foundation and three USA think-tanks (the Pacific Forum, the Center for a New American Security and American Enterprise Institute) cooperatively held three Japan-US dialogue conferences on sea power. Through dialogue, they discussed topics confronted by Japan-US Alliance, the methods and means to deal with marine issues and exchanged views. Ocean Policy Research Foundation integrated achievements of dialogues to propose the draft suggestion in the third Japan-US dialogue conference on sea power and submitted to Japanese Defense Minister the Japan-US Alliance on Sea Power on June 25, 2009 after getting consents from participants of Japan-US dialogue on sea power. the Japan-US Alliance on Sea Power does not only propose the concept of New Sea Power but also specific suggestion on expanding the Japan-US Alliance on Sea Power to both governments.

II. Specific Suggestion of Japan-US Alliance on Sea Power

In order to secure the freedom of navigation and environment guaranteeing the safety of sea lane, also prevent disputes resorting to forces related to marine rights and interests, foster sustainable marine development and build new sea power with joint efforts, Japan-US Alliance on Sea Power proposes suggestion to Japanese and American government. Meanwhile, both countries realized that the sea was an entirety and the resolution of marine issues needs comprehensive means, so it was more important to strengthen cooperation between ocean countries in fields of military and safety guaranty, resources and environment protection and scientific technology development and so on and the cooperation in these fields also tested wishes between Japan and the USA. The suggestion proposed by Japan-US Alliance on Sea Power to both governments is specified in the following aspects:

(I) Marine Defense and Security

The first one is the suggestion on further promoting global maritime cooperation in the Indian Ocean and the Pacific Ocean. It includes the following aspects: Japan and the USA shall strengthen their global marine cooperation in Indian Ocean and the Pacific; Japan and the USA shall make great efforts to develop their capabilities of identifying ocean area as international public properties; praise or appraise North-Pacific Coast Guard Forum Leaders' Meetings, similar meetings targeted at the Southeast Asia and activities led by Japan with aim to promoting international cooperation between coast guards of countries, meanwhile recognize the positive role of Western Pacific Naval Symposium; Japan shall grant support for navigation safety in Malacca, Singapore Strait and adjacent areas and extend such support to the Indian Ocean under the coordination of India. Japan shall participate in international coordinating activities for combating piracy in sea areas around Somalia, conduct direct or indirect cooperation with European Union, Russia and China on basis of Japan-USA cooperation; appraise the role of international marine organizations in coordinating marine security issues; Japan and the USA shall support developing countries in exploiting their coastal regions, ensuring navigation safety and order in international strait, protecting environment and other activities, educate and train coast guard staffs, expand diplomatic measures in sharing information relevant to marine security; the USA and Japan shall advance cooperation mechanism established for ensuring navigation safety and protecting environment in Malacca and Singapore Strait.

The second one is the suggestion on establishing a mechanism for jointly dealing with dangerous armed conflict events. It includes the following aspects: Firstly, Japan and the USA shall make prediction on possible conflict events between countries arising from resource contention and sea waters delimitation, so it is necessary to improve a mechanism for easing tension, preventing armed conflicts and enduring joint treatment at the time of conflict events. Secondly, in order to cope with unstable security environment resulted from unbalanced strength of countries who go into and out of the sea to seek hegemony, Japan and the USA shall act as allies to cooperate with other countries to improve works on information, surveillance and reconnaissance at the same time of maintaining and developing strong and solid marine defense. Thirdly, in order to implement ocean strategy including restraining other countries from improper ocean activities, carrying out forward movement to ensure quick and effective response and countermeasures, imposing ocean control and so on, discussions shall be made on roles, tasks and functions of Japan Maritime Self Defense Force, Japan Coast Guard, the USA Navy, Marine Corps and Coast Guard, as well as base improvement. Fourth, in order to defend important ocean facilities related to sea lanes, cope with missile defense in oceans, improvement must be made on utilizing relevant systems in ocean space, astrospace and cyberspace. Fifth, consideration must be given to events that climate changes result in deterioration of security environment and escalation of armed conflicts. Sixth, in order to responsibly carry out the aforesaid activities, Japan shall solve relevant issues concerning interpretation of its Constitution as soon as possible.

The third one is the consideration and suggestion on alliance of marine countries. It includes the following aspects: Firstly, Japan and the USA shall, through international coordination, make sure that Japan-US Alliance on Sea Power as an ocean security guaranty is closed but expandable, and together with other countries in favor of alliance on sea power, propose to gradually construct an alliance of marine countries. Secondly, in order to cope with wars made by armies of many countries against terrorist acts and international piracy, Japan and the USA shall strive to ensure the navigation safety of sea lanes from Indian Ocean to East Pacific. Thirdly, countries' smooth entry into the alliance of marine countries shall be conditioned on their compliance with international rules including freedom of high seas specified in the United Nations Charter and the United Nations Convention on the Law of the Sea and international coordination.

(II) Sustainable Development of the Sea

The first one is the suggestion on resource development, ocean technology development, investigation and research. Japan and the USA shall be well prepared for shortage of resources, energy and food in the world and play a lead role in utilizing non-living resources stored in the sea floor and the continental shelf, ocean living resources, seawater resources and ocean energy and so on. As for ocean space, exploration and exploitation of the sea and its resources shall be promoted at the same time of consideration being given to environment protection.

The second one is the suggestion on protecting ocean environment and coping with climate change. It mainly includes solving major projects in present ocean fields, marine surveillance system, ocean resources development, development of technology on coping with global warming and so on.

The third one is the suggestion on international order established by the United Nations Convention on the Law of the Sea and other relevant treaties. It mainly includes the trend of the USA being welcome to accede to the United Nations Convention on the Law of the Sea. Japan and the USA shall make joint efforts to establish international order on basis of the United Nations Convention on the Law of the Sea and other relevant treaties; Japan shall establish international order concerning issues related to development of resources in international sea floor, national acts of utilizing countries and adjustment of interest of coastal countries in economic exclusive zones.

III. Main Features of Japan-US Alliance on Sea Power

From its content, we can see that the Japan-US Alliance on Sea Power has mainly the following features: the first one is the comprehensiveness. Japan-US Alliance on Sea Power covers many aspects of marine issues and thus enjoys features of completeness and comprehensiveness. Especially it predicts possible marine issues arising in the future and their solutions with focus on preventive measures for non-traditional security threats. The second one is the openness. Japan-US Alliance on Sea Power not only allows allied nations to join but also invites other countries to join conditionally, which shows its feature of relative openness. The third one is cooperativeness. The implementation of suggestion in Japan-US Alliance on Sea Power will inevitably influence the development process of international new order including ocean blueprint in the future, while the realization of the ocean blueprint need cooperation and support at every level, otherwise marine issues can not be really solved. In other words, in coping with and handling marine issues, it strengthens peaceful cooperation mode through many channels such as dialogue, information sharing and exchange.

In short, we shall continue to research marine issues and their dangers and work out solutions including positive participation in various activities related to the sea to ensure China's marine rights and interests and provide guaranty for obtaining energy resources necessary for economic and social development.

This article was originally published on Page 4 of *China Ocean News* on Aug. 13, 2010

Origins and Trends of Disputes over Diaoyu Islands

The disputes over Diaoyu Islands between China and Japan have been in the escalating trend recently, what will such disputes lead to?

(1) It Can Be Proved by History, Geography and International Law that Diaoyu Island Is China's Inherent Territory

Q: What is the foundation for China to hold that Diaoyu Islands is China's inherent territory?

A: Diaoyu Islands have been China's inherent territory since ancient times which can be proved by history, geography and international law.

Firstly, Firstly, the earliest record of the discovery, naming and use of Diaoyu Island and its affiliated islands can be found in the book *Voyage with a Tail Wind* wrote by envoys sent by the imperial court to oriental and western countries in the first year of Yongle of Ming Dynasty (1403). Imperial envoys of Ming and Qing Dynasties went to Diaoyu Islands for many times in order to survey shipping line and adjust needle mark and they regarded these islands as shipping marks leading to Ryukyu. This constitutes a kind of inchoate title in the international law.

Secondly, the boundary between the kingdom of the Ryukyu and China has been determined clearly since Ming Dynasty. As for the boundary, from the perspective of China, it is Chiwei Yu; from the perspective of Ryukyu, it is Gumi Mountain (Kume Island). The separating line of the sea waters between China and the kingdom of Ryukyu lies in Hei Shui Gou (namely Okinawa Trough) between Chiwei Yu and Gumi Mountain.

Thirdly, the earliest record of placing Diaoyu Yu, Huangwei Yu and Chi Yu under Chinese administration can be found in *Map of Coastal Mountains and Sands*, the Volume I of *An Illustrated Compendium on Maritime Security* published at the beginning of the 41st year of Jiajing of Ming Dynasty (1562). In two maps of Fuqi and Fuba of *Map of Coastal Mountains and Sands*, Diaoyu Yu, Huangwei Yu and Chi Yu were clearly incorporated into the administrative jurisdiction of Fujian.

Finally, from the geological perspective, Diaoyu Islands, prolonged southeast from Chinese mainland, is a hump of the Continental Shelf of the East China Sea; from the perspective of tectonic structure, Diaoyu Islands belong to volcanic belt of Datun mountain in North Taiwan and Ryukyu Islands belong to volcanic belt of Kirisima. Meanwhile, there is the Okinawa Trough at a depth of 2700 meters between Ryukyu Islands and the Continental Shelf of China Sea.

It can be seen from the aforesaid analysis that the earliest discovery, the first naming, earliest development and administration of Diaoyu Island by China constitute China's territorial sovereignty over it in the sense of international law.

(2) The Foundation Alleged by Japan Is Illegal and Invalid because It Was Japan and the USA that Illegally Transferred China's Territory

Q: What is the foundation for Japan to allege its sovereignty over Diaoyu Islands?

A: The document in which Japan alleged its sovereignty over Diaoyu Islands is Basic View on the Sovereignty over the Senkaku Island (Japanese name of Diaoyu Islands) issued by Japan's Ministry of Foreign Affairs on March 8, 1972. Its main ideas include the following aspects: Firstly, from 1885 to 1895, after investigation on the spot, Japan thought Diaoyu Islands were desert island and had no signs of control by Qing Dynasty, therefore, its Cabinet passed a decision to build a signal and incorporate it into Japanese territory. This is the so called claim of terra nullius. Secondly, Diaoyu Islands were part of the Southwest Islands of Ryukyu, Japan, so it was not included in Pescadores, Formosa [Taiwan] or their affiliated islands which were ceded to Japan by the Qing government in accordance with the Treaty of Shimonoseki or included in the territory which Japan renounced under Article 2 of the Treaty of San Francisco. Thirdly, Diaoyu Islands were not part of

Taiwan.

In fact, Diaoyu Islands were China's territory rather than terra nullius in Ming and Qing Dynasties. They were not part of the Southwest Islands of Ryukyu but affiliated islands of Taiwan. This was not only recorded in Chinese official documents on titie conferring but also a consensus in international community. The historical book *A General Guide* (1708) which was the first one to record Diaoyu Islands and written by Cheng Shunze, a noted scholar and the Grand Master with the Purple-Golden Ribbon of Ryukyu, and *Illustrated Outline of the Three Countries* (1785) written by Japanese historian and geographer Lin Ziping and its attached Map of Three Provinces and Thiry-six Islands of Ryukyu clearly incorporated Diaoyu Islands into the territory of China. Maps published in European countries and Japan at that time marked Diaoyu Islands as China's territory rather than the Ryukyu Islands' territory.

Meanwhile, because Taiwanese fishermen frequently operated in and around Daoyu Islands, They have customarily been regarded as affiliated islands of Taiwan. This is a kind of natural formation through history and such historical formation in geography has been reflected in Chinese and Japanese documents and materials.

In reality, Japanese did not notice the existence of Diaoyu Islands until in about 1885 through western's Sea Chart (mainly the Sailing Directions of Britain). British navy learned the name of Diaoyu Islands through Fujianese and Taiwanese. In 1990, Japanese named Diaoyu

Islands Senkaku Islands.

After Japan's defeat and surrender in 1945, according to stipulations in the Cairo Declaration, the Potsdam Proclamation, Diaoyu Islands should have been returned to China as affiliated islands of Taiwan, however, the USA placed Ryukyu under its trusteeship according to the Treaty of San Francisco in 1951, incorporated Diaoyu Islands into the interzone line of the Ryukyu Islands and handed over Diaoyu Islands and the Ryukyu Islands together to Japan in 1972. Such backroom deal between the USA and Japan concerning China's territory Diaoyu Islands led to the situation that Diaoyu Islands are nowadays under illegal and actual control of Japan and resulted in 40 years-long territorial dispute over Diaoyu Islands between China and Japan.

To sum up, Japanese foundations and evidences for claim of sovereignty are illegal and invalid.

(3) Recent Dispute Escalation is Due to Japan's Violation of Consensus on Setting Aside Disputes

Q: Why the issue of Diaoyu Islands between China and Japan is gradually escalating and what is the reason?

A: Japan unilaterally has strengthened its wrongful words, conducts and measures concerning Diaoyus Islands and turned the dispute escalated recently due to two main reasons:

Firstly, the international background. With the growing strength of

China, especially the total economic volume of China surpassing Japan from 2010, development of Chinese ocean power alleged by Japan including increased access to the sea, development of navel power and China's strengthened administration on Diaoyu Islands, Japan creates unnecessary tension and anxiety and is afraid that further development of China in its strength will serve as an disadvantageous factor for Japan to exercise illegal and longtime occupation of Diaoyu Islands, so Japan hopes to initiate a dispute to win Diaoyu Islands before China fully develops to gain its strength. Meanwhile, the implementation of the USA's Asian-Pacific rebalancing strategy needs cooperation and assistance from Japan. Therefore, the tension resulted from the issue of Diaoyu Islands is beneficial to a strengthened alliance between the USA and Japan including the implementation of the USA's reloc ation of its base in Japan. Japan hopes that the USA may support it in terms of the issue of Diaoyu Islands and the USA's statement that the issue of Diaoyu Islands shall be governed by Article 5 of Treaty of Mutual Cooperation and Security between the United States and Japan further inspired Japan to choose a tough attitude towards the issue of Diaoyu Islands.

Secondly, domestic background. Since its ruling in 2009, Democratic Party has advocated the development of equal alliance relation between Japan and the USA, which resulted in collapse of Hatoyama administration. The later Naoto Kan administration, insisting on the politics-oriented guideline and ignoring officials' role, attempted to severely deal with the incident of illegal seizure of Chinese ships and captains by Japan Coast Guard (Sept. 7, 2010) according to Japanese domestic laws, thus breaking tacit understanding between China and Japan on the issue of Diaoyu Islands and resulting in serious regression of Sino-Japanese relations. The current Noda administration achieves nothing due to unsuccessful development of domestic economic and social issues, especially constraints and checks of the Senate. While right-wingers are dissatisfied with the government's policies or guideline on the issue of Diaoyu Islands and strengthen words, conducts and measures of administrating Diaoyu Islands, which push Noda administration to express its attitude and place the government in a dilemma. However, in order to maintain the ruling status of the Democratic Party, Japanese government adopts a moderately tough attitude towards China to try to balance the interest of each party and make the issue of Diaoyu Islands not influence the development of Sino-Japanese relation, especially activities celebrating 40th anniversary of normalized diplomatic relation between China and Japan.

The conduct that Japan has always relied on the US including the US's favoring Japan and the practice that Japan denies a dispute over Diaoyu Islands and refuses to negotiate with China are the main reason for the escalation of the issue of Diaoyu Islands.

Well, is there a consensus on Setting Aside Dispute? Although the term of Setting Aside Dispute did not appear in documents such as the China-Japan Joint Statement and the China-Japan Treaty of Peace and Friendship, answers made by Deng Xiaoping in Japan National Press

Club showed the fact that such agreements do not involve Diaoyudao Islands during the two countries' negotiation of normalizing Sino-Japanese diplomatic relations and signing Sino-Japanese Treaty of Peace and Friendship. In other words, leaders of China and Japan agreed to setting aside disputes over Diaoyudao Islands, otherwise, Japanese government could give different responses after Deng Xiaoping gave his answers in Japan National Press Club. However, they did not express any different or opposite opinions, which showed that Japanese government give tacit consent to Setting Aside Disputes. Afterwards, Japanese government handled Diaoyu Island issues according to the guideline of Setting Aside Disputes.

(4) Japanese Side Is Still Attempting to Purchase the Island, so China Will Definitely Take Countermeasures

Q: What is the outcome of Diaoyu Islands Dispute between China and Japan? Is it possible to result in large-scale conflict?

A: It is predictable that during the current Japanese administration or in the future Japanese administration, the so-called issue of Nationalization arising from island purchase concerning Diaoyu Islands will be continued because it is for interest of Japan and also a conduct due to lack of choice, a so-called measure to avoid escalating conflict on Diaoyu Islands issue. Of course, Japanese government has to confront China's response to and the USA's attitude towards the issue of Nationalization, so it is impossible to lead to military conflict due to Diaoyu Islands issue. China keeps a maximum restraint on this issue with the hope to solve it peacefully and stabilize and develop Sino-Japanese relations. However, it is an unavoidable issue to manage and instruct Diaoyu Islands Defending actitivities, so it is very necessary to develop persuasive publicity works.

At present, the issue of Diaoyu Islands arose and escalated unilaterally by Japan is continuing including the so-called investigation on island landing, promotion of nationalization conducted by Japan. Japanese right-wingers kidnap the government with the aim to push Japanese government strengthen management on Diaoyu Islands to show Japan's real control on it and request to severely publish Chinese who ascend the island including formulating laws and regulations regulating infringement of the so-called territorial sea. It should be mentioned that, it is true that such affirmative attitude of Japanese government towards the aforesaid behaviors will definitely affect and inspire firm resolution and will of Chinese government and people on defending national territory, and will give rise to strong opposition and countermeasures. It is predictable that non-governmental activities such as Defending Diaoyu Islands and legitimate activities by China such as official ships' enforcement and cruise will inevitably increase. Japan shall be responsible for any resulted serious conflicts because it is Japan that damages the existing situation concerning Diaoyu Islands between China and Japan. Of course, the possible development and outcome of Diaoyu Islands issue in the future is an important issue attracting attention of the international community, we will keep an eye on it and specially hope that Japanese government will honor history, facts and international law, carry out equal consultation and negotiation with Chinese government with the aim to resolve Diaoyu Islands issue peacefully.

This article was originally published in Page A26 of *XinMin Evening News* on Aug. 24, 2012

Japan Should End the Farce

Japan has been playing out a farce. It started with a plan to name (rather rename) some of the islets of the Diaoyu Islands. Then came its attempt to "buy" the islands from their supposed private owner, intend to "nationalize" them and conduct a joint landing drill with the United States, followed by the Tokyo metropolitan government's illegal survey around the Diaoyu Islands.

Japan's actions have infringed on China's territorial sovereignty and maritime interests, and poisoned bilateral relations, which could have reached a new height in the 40th year of the normalization of diplomatic relations between the two countries.

Despite facing an indifferent Japanese government (which is not bothered about frayed bilateral ties) and right-wing conspirators, China has adhered to the principles enshrined in the four political documents signed between Beijing and Tokyo, and maintained utmost restraint. It has done so in the hope that Japan would respect historical facts and international law, and hold talks under the existing bilateral mechanisms, such as the China-Japan high-level consultation mechanism on maritime affairs, to resolve the dispute. This would serve the interests of the two countries as well as regional peace and stability.

But there is no sign of Japan refraining from taking unilateral actions over the Diaoyu Islands.

The Diaoyu Islands have been part of China's territory since ancient times. That is proved by historical records, and confirmed by international law and many reputable Japanese scholars.

Japanese historian Kiyoshi Inoue (1913–2001) says in his works, published in the 1970s, that it is a well-known fact among Chinese, Ryukyuans and even Japanese that the Diaoyu Islands [(called Senkaku Islands in Japan) have belonged to China since the Ming Dynasty (1368–1644), and before Japan encroached on them, they were part of China's territory and not terra nullius (land belonging to no one)]. And Tadayoshi Murata, a professor at Yokohama National University, says that the Diaoyu Islands actually belong to China. Japan occupied them in 1895 during the Sino-Japanese War (1894–1895), which was nothing but a robbery.

Contradicting Japanese officials' claim that there is no dispute over the Diaoyu Islands, some former officials of Japan's Ministry of Foreign Affairs, including Ukeru Magosaki and Kazuhiko Togo, have admitted that there is one between China and Japan. They have even expressed concern over the unilateral actions of the Japanese side. These are views that Japan should respect.

Unfortunately, Japanese right-wing forces and some politicians have chosen to ignore the rational voices at home and are exploiting the The issue of Diaoyu Islands for their own gain. They stepped up their efforts recently mainly because of the challenges that Japan faces on the domestic as well as the international front.

Japan is worried that China's continued rise and the change in the regional power balance will end its illegal possession of the Diaoyu Islands and is thus eager to get an upper hand in the dispute.

Amid all this, the United States is implementing its back-to-Asia-Pacific strategy, for which it needs Japan's help. Washington is more than willing to muddy the waters to consolidate the US-Japan alliance, which will pave the way for a stronger American military presence in Japan. And the US says that the Diaoyu Islands fall within the scope of the US-Japan security treaty to encourage Japan to act more aggressively.

This is surprising because in its election campaign, the Democratic Party of Japan had vowed to rebuild the slumping Japanese economy and make Tokyo a more equal partner in the US-Japan alliance. But former prime minister Yukio Hatoyama couldn't do that and was replaced by Naoto Kan. Beijing-Tokyo relations were dealt a severe blow during the Kan administration, especially when Japan illegally detained Chinese fishermen in the waters off the Diaoyu Islands and insisted on pressing charges against them according to Japanese laws.

It has to be conceded, though, that Kan's successor Yoshihiko Noda dealt with Chinese activists who landed on the Diaoyu Islands with restraint last month. He just "deported" the Chinese nationals and urged everyone to keep the The issue of Diaoyu Islands under control, and even wrote a letter to President Hu Jintao emphasizing the importance of China-Japan "strategic and beneficial relationship".

But since the Noda government is troubled by economic and social problems at home and faces rising pressure, especially from rightists, to "act", it had to take a hard stance and announce that it planned to "nationalize" the Diaoyu Islands. Perhaps this is Noda's way of trying to prevent more Japanese right-wing activists from landing on the Diaoyu Islands and thus avoid provoking China further. But the "nationalization" plan also suits Japan's interests, for it will try to build a legal case on that basis.

Japan's efforts will be in vain, though, because it can't change the fact that the Diaoyu Islands belong to China. Illegal actions do not give one legal rights.

Japan should refrain from taking any more unilateral action if it doesn't want to bear the consequences of China safeguarding its sovereignty and defending its maritime interests.

China still hopes that Japan would respect historical facts and international law, and hold bilateral talks to resolve the dispute.

This article was originally published on Page 9
of *China Daily* on Sept. 5, 2012

China Should Be Well Prepared that The Issue of Diaoyu Islands Will Last for a Long Time

Starting from 2012, the conduct of island purchase for trying to strengthen the so-called management initiated by Japanese right-wingers and instigated by the government to realize national interest was concluded through a guideline of island purchase established by Japanese government on Sept. 10, 2012 (the so-called successful and stable maintenance and management of Diaoyu Island and other islands), signing of purchase contract on Sept. 11, 2012 and completion of land ownership registration formalities on Sept. 12, 2012, which seems natural and beyond reproach.

It must be pointed out that Diaoyu Island and its affiliated islands are lands with special features. They are not under sovereignty or ownership of Japan, so all acts and measures concerning Diaoyu Islands made by Japan unilaterally who has no sovereignty are illegal and invalid, which is the exact stance and attitude held by Chinese government and people all the time. In other words, Japan used its so-called domestic cabinet resolution (Jan. 14, 1895) by taking advantage of its victory in the Sino-Japanese War to secretly occupy Diaoyu Islands, it did not announce such resolution, so the public did not know such resolution. Especially, the so-called point of view of terra nullius in the Basic View on the Sovereignty over the Senkaku Islands (Mar. 8, 1972) was basically groundless. Because a lot of Chinese and foreign historical documents and maps clearly showed that the land boundaries between China and the Ryukyu were Chiwei Yu and Kume Island, the sea border was Okinawa Trough. At the same time, Diaoyu Island and other islands were not part of traditional territory of the Ryukyu but affiliated islands of Taiwan, which could be proved by means of history, geography, geology and the use. Japan, by taking advantage of Mudanjiang Incident （1876）, in order to occupy Taiwan, took occupation of Diaoyu Islands as its preliminary objective after occupying the Ryukyu in 1879 (the legal status of the Ryukyu was actually undetermined). Japan carried out the so-called three investigations on Diaoyu Island and other islands in 1885 and arrived at a conclusion that they were islands owned by Qing Dynasty (China), not only named but also used for a long time as navigation marks, so Japan did not take any action. Up to Dec. 1894, it was certain that China would be defeated in the Sino-Japanese War, officials of Japan cabinet began to discuss occupation of Diaoyu Island and conclude a so-called international resolution. That is to say, Japan claimed it had sovereignty over Diaoyu Islands before signing the Treaty of Shimonoseki (Apr. 17, 1895). Diaoyu Islands were not ceded to

Japan according to the Treaty of Shimonoseki but occupied according to the principle of terra nullius. For such kind of opinion, even some Japanese scholars, for example, deceased historians and professors Kiyoshi Inoueand Murata Tadayoshi (Yokohama National University) believed that Diaoyu Island and other islands were China's territory and they were secretly stolen and occupied by Japan by taking advantage of its victory in the Sino-Japanese War. It is not a legitimate and dignified sovereignty-obtaining act.

After World War II, according to the Cairo Declaration, the Potsdam Proclamation and the Japanese Instrument of Surrender and the Treaty of Shimonoseki and so forth, from the legal perspective, Japan has already returned all islands of Taiwan and all affiliated islands including Diaoyu Island and its affiliated islands to China. However, because the USA placed the Ryukyu under its trusteeship according to the Treaty of San Francisco (Sept. 8, 1951) and promulgated a proclamation on geographic limites of the Ryukyu Islands (Decree No. 27, Dec. 25, 1953) through trustee (The United States Civil Administration of the Ryukyu), wrongly delimited the geographic scope of the Ryukyu Islands according to astronomical standard of boundary and geometric standard of boundary to make interzone line of the Ryukyu Islands include Diaoyu Island and other islands, which has become the foundation for Japan to claim its sovereignty over Diaoyu Island and other islands.

In reality, the USA ignored the most important principle of physiographic standard of boundary when it acted as a trustee to delimit geographic boundary of the Ryukyu. Meanwhile, The United States Civil Administration of the Ryukyu could not apply the regime of archipelagic baselines to determine the geographic boundary of the Ryukyu. Because the Ryukyu was not a archipelagic state, Diaoyu Island and other islands were not uniform in geography nor shared completeness in politics with the Ryukyu archipelago, elements of archipelagic baselines were not satisfied. Therefore, the geographic boundary of the Ryukyu delimited by The United States Civil Administration of the Ryukyu was invalid. In other words, China was not able to exercise jurisdiction over Diaoyu Island and other islands due to the USA's trusteeship.

Afterwards, the USA and Japan wrongly returned administration over Okinawa, Diaoyu Island and other islands to Japan through the Okinawa Reversion Agreement (June 17, 1971) by violating the aim of the UN trusteeship system (Article 76 of the United Nations Charter) and without approval of major powers of World War II, which resulted in the actual situation that China was not able to exercise management on Diaoyu Islands and other islands again and the territorial dispute over Diaoyu Islands issue between China and Japan for as long as 40 years.

With the further development of China's national power, Japan has gained strategic anxiety and tried to seize the opportunity of the USA's Asian-Pacific rebalancing strategy, by taking advantage of the USA's seeking help from Japan, to occupy Diaoyu Island and other islands as soon as possible with the partial protection of the USA. In other words, Japan holds that the tension arising from the issue of Diaoyu Islands is beneficial to promoting the US-Japan alliance including relocation of the American military base in Japan, deployment of Ospreys helicopters, so there were farces starting from the beginning of this year such as congressmen's landing on Diaoyu Island, island re-naming, Diaoyu Island purchase plan, nationalizing Diaoyu Island, defending Diaoyu Island with forces, landing on Diaoyu Island to seize Chinese people, conforting spirits by investigating Diaoyu Island, drill of occupying Diaoyu Island, landing on Diaoyu Island to conduct investigation, adopting a resolution to defend Diaoyu Island, complete registration to manage Diaoyu Island and so forth to show the so-called effective administration and reflect the trend of nationalization, habitalization, undesertedness, military involvement and development.

Japan's series of unilaterally wrongdoings concerning Diaoyu Island and other islands include distorting facts and international law and denying existence of dispute since a long time ago. Japan pursues the political party's and individual interests due to domestically political need and shows its short-sightedness. Japanese government ignores Sino-Japanese relations and its own long-term interests, arbitrarily decided to change current situation of Diaoyu Island and other islands without any repentance after China gave several pieces of advice and warning. Japan's such conducts and measures greatly infringe China's sovereignty and territorial integrity and seriously damage Chinese people's feeling. Therefore, China has expressed strong protests and solemn statements at various levels, especially adopt powerful legal countermeasures showing

Chinese government and Chinese people's will and determination in firmly defending national sovereignty and territorial integrity.

The author holds that China has gained the initiative on the issue of Diaoyu Islands (Diaoyu Island and its affiliated islands) and changed the long-lasting passive situation and circumstance. The main signal was that Chinese government published a declaration on the baseline of the territorial sea and announced the geographic coordinate taking Diaoyu islands as base points on Sept. 10, 2012, thus establishing and specifying the regime of the territorial sea and the scope of jurisdiction over other sea waters of Diaoyu Islands on basis of Straight baselines, and submitted duplicates of relevant charts and lists of geographical co-ordinates to the General-Secretary of the United Nations on Sept. 13, 2012, thus completing domestically and internationally legal formalities. The announcement of its baseline of the territorial sea by Chinese government is a subsequent measure following the announcement of names of Diaoyu Island and part of affiliated islands by State Oceanic Administration and Ministry of Civil Affairs of People's Republic of China on Mar. 3, 2013 upon approval and authority of the State Council, a decision made according to the system on the law of the sea of China with the aim to improve legal system of China on the sea and safeguard the territorial integrity and marine rights and interest of China.

Since always, Chinese government and People, taking into consideration the importance of development of Sino-Japanese friendly relations, have adhered to political understanding (Setting

Aside Dispute) on the issue of Diaoyu Islands reached by Chinese and Japanese leaders all the time, strictly complied with principles and sprits of four documents between China and Japan, exercised maximum restraint and hoped to deal with the issue of Diaoyu Islands in the mode of joint exploitation.

At present, Chinese government has announced the baseline of the territorial sea of Diaoyu Islands at a proper time in order to respond to Japan's nationalization of Diaoyu Islands and follow-up. Therefore, in terms of law, Chinese government and people have the legal responsibility to safeguard the land and surrounding sea waters especially the territorial sea of 12 nautical miles of Diaoyu Islands. If Japanese warships enter the territorial sea of Diaoyu Islands without approval of Chinese government, China may exercise its right of self-defense because Chinese territory and sovereignty are infringed. It can be predicted that conflicts and disputes even such as collisions between various types of ships of China and Japan will increase under such situation that Japan Coast Guard still continues to maintain the guarding system for the territorial sea, therefore it is of special significance that China formulates and improves relevant domestic laws and regulations for example regulation on law enforcement and management of cruise in sea waters governed by China and punishment, system and rule on innocent navigation of foreign ships in the territorial sea of China.

According to the development trend of the issue of Diaoyu Islands at present, the nationalization of Diaoyu Islands by Japan has been conducted and there is no possibility for its revocation and correction but a trend of advancement of its follow-up, so Chinese government has the initiative of whether to adopt a countermeasure, how to adopt a countermeasure, when to adopt a countermeasure and what is the countermeasure. When China adopts a comprehensive countermeasure, it shall make sure that Japan can thoroughly and deeply sense China's firm will and determination to resolutely maintain the sovereign and territorial integrity and recognize that any conducts or measures challenging China's core interests will definitely result in severe sanction and damage and seriously influence comprehensive relations between China and Japan including damaging nationals' emotion. One of China's objectives of adopting these measures is to impose deterrence on other countries and to prevent them from initiating disputes rashly. This is to say, China needs to build up authority and prestige among neighboring countries in order to better protect its core interests and ensure marine rights and interests.

Finally, it should be noted that the issue of Diaoyu islands is sensitive and complex due to history and national emotion, relating to sovereignty and security as well as involving the USA and cross-straits relations, so there are a lot of difficulties at present in actually resolving it and China needs to be aware that it is a long-term struggle. However, it is especially significant for China to make some preparation including organizing national strength to strengthen comprehensive research into the issue of Diaoyu Islands, hold academic seminars, publish relevant papers and books, enhance cross-straits exchange and cooperation, set up websites for publicity and so forth. In recent time, regarding marine issues confronted by China at present, it is very important to formulate and implement a national marine development strategy with the aim to improve the system and mechanism on the sea, make clear China's marine strategy and objective, etc., and carry out publicity in order to efficiently and effectively deal with and coordinate various marine issues.

This article was originally published on Page A16 of *Dongfang Daily* on Sept. 18, 2012

China and Japan Shall Accelerate Their Paces in Negotiation on Maritime issues

Since 2012, Japanese government have done nothing and even incited right-wingers to carry out wrongful words, conducts and measures concerning Diaoyu Island and its affiliated islands (hereinafter referred to as Diaoyu Islands) again and again and strengthened unilateral behaviours on Diaoyu Islands especially the so-called Nationalization and the follow-up, which seriously damages the national sovereignty and territorial integrity of China, therefore, China has taken a series of legal countermeasures which showed the firm will and determination of China to safeguard the sovereignty, territorial integrity, marine interest and rights of China.

The main legal countermeasures adopted by China in dealing with the issue of Diaoyu Islands are as follows: on Sept. 10, 2012, Chinese government published a declaration on the baseline of the territorial sea of Diaoyu Islands and announced the geographical coordinates which take Diaoyu Islands as base points, thus establishing and making clear the regime of the territorial sea and jurisdiction over other sea areas of Diaoyu Islands on basis of the straight baseline; on Sept. 13, 2012, Envoy Li Baodong, the Permanent Representative of China to the United Nations, submitted lists of geographical co-ordinates of base points and the baseline of the territorial sea of Diaoyu Islands and charts to the General-Secretary of the United States; on Sept. 18, 2012, Sino Maps Press published a thematic map on Diaoyu Islands according to Regulations of the People's Republic of China on the Management of the Map Drawing and Publication. China has went through all legal systems for exercising sovereignty and jurisdiction over Diaoyu Islands including legal substantive and procedural issues, thus refuting the fallacy proposed by Japanese government in disregard of facts and international laws that there is no territorial disputes on Diaoyu Islands between China and Japan, and fighting against the sinister motives of Japan to attempt to challenge the world order especially the territorial scope established after the World War II.

More encouragingly, Ministry of Foreign Affairs of China decided on Sept. 16, 2012 to submit an application for delimitation on the continental shelf beyond 200 nautical miles in East China Sea to Commission on the Limits of the Continental Shelf of the United Nations. Such delimitation application submission will further enrich China's legal proposition on delimitation of natural prolongation of the continental shelf in East China Sea. Although it will be a long period from the submission of such delimitation application to advice made by the Commission but such submission will play a big positive role in refuting Japan's long-lasting proposition of delimiting sea areas in East China Sea by the Median Line (the exclusive economic zone and the continental shelf). In other words, this is good for China's principle and proposition on the delimitation in East China Sea especially the delimitation of continental shelf and also advantageous for China to refute Japan's wrong opinion that the regime of the continental shelf is absorbed by the regime of the exclusive economic zone. Of course, China's submission of application for delimitation of outer continental shelf in East China Sea is also a follow-up of the Preliminary Information of China on Determining the Delimitation of the Continental Shelf beyond 200 Nautical Miles submitted to the General-Secretary of the United Nations on May 11, 2012. China strictly keeps to its words and all those conducts are in compliance with relevant legal requirements.

Till now we may conclude that the improvement and implementation of China on relevant legal policies and measures concerning Diaoyu Islands have changed China's long-lasting positive situation regarding East China Sea issue especially the issue of Diaoyu Islands and obtained initiative for China, which is of great significance and plays a big role in actually resolving disputes over East China Sea issue.

Since the outburst of East China Sea issue in May 2004, China and Japan have conducted 11 negotiations on marine issues but achieved no real progress including failure to reach any compromise and understanding due to serious disagreement and opposition in the principle and method of delimitation in East China Sea. Afterwords, in order to realize the political wish of turning East China Sea into the sea of peace, cooperation and friendship reached by Chinese and Japanese learders, Chinese government pays attention to the interests of the whole and make concessions for continued enrichment and development of Sion-Japanese relations. Therefore, ministries of foreign affairs of China and Japan announced the Sino-Japanese Principled Consensus on the East China Sea Issues (hereinafter referred to as Principled Consensus) on June 18, 2008.

From the context of the Principled Consensus, we can conclude that China and Japan agree to formulate rules on steps and requirements of joint exploitation in specified areas and cooperative exploitation in Chunxiao Oil and Gas Field without prejudice to legal statuses of both parties during the transition period before delimitation in East China Sea. but the Principled Consensus does not cover the issue of delimitation in East China Sea especially the issue of Diaoyu Islands. Therefore, China and Japan shall continue to carry out consultation and negotiation on the issue of delimitation in East China Sea in order to resolve it peacefully.

Since the announcement of the Principled Consensus, China and Japan held the first governmental negotiation with exchange of notes on the principled consensus in July 2010 and stopped the process because Japan Coast Guard illegally seized Chinese fishing ships and fishermen in waters adjacent to Diaoyu Island on Sept. 7, 2010. That is to say,

Japan's conduct attempting to deal with Chinese fishermen by use of the so-called domestic laws damaged the political atmosphere for both parties to hold the second governmental negotiation with exchange of notes on the Principled Consensus, thus resulting in no progress till now. Of course, both parties' different understanding of the Principled Consensus is also a reason for failure to achieve progress in negotiation.

It should be noted that the main reasons why China and Japan could not achieve real progress on the issue of delimitation in East China Sea are that Japanese government denies the existence of disputes over Diaoyu Islands and refuses to conduct negotiation for a long time and utilizes the so-called guarding system of Japan Coast Guard to illegally control and punish Chinese fishermen and so forth, which are key elements causing the failure in settlement and constant outburst and escalation of the issue of Diaoyu Islands. Such measures and conducts disregard facts and violate the international law, so Japan must make modification as soon as possible. Of course, the USA's partial remarks that Treaty of Mutual Cooperation and Security between the United States and Japan is applicable to Diaoyu Islands in order to conform to the so-called Asian-Pacific rebalancing strategy and satisfy the interest of the US-Japan alliance are also external elements escalating the issue of Diaoyu Islands.

It should be specially emphasized that the so-called Nationalization and its follow-up carried out by Japanese government under the kidnapping of Japanese right-wingers share the same interests in essence, i.e. the so-called sovereign interests in Diaoyu Islands, in order to strengthen the so-called actual and effective administration to reflect the jurisdiction and try to consolidate the foundation for judicial resolution. Meanwhile, Japan is seeking more interests in delimitation in East China Sea including taking Diaoyu Islands as base points to claim jurisdiction over sea areas, adopting the Median Line to conduct delimitation to let it play its effective role in delimitation in East China Sea.

In view of the political wish of Chinese government to resolve Diaoyu Islands by means of peaceful negotiation, Japanese government shall take initiative to carry out equal negotiation on Diaoyu Islands with China including disputes resolution in the mode of Setting Aside Dispute and Seeking Joint Development. This corresponds to opinions and wishes of some Japanese with insight and also is compliance with the long-term interest of Japan.

If Japan denies the existence of disputes over Diaoyu Islands, refuses to carry out consultation and negotiation with China again, showing its short-sightedness, China may adopt comprehensive strengths and measures to recover administration and control over Diaoyu Islands. As mentioned above, China has announced the baseline of the territorial sea of Diaoyu Islands and made clear the scope of the territorial sea, so it is mainly up to China to decide whether to carry out joint exploitation in sea areas adjacent to Diaoyu Islands. Because according to Law of China on the Territorial Sea and Contiguous Zone (Article 2) and the recent declaration on the baseline of the territorial sea of Diaoyu

Islands, Diaoyu Islands and the territorial sea are China's territory and sea areas under China's jurisdiction. Japanese government and people must have a clear understanding of this, otherwise it is unavoidable to see ship collision or disputes even greater conflicts in sea areas adjacent to Diaoyu Islands, from which all damages and losses resulting shall be borne by Japan.

In order to maintain regional peace and security, and stabilize Sino-Japanese relations, the tension and dispute over Diaoyu Islands between China and Japan shall be eliminated and resolved as soon as possible, therefore, it is very urgent for both parties to initiate the existing bilateral mechanisms (for example, Sino-Japanese high-level consultation mechanism for marine issues, Sino-Japanese strategic diolague mechanism) and accelerate consulation process. This is undoubtedly an effective way to ease and resolve disputes over Diaoyu Islands which deserves our attention and appreciation.

This article was originally published on Page A20
of *Dongfang Daily* on Sept. 20, 2012

Necessities for China and Japan to Reiterate the Principles of China-Japan Treaty of Peace and Friendship

China and Japan must enhance communication and coordination, bridge gap, seek common ground while reserving differences, strengthen comprehensive cooperation, expand common interests, boost trust and realize peaceful development through diolague and consultation to make contributions to ensure regional and world safety and development. This is the important guaidline and basic stance for both governments to comply with without violation and disregard. China and Japan must not stand against or oppose each other, otherwise Sino-Japanese relations will be set back, resulting in confrontation and mutual damage.

Oct. 23, 2013 was the 35th anniversary of the effectiveness of the China-Japan Treaty of Peace and Friendship (signed on Aug. 12, 1978 and became effective on Oct. 23, 1978). Against the present background, it is of special value and significance to commemorate of the China-Japan Treaty of Peace and Friendship, which will paly a big and positive role in improving the present Sino-Japanese relations featuring frozen political relations and warm economic relations. In view of the present Sino-Japanese relations, it is necessary to review principles and guidelines of four important documents between China and Japan including the China-Japan Treaty of Peace and Friendship to understand their connotation and use them to give instruction on Sino-Japanese relations to ensure the drawing of the big picture of Sino-Japanese which means further deepening mutual reliance beween both parties on basis of economy and promoting sustainable and friendly development of Sino-Japanese relations.

From the essense and context of four political documents between China and Japan (China-Japan Joint Statement, the China-Japan Treaty of Peace and Friendship, the China-Japan Joint Declaration, Sino-Japanese Joint Statement on All-round Promotion of Strategic and Mutually Beneficial Relations), we can learn that the following important principles are contained in Sino-Japanese relations for both parties' adherence and compliance.

Firstly, the objective of development of Sino-Japanese relations has been constantly promoting and upgrading from Developing Good-Neighbor and Friendly Relations (Paragraph 5 of the Foreword of China-Japan Joint Statement), Establishing Long-term Peaceful and Friendly Relations (Article 6 of China-Japan Joint Statement), through Developing Long-term Peaceful and Friendly Relations (Paragraph 1 of Article 1 of the China-Japan Treaty of Peace and Friendship, Paragraph IV of Part III of China-Japan Joint Declaration), Development and

Establishing Friendly and Cooperative Partnership Devoted to Peace and Development (Paragraph I of Part III of China-Japan Joint Declaration), to Comprehensively Advancing Sino-Japanese Strategic Relations with Mutual Benefits (Article 1 of Sino-Japanese Joint Statement on All-round Promotion of Strategic and Mutually Beneficial Relations), in order to realize the lofty objectie of both parties of peaceful coexistence, friendship for generations, mutual benefits and cooperation and common development. Obviously, the definition of Sino-Japanese relations was constantly improved and enriched in such four poticial documents.

Secondly, the status of Sino-Japanese relation is basically determined: Sino-Japanese relation is one of the most important bilateral relations for both countries. For example, Paragraph I of Part III of China-Japan Joint Declaration states that both parties confirm Sino-Japanese relation is one of the most important bilateral relations for both countries. Article 1 of Sino-Japanese Joint Statement on All-round Promotion of Strategic and Mutually Beneficial Relations stipulates that both parties unanimously believe Sino-Japanese relation is one of the most important bilateral relations for both countries. In other words, both parties confirm the important status of the other party.

Thirdly, the anti-hegemonism principle is upheld. For example, neither party shall seek hegemony in Asian-Pacific region and either party opposes any other country's efforts to establish such hegomony (Article 7 of China-Japan Joint Statement and Article 2 of the China-Japan Treaty of Peace and Friendship). Paragraph II of Part II of China-

Japan Joint Declaration states that both parties reiterate maintenance of regional peace and promotion of regional development are basic guidelines firmly held by both parties who will not seek hegemony in this region. Paragraph 1 of Article 4 of Sino-Japanese Joint Statement on All-round Promotion of Strategic and Mutually Beneficial Relations stipulates both parties confirm they are partners and will not impose threats to each other; both parties reiterate mutual support for peaceful development of the other party. Therefore, both countries shall actively support peaceful development process of the other party and oppose all kinds of measures and conducts making efforts to seek and establish hegemony including cooperation with some other countries to respond to other countries.

Fourthly, the principle of peaceful settlement of disputes is upheld. For example, both governments confirm to settle all disputes in their mutual relations by peaceful means without resorting to the use or threat of force (Article 6 of China-Japan Joint Statement and Paragraph 2 of Article 2 of the China-Japan Treaty of Peace and Friendship); both parties reiterate that they will not use force or the threat of force and advocate settlement of all disputes by peaceful means (Paragraph II of Part II of China-Japan Joint Declaration); Paragraph 4 of Article 4 of Sino-Japanese Joint Statement on All-round Promotion of Strategic and Mutually Beneficial Relations stipulates that both parties insist on settlement of issues between them through consultation and negotiation.

Fifthly, the spirit, principle, content and mode of developing

Sino-Japanese relations are determined. For example, Article 3 of the China-Japan Treaty of Peace and Friendship states that both parties will make efforts to further develop economic and cultural relations between them and promote exchance between their people in the spirit of good neighborliness and according to princples of equality, mutual benefit and non-interference with domestic affairs. Paragraph V of Part I of China-Japan Joint Declaration points out that both parties will enhance coordination and cooperation in fields such as international politics, economics and global issues to make positive contribution to world peace and development as well as cause of human progress including that both parties will actively take part in various multiple activities in the region such as ASEAN regional forum and carry out coordination and cooperation, support all measures benefiting promotion of understanding and trust (Paragraph IV of Part II of China-Japan Joint Declaration); both parties confirm to make mutual leaders' visit alternately and by turn every year, build Sino-Japanese governmental hotline between Beijing and Tokyo, and enhance exchange at all levels especially between teenagers shouldering future development of both countries (Paragraph VI of Part III of China-Japan Joint Declaration); both parties shall, on basis of equality and mutual benefits, establish long-term and stable economic and trade cooperation relations, further expand their cooperation in high-tech, information, environment protection, agriculture, infrastructure and other fileds (Paragraph VII of Part III of China-Japan Joint Declaration). Both parties have decided to establish diolague and cooperation framework and carry out cooperation in the following five fields: promotion of political mutual trust; increase of cultural exchange and enhancement of national friendship and emotion; expansion of mutual benefits and cooperation; common efforts in development of Asian-Pacific region, joint response to global issues (Article 6 of Sino-Japanese Joint Statement on All-round Promotion of Strategic and Mutually Beneficial Relations).

According to the aforesaid basic principles of four important documents dealing with Sino-Japanese relations, both countries shall develop sustabinable and amicable relations in order to realize the objective of peaceful coexistance, win-win through cooperation and common development. We must deeply understand and acquire the nature and requirements.

Both countries enhance communication and coordination, bridge gap, seek common ground while reserving differences, strengthen comprehensive cooperation, expand common interests, boost trust and realize peaceful development through diolague and consultation to make contributions to ensure regional and world safety and development. This is the important guaidline and basic stance for both governments to comply with without violation and disregard. China and Japan must not stand against or oppose each other, otherwise Sino-Japanese relations will be set back, resulting in confrontation and mutual damage.

Therefore, specific and practical measures shall be taken to try the best to ease and improve Sino-Japanese relations, including further enrichment and improvement of connotation of Sino-Japanese relations, make effors to develop and establish comprehensively strategic and mutually beneficial relations between China and Japan for protecting the overall situation of Sino-Japanense relations. This is the requirment and call of the era.

In short, powerful steps and measures shall be taken including making efforts to see beyong small issues and protect the overall situation through dialogue and consultation in order to further deepen and solidify the comprehensively strategic and mutually beneficial relations between China and Japan and make both countries' contribution to regional and world peace and development.

This article was originally published on Page A16
of *Dongfang Daily* on Oct. 25, 2013

Defuse Dangerous Tensions between China and Japan

Japan's provoking of China in its bid to get a full-fledged military is a dangerous gambit that could go too far.

Since the Japanese government's illegal "purchase" of parts of China's Diaoyu Islands last September, relations between Japan and China have continued to sour, and tensions are high after a Japanese warship and military plane intruded into a naval exercise being conducted by China on the open sea of the West Pacific.

The intrusion is a dangerous provocation that might lead to immediate military confrontation. Every country is entitled to hold military drills on the open seas, and the ships and planes of other countries are advised to stay out of the exercise area. When holding naval exercises, the country concerned should consider other countries' navigational freedom and alert foreign vessels and planes and make sure they are well informed. However, the country retains the right to send up a flare or even eject the foreign vessels and planes if they refuse to leave the area.

Chinese authorities publicized the exercise areas via international maritime organizations in accordance with international custom. However, Japan's military vessel and reconnaissance aircraft remained in the zone for an undue length of time. And ignoring an alert from China, they monitored Chinese activities at close distance and seriously disrupted the naval drill. Japan's act is in severe violation of international law and practice.

For decades, Japan has been aspiring to become a "normal country", one that can regain clout not only with a revived economy but also with a full-fledged military. In the eyes of Japanese politicians, the need to gain the status of a normal country seems particularly urgent in the context of Washington's strategic rebalancing toward the Asia-Pacific, the prolonged tensions over regional territorial disputes, and also the new arms race in Asia. Japan is counting on the US' wish for it to play a bigger role in the region as an ally. China's rapidly growing strength and its firm stance over the Diaoyu Islands is also being drummed up by Japan as an excuse to further boost its military capabilities.

There has been resistance at home and beyond as Japan inches toward revising its pacifist constitution and establishing a full-fledged military. To overcome this resistance, Prime Minister Shinzo Abe and his supporters are overplaying external threats. The recent intrusion of the Japanese warship and military plane into China's drill zone is just part of the long-standing pattern of Tokyo provoking and stirring up trouble to fan the flames of nationalist sentiment at home and seek support for its military buildup.

Such acts based on self-interest will do no good to regional stability. It is in the fundamental interests of both sides to ease the tension and improve and stabilize bilateral ties by adhering to the principles and spirit enshrined in the four political documents between China and Japan.

To this end, it is all the more essential to realize that the souring of bilateral ties is not simply because of the territorial dispute. Given the complexity of the issues, the two countries will not be able to come up with any quick fix and thus should remain coolheaded and seek a viable solution in the long run.

Tokyo should withdraw from its conspiracy of playing up the islands dispute and broaden its perspective on bilateral ties. After all, the overall interests of the bilateral relations lie in their interdependency especially on the economic front, and it is of mutual benefit for the two countries to shelve the dispute over the Diaoyu Islands and seek cooperation in other areas.

Japan should also understand and respect China's maritime needs. The 30-plus years of reform and opening-up have equipped China with the economic foundation and technological conditions needed for its maritime development, which remains rather backward. The country's maritime activities including its naval drills will become more regular, though still not comparable with the many drills conducted by Japan and the United States, and Tokyo should be aware of that.

Moreover, considering that bilateral tensions have escalated from the level of maritime law enforcement to military confrontation, the two countries should set up a bilateral maritime emergency management mechanism. They should also standardize the notification system to inform each other of their major maritime activities, so as to enhance communication and avoid misunderstandings and miscalculations.

The resumption of the Sino-Japanese maritime consultation and negotiation process is also of great necessity. Beijing and Tokyo reached a principled consensus on the East China Sea issue in June 2008 through consultations on an equal footing. However, they stalled after the detention of a Chinese trawler captain by the Japanese coast guard in the contested waters in 2010. Of course, even with the resumption of the process, bilateral differences will persist and they will find it hard to reach a consensus. Still, the resumption of bilateral negotiations will be a key step toward easing tension over the islands and boosting mutual trust.

China, meanwhile, should attach great importance to its policy toward Japan. China surpassed Japan in nominal GDP in 2010, and after three more years of development, the country has gained a competitive edge over Japan not only on the economic front but also in many other areas. Japan remains pessimistic about the future of its economy. Today these feelings have gone from bad to worse because of its rising neighbor, which is likely to undermine the development of bilateral ties. That is why China must accurately define bilateral relations and analyze Japan's role and influence in the process of China's peaceful development.

China's rise is inevitable, and Beijing should promote the fact its rise is peaceful to dispel the concerns of other countries, including Japan. It is equally important to enhance communication and consultation with Washington, as it plays a key role in influencing Japan's policy initiatives, and hence can make efforts to prevent a military clash between China and Japan.

This article was originally published on Page 8 of *China Daily* on Nov. 22, 2013

Several Thoughts and Suggestions on Improving Sino-Japan Relations

At present, the intense rivalry between China and Japan concerning Diaoyu Islands, which have brought Sino-Japanese relations into the nadir after the normalization of diplomatic relation between China and Japan (China-Japan Joint Statement, Sept. 29, 1972), seriously go against the supposed status and aim of Sino-Japanese relations. It is an important issue for both coutries to consider that how to deal with Sino-Japanese relations according to principles and spirits determined in four political documents between China and Japan including enrichment and development of sustainable and amicable cooperation relations between China and Japan, realization of comprehensively strategic and mutually beneficial relations, protection of regional and world peace and development.

Sino-Japanese relation has been increasingly deteriorated since Sept.11, 2012 when Japanese government adopted the policy of naturalizing Diaoyu Islands and afterwards China took powerful measures to maintain its sovereignty. The two countries' official ships stood off at the time of cruise and law enforcement. Meanwhile, unapproved entry of warships and aircrafts of Japan Self-Defense Force into China's designated military drill areas of Western Pacific increased the possibility and dangerousness of military conflicts between China and Japan.

It is generally believed that every country has the right to conduct military drill in high seas which is regarded as part of traditional freedom of high seas. Relevant countries shall try to keep away including no operation and activity in such drill areas. Of course, when exercising such right, the country shall give consideration to other countries' interests in utilizing the freedom of high seas. Therefore, when ships or planes of other countries go into the military drill areas, reminding information and requests for avoidance shall be issued and be surely heard or seen by such ships or planes. If warships and aircrafts of other countries are still unwilling to leave the military drill area after such information or requests are issued, signal flare can be fired and measures such as eviction and force can be taken.

Although Japan has the right to pay attention to other countries' military drill in sea areas surrounding its territory, but its conduct of stubborn retention of warships and aircrafts in China's military drill areas designated according to proper procedures is obviously not compliance with international law especially international practices. Because such conduct is dangerous, serously influencing peace and safety, clearly disturbing and hindering China's normal conduct of military drill programs, it shall be corrected and not be allowed to occur any more.

In addition, Ministry of National Defense of China, based on the safety in East China Sea, especially the flying safety, and for protection of sovereignty of Diaoyu Islands and legitimate rights and interests of surrounding sea areas, established Air Defense Identification Zone in East China Sea on Nov. 23, 2013 and issued rules on identifying aircrafts in Air Defense Identification Zone of East China Sea. However, because the Air Defense Identification Zone of China and that of Japan overlap a lot, Japan made protests. It should be said that it is very necessary to make further communication to let Japan respect China's concerns and conducts.

At present, there is a trend of armament races in East Asia. The United States, under the situation of declining strength and failure to impose control independently, needs to further take advantage of roles of its allies, especially Japan in defense to maintain its directing position in Asian Pacific. Japan holds the opinion of accelarating development of defense power to safeguard its interests and realize its objective of being a normalized country. But the development of Japanense defence power is limited by international and demostic factors, so against the background that it is unable to demostically promote development of defence power as soon as possible and amend the Consitution Law, it becomes an important option to create and utilize threats of external factors. The forcible entry of warships and aircrafts of Japan

Self-Defense Force into China's military drill areas is a provocative and dangerous conduct trying to create an accident with conflicts, arouse domestic national emotion, add to its excuse for improving defense power to develop and expand military strength to respond to "Challenges" from China. Moreover, the entry Japanese warships and aircrafts into China's military drill areas without permission was partly due to the intention of collecting information on the real strength of China Navy and testing China's bottom line.

What shall China and Japan do to stabilize their relations and avoid military conflicts, accident even war.

Firstly, both parties shall fully understand the sensitivity of the issue of Diaoyu Islands and deal with it properly. The issue of Diaoyu Islands is very complicated and sensitive and both countries have no space for making compromise, so there is still difficult to settle the issue of Diaoyu Islands in recent times. Under this situation, both parties shall calmly deal with the issue of Diaoyu Islands in low key, especially Japan shall give up its policy and thought of speculating and amplifying the issue of Diaoyu Islands to realize its objective of military development, to try their best to make Diaoyu Islands impose no adverse influence on the overall target of Sino-Japanese relations. The so-called overall target of Sino-Japanese relations means that both parties shall further deepen their mutual dependent relations on basis of economy and realize the objective of good neighborliness and long-term development.

Secondly, China and Japan shall fully understand the inevitability of China's reliance on the sea and China's reasonable requests. The achievements of more than thirty years' reform and opening-up have equipped China with economic basis and technological conditions for getting access to and exploiting the sea as well as strategizing on and managing the sea. Meanwhile, it is necessary and reasonable for China to rely on the sea and need ocean resources for further development. China will inevitably strengthen its marine activities including military drills, so Japan shall fully understand the inevitability of China's activities of going in and out of the sea and maintain a normal attitude. For this, it is of special significance for China and Japan to further enhance communication and coordination.

Thirdly, both parties shall build Sino-Japanese ocean crisis management mechanism. Recently, there has been a trend for ocean conflicts between both China and Japan developing into military conflicts from law enforcement conflicts. In order to avoid military accident and collision of law enforcement ships, both parties shall build Sino-Japanese ocean crisis management mechanism as soon as possible including dialogue and consultation mechanism at law enforcement level (China Coast Guard and Japan Coast Guard) and military level (Chinese People's Liberation Army and Japan Self-Defense Force). Especially both parties shall regulate the notification system on major ocean activities in Sino-Japanese ocean crisis management mechanism to enhance communication and exchange, avoid unnecessary accident and wrong interpretation due to misreading and misunderstanding.

Fourthly, both parties shall resume negotiation on Sino-Japanese marine issues. China and Japan have established the high-level marine issue consultation mechanism participated by many sea-related agencies, but due to the incident of collision of ships in sea areas surrounding Diaoyu Islands and the seizure of Chinese captains (Sept. 7, 2010), consultation and negotiation on Sino-Japanese marine issues between China and Japan were suspended. In order to reasonably deal with Sino-Japanese marine issues and disputes including the issue of Diaoyu Islands, it is an urgent task to resume negotiation on Sino-Japanese marine issues for discharging obligations under the document.

Fifthly, both parties shall fully understand that competition between them will be long-term and tough. Since China surpassed Japan in GDP in 2010, there has been a sense of loss and pessimism in Japan. This situation can not be changed in recent times, therefore, China must attach great importance to policies on Japan from the strategic perspective including correctly defining Sino-Japanese relations and analyzing Japan's status, role and effect in China's peaceful development, practically enhance research into Japan and make suitable response, try its best to avoid events that Japan may provoke China to use force, proactively and actively utilize media resources to publicize its policies including reasonably and moderately instructing media reports. This is very important.

It is an irresistible trend for China to make development. In order to make other countries understand China's policies on peaceful development more including activities and conducts of peaceful utilization of the sea and ocean resources, China shall create conditions for building Sino-Japanese foreign and defense ministers consultation mechanism (" 2+2 " conference) to make comprehensive communication on policies on foreign affairs and national defenses, seek moderate understanding and support, provide guaranty for sustainable enrichment and development of Sino-Japanese friendship. In addition, the attitude of the United States and its control over Japan are key to the occurrence of military conflicts and avoidance of accident between China and Japan. Therefore, it is also crucial for China to enhance communication and coordination with the United States.

This article was originally published on Page A15
of *Dongfang Daily* on Dec. 5, 2013

China Should Improve Law Enforcement System for Sea and Air Security of East China Sea

Decision of the Central Committee of the Communist Party of China on Some Major Issues Concerning Comprehensively Deepening the Reform (hereinafter referred to as Decision) points out that (China) will establish National Security Commission of the Communist Party of China, improve national safety system and strategy to ensure national security; China shall increase law enforcement power in major fields such as sea areas and islands and improve law enforcement level.

At present, against the background that sea and air security issue of East China Sea is especially outstanding, China must make every effort to improve law enforcement system for sea and air security of East China Sea and further strengthen out China's system and mechanism on management of marine issues and defense security to ensure national security.

Firstly, from the perspective of sea areas of East China Sea, China shall improve law enforcement system in sea areas surrounding Diaoyu

Islands to maintain security and order of sea areas of East China Sea and ensure marine rights and interests.

After Japan "nationalized" three islands of Diaoyu Islands, China published the baseline of the territorial sea of Diaoyu Island and its affiliated islands on Sept. 10, 2012. Since then, China has realized its normalized management system in sea areas surrounding Diaoyu Islands. Therefore, under the premises that both parties make no compromise, the rate of incidents of collision and conflicts between Chinese and Japanese law enforcement vessels is rising. Japan did not only amend Law on Japan Coast Guard and Law on Foreign Ship's Navigation in Areas including the Territorial Sea, endowing law enforcers of Japan Coast Guard with police power over island landers, foreign ships and crews in sea areas surrounding Diaoyu Islands, that is to say, strengthening the so-called countermeasures, but also formulated Basic Plan on the Sea (2013–2017), reorganizing new security policies and measures with focus on strengthening the "management" over Southwest islands. Against such background, it is insufficient for China to just announce the baseline of the territorial sea of Diaoyu Island and its affiliated islands, it is also necessary to improve systems of law enforcement in neibourghering sea areas, including a system of foreign ships' navigation in waters surrounding Diaoyu Islands, a stystem of cruise and law enforcement in sea areas governed by China with focus on specifying the authority of ocean management organ and punitive measures in order to deal with illegal activities discovered in the course of law enforcement.

Secondly, from the perspective of airspace of East China Sea, China shall mainly improve the law enforcement system of Air Defense Identification Zone for stabilizing security and order of airspace of East China Sea and ensure the safety of air space.

In order to guarantee the aviation safety in airspace of East China Sea including sea areas surrounding Diaoyu Islands, avoid such incident as entry of Japanese warships and aircrafts without permission into China's military drill sea areas and airspace designated according to international rules, as emergency and counter measures, Ministry of National Defense of China announced Air Defense Identification Zone and published rules on identifying aircrafts on Nov. 23, 2013 in order to impose further control over the order and aviation safety in airspace of East China Sea. However, because Air Defense Identification Zone of China and that of Japan (announced on Apr. 29, 1969, amended on May 10, 1972 and June 30, 1973) overlap a lot, the probability of conflicts and accidents made by aircrafts, especially military aircrafts of both countries in overlapped zone has been increased. Under such situation especially when aircrafts of the other party fail to comply with rules of China on identifying aircrafts in East China Sea, China shall further improve law enforcement system including formulation of detailed regulations for rules on identifying aircrafts in Air Defense Identification Zone of East China Sea, implementation of differentiated management system in airspaces with different natures to ensure ordinary operation and reasonable management of Air Defense Identification Zone of East

China Sea.

Thirdly, China shall further accelerate its steps in developing ocean system and mechanism with focus on formulating and implementing the Basic Law of the Sea.

Taking into consideration that management organs maintaining sea and air safety of East China Sea include State Oceanic Administration of People's Republic of China and Ministry of National Defense of China, it is important to coordinate their authorities. Therefore, China shall take the current reorganization of State Oceanic Administration of People's Republic of China and establishment of National Ocean Commission as an opportunity to enhance the mechanism of unifying and coordinating ocean issues. The specific suggestion is to further strengthen out ocean mechanism and system under the National Security Commission (Leading Group Office for Works Concerning Marine Rights and Interests, Ocean Commission, State Oceanic Administration and China Coast Guard) to clear their respective powers and functions and realistically promote the unification and coordination of marine affairs, also strengthen contacts with Ministry of National Defense including information communication, and coordinate with Ministry of Foreign Affairs to give unified statement and explanation in time and realize the objective of comprehensive coordination and management.

From the perspective of maintaining sea and air security of East China Sea, China and Japan shall further enhance information communication and coordination mechanism for major sea and air activities including the management mechanism for sea and air crisis between Ministry of National Defense of China and Ministry of Defense of Japan and between China Coast Guard and Japan Coast Guard in order to avoid occurrence of major sea or air accidents. Therefore, both parties shall create good basis and conditions for building the aforesaid mechanism, especially they shall improve political atmosphere between China and Japan.

From the domestic level, China shall formulate and implement the Basic Law of the Sea to further strengthen out authorities of the aforesaid organs, including making clear the composition and tasks of Leading Group Office for Works Concerning Marine Rights and Interests and Ocean Commission in the Basic Law of the Sea, in order to organize strength to deal with marine issues in an unified and coordinated way, increase efficiency, protect marine rights and interests and ensure national security.

This article was originally published on Page A10 of *Dongfang Daily* on Dec. 17, 2013

Work to Make a Sea Change

China and Japan must increase communication and establish coordination to prevent untoward incidents in East China Sea.

A State security committee will be set up to improve systems and strategies to ensure national security, according to the Decisions on Major Issues Concerning Comprehensively Deepening Reforms, issued by the Third Plenum of the 18th Communist Party of China Central Committee in November. The plenum document also calls for bolstering maritime law enforcement in China's territorial waters, including around islands.

National security includes maritime security, which has a direct bearing on China's strategy of becoming a sea power through peaceful development. Given the increase in sea and air safety related problems in the East China Sea, China must expedite efforts to secure its maritime territory, exercise its territorial rights in the East China Sea, especially in the waters surrounding the Diaoyu Islands, and strengthen the management and mechanism of maritime affairs to safeguard national security and protect its overall maritime rights and interests.

After Japan "nationalized" the Diaoyu Islands in September 2012, China announced the baselines of its territorial waters, which covers the Diaoyu Islands and their affiliated islets, enforced its maritime law and regularized patrol missions near the islands. Since neither China nor Japan is ready to make any concession, the risk of the two countries' patrol vessels colliding has increased.

Moreover, Japan has empowered its Coast Guard to police the waters off Diaoyu Islands and arrest anyone who sets foot on them. It also has developed a five-year basic plan for ocean policy to integrate new security policies and measures with focus on strengthening the "management" of the Diaoyu Islands.

It is thus not enough for China to only announce the baselines of its territorial waters around the Diaoyu Islands and their affiliated islets. It also has to strengthen measures to enforce its maritime laws, which should include intensified patrolling of the surrounding waters with emphasis on defining the functions, powers and punitive measures of maritime management organizations.

To ensure airspace safety over and maintain order in the East China Sea, China should more firmly enforce the laws of its new Air Defense Identification Zone. To guarantee the safety of flights within the ADIZ, including the area over the Diaoyu Islands, and strengthen control over the East China Sea airspace, the Ministry of National Defense has issued the aircraft identification rules.

Because of the large overlapping area of the ADIZs of China and

Japan, there is increased fear of the two countries' aircraft, especially warplanes, clashing. Making matters worse is Japan's adamant stance not to abide by China's ADIZ rules.

Therefore, China should take steps to bolster the enforcement of its ADIZ rules, including formulating detailed regulations for aircraft identification, applying different management tactics for different areas of the airspace, to ensure the normal operation of its airspace over the East China Sea.

China should further strengthen its maritime defense system, for which a key step should be the formulation and implementation of the basic law of ocean. Considering that the State Oceanic Administration and the Ministry of National Defense are the main departments in charge of maintaining sea and air safety in the East China Sea, it is very important that they establish a sound coordination mechanism for the sharing of functions and powers.

The development in the East China Sea is a good opportunity for China to restructure the State Oceanic Administration and establish a national ocean council, and set up a unified coordination mechanism for maritime affairs.

The leadership of the proposed State security committee should help streamline the maritime defense system, define the specific functions and powers of different departments (including a leading central group on maritime rights and interests, national ocean council, State Oceanic Administration and China Coast Guard), promote coordinated action in dealing with maritime affairs and strengthen cooperation with the Ministry of National Defense, including sharing of information and intelligence.

The proposed council should also coordinate with the Ministry of Foreign Affairs to ensure that all departments speak in one voice when it comes to defense matters.

But it is absolutely necessary that China and Japan increase communication and strengthen their coordination mechanism over major sea and air activities to maintain sea and air safety, prevent accidents and respond to emergencies in the East China Sea.

The coordination mechanism should include the establishment of a sea and air crisis management system between China's Ministry of National Defense and the Japanese Ministry of Defense and between the Coast Guards of the neighboring countries.

This article was originally published on Page 8 of *China Daily* on Jan. 8, 2014

On Connotation of Japanese So-called "Inherent Territory"

As for the issue of Diaoyu Islands, Japanese government holds that Diaoyu Island and its affiliated islands known as Senkaku Islands in Japan is the Inherent Territory of Japan. Even representative documents of Ministry of Foreign Affairs of Japan on Senkaku Islands (for example, the Basic View on the Sovereignty over the Senkaku Islands published by Ministry of Foreign Affairs of Japan on Mar. 8, 1972, "Three Truths" about the Senkaku Islands on Oct. 4, 2012 and Senkaku Islands Flyer in Oct. 2013) call it "Inherent Territory" of Japan. Therefore, it is necessary to discuss the connotation of inherent territory including the time of using such term, its origin and changes and its meaning.

I. Initial Appearance and Frustration of the Concept of "Inherent Territory"

The Origin of the term Inherent Territory is Inherent Land which first appeared in Konoe Peace Plan about territorial issues between Japan and Soviet prior to the end of World War II. On July 10, 1949, in order to seek Soviet's compliance with Japan-USSR Neutrality Treaty and try to maintain peace relations with the United States and Britain, Fumimaro Konoe, a special envoy dispatched by Japan proposed the concept of Inherent Land in a plan to Soviet made with the help of his brain truster Koji Sakai, a lieutenant general. In this plan to Soviet recognized by Japanese Emperor, the text regarding Inherent Land is as follows: the scope of Japanese territory shall be determined as possible as we can in a way that is beneficial for further negotiation. At least it shall satisfy the requirement of Inherent Land. The so-called Inherent Land refers to the bottom line of giving up Okinawa, Bonin Islands and Karafuto but at least keeping the southern half of Kurile under its territorial scope. It is obvious that the territory of the South Kuril Islands is the Inherent Land of Japan. The Inherent Land hereby is only a concept for Japanese government to propose for trying the best to retain a land as territory of Japan in negotiation.

The term of Inherent Territory was proposed by foreign minister as a basis for Japan to claim recovery of Northern Territories in an intense debate in congress during the negotiation of normalization of Japan-Soviet relations. The foreign minister of Japan Mamoru Shigemitsu maintained that the South Kuril Islands were Inherent Territory of Japan (Nov. 30, 1955). From the perspective of history, the fact that the South Kuril Islands are the territory of Japan was undoubted, so it could be claimed for recovery as Inherent Territory of Japan (Dec. 16, 1955). We can see from the above-mentioned that the term of Inherent Territory was a new concept proposed as a basis for recovery of Northern Territories. This new concept of Inherent Territory was appeared in foreign situation in the summer of 1956 for the first time when the foreign minister of Japan Mamoru Shigemitsu as a plenipotentiary went to Moscow to negotiate with Soviet on normalization of Japan-Soviet relations. The foreign minister of Japan Mamoru Shigemitsu pointed out that Kunashiri and Etorofu-Shima in the Northern Territories are permanent territory of Japan in the past and at present which will not given up by Japan forever. In other words, Japan proposed the concept of Inherent Territory in foreign situation for the first time. However, this opinion was not affirmed by Soviet in the negotiation. So the foreign minister of Japan Mamoru Shigemitsu withdrew such proposition and turned to preparation for conclusion of treaty on peace for recovering Habomai and Shikotan in Northern Territories. It is clear that the concept of Inherent Territory is just a bargaining chip for diplomatic negotiation and an irrational proposition which could not be accepted by the other party.

II. The Revival and Variance of the Concept of Inherent Territory

In order to conclude a treaty with Soviet on recovering two islands in the Northern Territories, Ministry of Foreign Affairs of Japan consulted the United States that whether it was ok to hold that the Kurile islands given up by Japan in the Treaty of San Francisco excluded Kunashiri and Etorofu-Shima in the Northern Territories when Japan requested Soviet to return the Northern Territories. For this question, the United States responded that it was welcome for Japan to request the Northern Territories from Soviet but the United States could not make public explanation that the Kurile islands given up by Japan in the Treaty of San Francisco only included two islands. This ambiguous response stopped the process of signing treaty on peace between Japan and Soviet for returning land including the aforesaid two islands. Afterwards, the United States published memorandum supporting Japan's request for the Northern Territories on Sept. 7, 1956, which pointed out that Kunashiri and Etorofu-Shima constituted an inherent part of Japan proper, so they were definitely territory under Japan's sovereignty. Japan translated the Japan proper in the memorandum of the United States as Inherent Territory of Japan, so the concept of Inherent Territory revived magically and became correct remark of Japan-USA cooperation. However, this is a false translation. It mainly refers to Japan proper, so the concept of Inherent Territory means nothing in diplomatic negotiation.

III. The Varied Translation of the Concept of Inherent Territory

The Japanese government used the concept of Inherent Territory in the issue of Takeshima / Dokdo between Japan and South Korea. For example, Ministry of Foreign Affairs of Japan pointed out at the time of South Korea's issuance of new opinion on the issue of Takeshima that Takeshima was clearly Japan's Inherent Territory even according to historical facts and from the perspective of international law (July 13, 1962). Hereby Japan translated the concept as Japan's inherent territory. For this, South Korea orally responded on Feb. 25, 1963 that Dokdo was an integral part of the Korean territory, the English translation version of which is still used by the Korean government nowadays. Afterwards, Japan changed its translation into a part of Japanese territory by reference to translation by South Korean and now translates it as an inherent part of Japanese territory. It is clear that the translation of the concept of Inherent Territory made by Japan is constantly changing.

IV. Role and Meaning of the Concept of Inherent Territory

Inherent Territory is not a legal term because such term does not appear in documents of international law. For example, Paragraph 4 of Article 2 of the Charter of the United Nations states that All Members shall refrain in their international relations from the threat or use of force against the territorial integrity or political independence of any state. At the same time, there is no such term or explanation in various legal dictionaries. The concept of Inherent Territory is just a political word with the purpose of enhancing Japan's proposition on territory but achieving nothing in negotiation on territorial disputes. Therefore Japan shall try its best to use less or even do not use the term of Inherent Territory in order to avoid encouragement of nationalist sentiment and difficulties in settlement of territorial disputes.

This article was originally published on Page A11 of *Dongfang Daily* on Feb. 18, 2014

China Should Re-define Sino-Japan Relations

Since Japanese Prime Minister Abe Shinzo took office, in order to cater to Japanese national's sense of panic, he has adopted all-round right-deviated policies and measures to ensure Japan's international status and accelerate Japan's process of normalization. In terms of economy, his administration has proactively promoted Abe Economics and further enhanced the US-Japan alliance in terms of security.

Japan preaches the security threats of China through speculating China's law enforcement activities in sea areas and airspace of Diaoyu Islands including fire-control radar irradiation incident and aircraft approaching incident to create a false image that China unilaterally changes the current situation by use of force or duress, thus gaining support and assistance from the United States to strengthen the US-Japan alliance.

To this end, the United States did not only pass National Defense Authorization Act for Fiscal Year 2013 in the congress officially announcing the act that includes the content of Diaoyu Islands defense by the United States, but also spared no efforts to welcome and support Japan in lifting the ban on collective right of self-defense. According to reports of Kyodo News Agency, regarding the issue of adding the provision that the Self-Defense Force supports the United States Army in Guidelines for Japan-U.S. Defense Cooperation amended in 2014, Japanese and the USA governments have basically decided to expand the scope of areas for logistic support which are no longer limited to those areas without possibility of war when Korean Peninsula incident or other surrounding area incident happens. There is also a plan in the new guidelines to enhance warning and surveillance operation in Southwest Islands and meanwhile promote the joint utilization of bases and facilities between Japan and the United States.

In addition to this, Japan has also enhanced cooperation with some ASEAN countries, Australia and India including trying to strengthen marine cooperation with ASEAN Member States especially those having disputes over marine issues with China through flexible utilization of Official Development Assistance (ODA) to improve their marine law enforcement and surveillance capability to deal with the so-called challenge from China. The strategic aim of Abe administration is not only a normal country and a political power, but also a military power, as well as hoping Japan to become a globally comprehensive power after the USA to direct the Asian progress.

It should be said that there are still some obstacles for Japan to realize such objectives including differences in strategic aims with the United States, influences of its attitude towards World War II only limited to East Asian Region, as well as the world's acceptance of Japan. Even in Japan, there are different voices. If those can not be handled properly, there will be regime risks. The opposition against China will influence economic interests of Japan and the domestic economic development of Japan is of great importance for the continued existence of Abe administration. At the same time, it is resistible for China to enjoy development and raise influence, and there are risks and challenges in Japan's attempts to establish encirclement to defer China's development. Therefore, it is possible for Abe to adjust diplomatic policies for interest balance.

In order to respond to Japan's powerful right-deviated measures and achieve relatively advantageous status in all-round confrontation and competition between China and Japan, China shall mainly adopt the following strategies:

The first one is to strengthen research into the issue of Diaoyu Islands from the perspectives of the public opinion and the law. China shall conduct specific study on detailed issues of Diaoyu Islands, especially give active response to Japan's policies and legal propositions, including publishing Suggestion on China's Policies on the Issue of Diaoyu Islands (academic edition) in sutiable time to give powerfully response in the public opinion war. Meanwhile, China shall also have a stimulation of and give response to resolving the issue of Diaoyu Islands by legal means and make good preparation for lawsuit initiated by Japan in International Court of Justice.

The second one is to enhance sea and air security control effect in Diaoyu Islands. Although China Coast Guard has entered into the territorial sea of Diaoyu Islands and implemented normalized cruise system, this just shows the existence and announcement of China's sovereignty and fails to embody the practical jurisdiction. Therefore, cruise activities shall be made with the aim to decrease behaviors such as innocent passage and improve the legal effect of cruise made by China Coast Guard. To this end, China shall make clear powers and functions of China Coast Guard including enactment of Law on Structure of China Coast Guard. In addition, China shall further improve the system of Air Defense Identification Zone in East China Sea including formulation of detailed regulations on implementation of rules on identifying aircrafts in Air Defense Identification Zone of East China Sea with the aim to enhance control and deal with challenges.

Thirdly, China shall strengthen functions of marine mechanism and system. Although China has established Leading Group for Works Concerning Marine Rights and Interests, its Office and Ocean Commission and reorganized State Oceanic Administration, special arrangement and plan shall be made to practically promote and instruct marine works and ocean issues, including enactment of the Basic Law of the Sea as soon as possible to comprehensively regulate marine affairs, imposing emphasis on making clear powers and functions of each relevant authority, expounding China's marine policies and stances in order to realize the objective of national comprehensive coordination and management of marine affairs.

The fourth one is to make good and detailed preparation for Sino-Japanese negotiation. It is deniable that Sino-Japanese relation is an important bilateral relation, so it is of special significance to utilize dialogue and negotiation to further strengthen out Sino-Japanese relations, eliminate obstacles and doubts, enhance mutual trust according to principles and spirits of four political documents. For this reason, China shall make deployment and plans as soon as possible on various preparatory works for negotiation with Japan. At the same time, China and Japan shall make plans on enrichment and development of strategic relation with mutual benefits at the strategic and tactical levels with focus on creating conditions for planning the future of Sino-Japanese relations including exploration of possibility of formulation of the fifth political document in order to redefine Sino-Japanese correctly.

The fifth one is to correctly handle relations with the United States. China must not exclude the role played by the United States in the issue of Diaoyu Islands because the United States is an important factor and element in arousing, returning, manipulating and resolving the issue of Diaoyu Islands, so China shall utilize the contradiction between the United States and Japan, especially the United States' stance on Diaoyu Islands and shall not push the USA to the side of Japan completely which will create a passive situation and disadvantageous status for China in marine strategy. At the same time, China shall keep an eye on Japan and the USA to eliminate influence on resolving South China Sea issues when Japan and the USA take amendment to Guidelines for Japan-U.S. Defense Cooperation as an opportunity to expand the scope of the so-called defense cooperation.

Finally, it should be pointed out that the competition between China and Japan will be comprehensive, long-term and tough, so China shall have full understanding and preparation in mind. The key is to define Sino-Japanese relations correctly that what role Japan plays in China's development, challenger, threat imposer, cooperator? In other words, China shall evaluate whether it can assume the adverse influence of a totally broken Sino-Japanese relations in order to establish definition of Sino-Japanese relations and responsive strategy.

This article was originally published on Page A17
of *Dongfang Daily* on June 23, 2014

South China Sea Review

China Should Deal with South China Sea Issues Tier by Tier

South China Sea issues become one of highlights in ASEAN regional forum held recently.

Regarding disputes over islands and reefs in South China Sea, China proposed the policy of Setting Aside Dispute and Seeking Joint Development and signed Declaration on the Conduct of Parties in the South China Sea with ASEAN. However, some countries did not respect and honor the aforesaid policies and relevant documents. For example, the Congress of Philippines adopted Law on Baseline of the Territorial Sea on Feb. 17, 2009 incorporating China's Huangyan Island and some islands and reefs of Nansha Islands into Philippine territory; Malaysian Prime Minister landed onto Swallow Reef declaring sovereignty over such reef and surrounding sea waters on Mar. 5, 2009. Therefore, Chinese government urges all countries to act in compliance with Declaration on the Conduct of Parties in the South China Sea and not to take actions which possibly make disputes more complicated and expanded so as to jointly maintain peace and stability in South China

Sea region.

In South China Sea, a large area of sea waters belonging to China has been delimited into the exclusive economic zone of other countries. Other countries and transnational enterprises of European-American countries have greatly developed resources of South China Sea. At the same time, some ASEAN Member States have often illegally controlled normal operation of Chinese fishermen and make them suffer undue treatments. The main reason for these is that oil, gas and fishery resources become a target for countries to competition for occupation. It is said that sea waters surrounding Nansha Islands in South China store submarine resources equaling to oil in Kuwait in amount.

In addition to this, South China Sea is also an important passage lane for international navigation because the total tonnage of ships passing through Nansha accounts for half of the total tonnage of world ships. The traffic volume in South China Sea is two times of that in Suez Canal and three times in the Panama Canal. It should be mentioned that peace and stability maintenance in South China Sea especially sea waters surrounding Nansha Islands is in compliance with common interests of all countries including the United States. Especially for East Asia with rapid economic development and increasing demand for energy resources, the transportation security in the passage lane of such sea waters must be ensured.

The Unites States' interest in South China Sea is mainly embodied in the freedom of military survey activities in and flight over the exclusive economic zone of China, which is in serious contradiction with China. For example, incidents of military survey activities of USNS Impeccable and plane collision of EP-3 are occurred due to disagreement between China and the United States in understanding military activities and reconnaissance in the exclusive economic zone of China. As for the reconnaissance made by the military plane over the exclusive economic zone of China, the United States holds it is a kind of freedom of flight, inter alia, freedom of high seas, but China maintains it is a kind of unfriendly behavior far beyond freedom of flight and an abuse of right. Other countries must take into consideration interests of coastal states when utilizing the sea and such utilization of the sea must be used for peaceful purpose. Similarly, as for military survey activities in the exclusive economic zone of China, the United States holds it is unnecessary to get permission from coastal states in advance due to freedom of such activities, so their activities are legal. China maintains survey activities in the exclusive economic zone of China (no matter marine scientific research or military survey activities) must get permission from coastal states, otherwise they are illegal.

It is obvious that there are not only disputes concerning ownership over islands and resources development but also opposite and different understanding in survey activities and other issues in South China Sea. Their natures and scopes are different, so solutions are different. The former disputes are between China and some countries of ASEAN, but the latter are between China and a major marine power the Untied States on marine defense security arising from survey activities. The former may be resolved through applying and improving regional system (including formulating a system such as A Code of Conduct of Parties in the South China Sea according to Declaration on the Conduct of Parties in the South China Sea) or bilateral consultation. The latter may be resolved with the help of international community including amending systems concerning marine scientific research and adding systematic rules on military activities in the United Nations Convention on the Law of the Sea and through consultation by means of bilateral mechanism on marine security.

As for South China Sea issue, China may take the following responses and measures: to enhance cruise and law enforcement in South China Sea especially sea waters surrounding Nansha Islands so as to discover problems and take prompt measures; to enhance survey and investigation in Nansha Islands and announce the baseline of the territorial sea of Nansha Islands of China at the right moment; to resolve disputes over islands and reefs with other countries by insisting on principles of documents such as Declaration on the Conduct of Parties in the South China Sea and the United Nations Convention on the Law of the Sea, including resolving issues of delimitation of sea areas through consultation, enhancing communication and coordination to search new mechanism of joint exploration and exploitation of submarine resources of South China Sea, making research into cooperation mechanism on South China Sea issues between cross-straits, enhancing comprehensive research into South China Sea issues including holding academic seminars and publishing important papers and books on South China Sea and so forth.

This article was originally published on Page A15 of *Dongfang Daily* on July 29, 2010

For Order in South China Sea

The root of the ongoing South China Sea dispute is the unilateral actions of Vietnam and the Philippines. The two countries have intensified their efforts to exploit resources and occupy parts of Nansha and Xisha islands, and dismantled plaques China had set up on the Nansha Islands to signify its maritime boundary.

The United States, which is not part of the region, has added fuel to fire by demanding freedom of navigation and holding joint military exercises in the seas off China.

Therefore, resolving the South China Sea issue, especially the jurisdiction of the Nansha Islands, with reason and guaranteeing navigation security and freedom are a challenge that the international community faces. To maintain order and ensure that the situation does not deteriorate further, all parties to the dispute should abide by the 1982 United Nations Convention on the Law of the Sea (UNCLOS) and the 2002 Declaration on the Conduct of Parties in the South China Sea.

Since the shift in global economic activities to the Asia-Pacific region has increased Asian countries' need for energy and resources, some players in the region are trying all means to exploit sea resources and seize the Nansha Islands.

Navigation safety has become a big concern in the South China Sea, which is an important waterway for merchant vessels. The gross tonnage in the waters around the Nansha Islands is half of the world total, and two and three times that of the Suez Canal and the Panama Canal. It is, therefore, in the interest of all countries, including the US, to maintain peace and stability in the South China Sea, especially in the waters around the Nansha Islands.

But the developments in recent times, thanks to some countries' actions, have been to the contrary. The US consolidated its alliance with South Korea and Japan during the Cheonan incident in March last year and after a Chinese fishing trawler collided with two Japanese coast guard vessels near Diaoyu Islands in September. The US has strengthened its strategic arrangements in East Asia, and is more interested in regaining its strategic position in the Asia Pacific than in resolving the issue.

For demarcation of outer continental shelves of countries, the South China Sea dispute has to be resolved immediately. The deadline for countries to submit their outer continental shelf delimitation applications to the Commission on the Limits of the Continental Shelf (CLCS), formed by the UN for the purpose, was May 13, 2009. Vietnam submitted its application on the South China Sea on May 7, 2009, and Malaysia and Vietnam made a joint submission on their claim on the southern part of the South China Sea a day earlier.

Both the submissions violate sovereignty rights and jurisdiction in the South China Sea. The CLCS would consider a submission on the premise that there is no controversy or dispute between or among countries on the issue and in case of any, it will not examine the controversial or disputed parts.

Some Asian countries have taken unilateral action because there are loopholes in international and regional regulations. Though China and Southeast Asian countries signed the Declaration on the Conduct of Parties in the South China Sea on Nov. 4, 2002, the declaration is one of principle and lacks a specific code of conduct, especially on the measures to be taken against countries that violate it.

Countries will always put forward arguments in their own favor, creating conflicts and disputes, and even take actions in pursuit of bigger interests. Worse, whether unilateral or joint actions of countries in the South China Seas have complicated, magnified or harmed regional peace and stability cannot be determined or judged.

For example, the joint war games held in the South China Sea, especially in the waters off the Nansha Islands, are against UNCLOS regulations, and their frequency and purpose have violated the goal of peaceful use of marine resources, which should be opposed.

For the resolution of the maritime disputes between China and some Southeast Asian nations, it is necessary that they clarify their claims, spell out their interests and positions, and hold dialogues.

And to oppose US-led military exercises and joint drills in the region, China should urge the international community to revise the UNCLOS and add specific regulations on military activities. This is important to safeguard common interests such as flights and ships. If international or regional regulations cannot be made specific, China should let its policies be known to the international community.

First, China should tell the international community clearly and confidently what its stand on the South China Sea issue is to ensure that other countries in the region do not misunderstand or misjudge it.

Second, China should stick to the principle of "joint development despite controversies" and despite setbacks. The urgent mission is to identify the controversial regions whose development is acceptable to all parties.

Third, the Chinese government has to set up a higher-level body on maritime issues that would coordinate among related departments to decide on joint actions. It should spell out its territorial "nine-dash" U-shaped baseline in the South China Sea, too, to solicit legal support.

China hopes to resolve the South China Sea disputes without exaggerating or magnifying them. The best way is to establish and maintain mechanisms in the region, and ensure that order and stability in the South China Sea are not harmed and the common interest of the international community is not undermined.

This article was originally published on Page 9 of *China Daily* on June 22, 2011

Peaceful Resolution of South China Sea Issues in Accordance with International Law

Recently, South China Sea issues have attracted attention from the international community and enjoyed a trend of escalation. Such issue was originated from unilateral behaviors and conducts of some countries including expansion of resources development, invasion of part of islands and reefs of Nansha, removal of China's boundary marker in Nansha Islands and Reefs and attempts to "safeguard" rights and interests in South China Sea by use of force. In addition, foreign powerful countries insist on freedom of flight, constantly carry out jointly military drill and desire to participate in dispute settlement, which are also reasons for escalation of South China Sea. Therefore, it is a major project confronted by the international community to further reasonably deal with South China Sea issues especially the issue of sovereignty over islands and reefs of Nansha Islands and ensure the navigation and passage safety and freedom. We must insist on and make efforts in resolving South China Sea issues by peaceful means according to rules of international relations and international laws including the

United Nations Convention on the Law of the Sea and Declaration on the Conduct of Parties in the South China Sea, so as to avoid deterioration of the situation.

I. Taking International Law and International Relations as Guiding Principles

The author suggests that reasons for increasing intension of South China Sea are as follows:

(1) Economical Aspect: The core of world economy has been shifted to Asian-Pacific region. Asian countries need more and more energy resources, so their demands for ocean resources are increasing. In other words, countries further expand their exploration and exploitation of marine resources including enhancing their efforts in occupation of Nansha Islands and Reefs.

(2) Passage Safety Aspect: South China Sea is an important passage lane for international navigation because the total tonnage of ships passing through Nansha accounts for half of that of the whole world ships. The traffic volume in South China Sea is two times of that in Suez Canal and three times in the Panama Canal. Therefore, peace and stability maintenance in South China Sea especially sea waters surrounding Nansha Islands is in compliance with common interests of all countries including the United States.

(3) Regime of Outer Continental Shelf requires resolution of

South China Sea disputes as soon as possible. Vietnam independently submitted application for delimitation of outer continental shelf of Vietnam in South China Sea on May 7, 2009; Vietnam and Malaysia submitted application for delimitation of outer continental shelf in southern area of South China Sea on May 6, 2009. These submissions seriously damaged China's sovereignty, sovereign rights and jurisdiction over South China Sea. However, the prerequisite for Commission on the Limits of the Continental Shelf to deliberate a country's application for delimitation of outer continental shelf is that there is no dispute with any country regarding the deliberation. If there is any dispute, any issue related to such dispute will not be deliberated. Meanwhile, some East Asian countries attempt to race to control and occupy part of islands and reefs and their resources in South China Sea, especially Nansha Islands before China have made further development in power, and hope that foreign powers especially the USA take part in resolution of disputes between them and China, including utilizing joint military drills to curb and reduce China's influence in a bid to earn more interests in South China Sea.

(4) Loopholes of relevant international and regional system utilized for carrying out unilateral actions. China signed Declaration on the Conduct of Parties in the South China Sea with Southeast Asian countries on Nov. 4, 2002, but it is a principled declaration without specific conduct rules, especially being lack of corresponding organizational structure and sanction measures for breaching such declaration. What

is more, it is impossible to make judgment on countries' unilateral or joint actions, so it is impossible to tell whether such conducts or actions make disputes more complicated or escalated and whether they influence peace and stability. For example, there is no systematic regulation on the multiple-national joint military drills in South China Sea especially sea areas surrounding Nansha Islands in the United Nations Convention on the Law of the Sea, but due to the frequency and clear objective of joint military drills, they are obviously in breach of the purpose and aim of peaceful use of the sea, so they should be opposed.

It is predicted that if the aforesaid reasons resulting in South China Sea issues and disputes cannot be dismissed, there is also possibility of disputes even armed conflicts in South China Sea. Disputes over sovereignty of Islands and Reefs in South China Sea may be solved by applying and improving regional system including formulation of legally binding systems such as A Code of Conduct of Parties in the South China Sea according to Declaration on the Conduct of Parties in the South China Sea, or by bilateral or limited multiple consultation, with focus on specifying countries' stances and prepositions in South China Sea, scope and nature of disputes, and establishing corresponding organizational structure.

II. Disputes over Sovereignty of Islands and Reefs in South China Sea

The opposition and disagreement between China and the USA

concerning military survey activities and freedom of flight over and jointly military drills in the exclusive economic zone may be resolved with the help of international community including amending systems concerning marine scientific research and adding systematic rules on military activities in the United Nations Convention on the Law of the Sea and through consultation by means of bilateral mechanism on marine security to jointly maintain common interests such as navigation and flight in South China Sea. In a word, regarding the two issues with different natures in the South China Sea, their solutions and resolution means are different.

Under the situation that it's hard to formulate or amend relevant international and regional systems, the key is to promptly announce China's policies on South China Sea issues to clarify the legal system of China on South China Sea. The main aspects are as follows:

Firstly, Chinese government shall collect and sum up preposition on and attitudes towards South China Sea issues in long time, promulgate documents such China's policy and stance on South China Sea issues and publicize them to let international community understand China's policies in a bid to avoid misunderstanding and misjudgment.

Secondly, China shall continue to adhere to the stance and principle of Setting Aside Dispute and Seeking Joint Development. Although this policy confronts a certain degree of frustration and its effect is not obvious, it is still an important principle for Chinese government to solve marine issues including South China Sea issues. The key point is to find out disputed areas accepted by multiple parties to carry out joint development.

Thirdly, China shall establish national marine management authority and improve relevant legal system. The comprehensiveness, complexity and sensitivity of marine issues require a comprehensive solution especially establishment of comprehensive management authority for marines issues (for example, National Marine Affairs Management Commission) to clarify authority of each agency related to the sea, reasonably deal with marine issues and carry out the connection mechanism featuring leading public opinion first, then law enforcement followed and navy offering protection. The important thing is to announce the baseline of the territorial sea of China in South China Sea and specify the legal status of nine-dotted line of South China Sea of China.

III. Utmost Efforts Disputes by Peaceful Means

In short, Chinese government hopes that there is no deterioration, more complexity and escalation of South China Sea issues, no adverse influence in relations between China and Southeast Asian countries, no damage to international and regional security and peaceful environment. Chinese government tries its best to resolve South China Sea issues and disputes by peaceful means, makes efforts to formulate and improve relevant international and regional systems and rules to maintain common interests of international community and ensure stability and order in South China Sea.

This article was originally published in Page A14 of *Sing Pao Daily News* (Hongkong) on June 26, 2011

How to Resolve the South China Sea Issue

China has been making continuous efforts to defuse the tension over the South China Sea issue, even though some countries have taken unilateral actions to meet their interests.

The South China Sea issue is complicated with legal disputes, which should be solved within the framework of international laws, including the Charter of United Nations, the 1982 UN Convention on the Law of the Sea (UNCLOS) and the 2002 Declaration on the Conduct of Parties in the South China Sea.

The legal disputes can be divided into two parts: China's territorial disputes with some Southeast Asian countries, and its disagreements with the US on military action in the region. The US claims to defend free navigation in the South China Sea, but actually it is defending its own military interests.

The disputes between countries can be resolved peacefully either politically or diplomatically, or through legal procedures.

The key to solving the territorial disputes over the islands, islets and reefs in the South China Sea through political means lies in related countries' (such as the Philippines and Vietnam) willingness to "shelve the disputes" and consent for "joint development". Since some countries are already exploiting many of the islands, it is very difficult to define the sea areas which need to be jointly developed and help resolve the disputes politically.

It is difficult to resolve them by using international laws, too, because neither China nor Vietnam has accepted the jurisdiction of the UN's International Court of Justice (ICJ) without reservations. The Philippines has accepted the ICJ's jurisdiction but has reservations on its jurisdiction over sea and land territorial disputes. Thus the possibility of solving the problem through the ICJ can also be ruled out.

Besides, according to Article 298 of UNCLOS, China made a statutory declaration on Aug. 25, 2006 to the UN secretary-general that it doesn't accept any international court or arbitration in disputes over sea delimitation, territorial disputes and military activities. So the International Tribunal for the Law of the Sea cannot intervene in the South China Sea disputes between China and some Southeast Asian countries.

Moreover, without an agreement among the relevant countries, no arbitration organization can deal with the disputes. Therefore, the disputes cannot be resolved politically any time soon.

But there are some good examples of success. On June 30, 2004, the China-Vietnam Agreement on the Demarcation of the Beibu Gulf and the Beibu Gulf Fishery Cooperation Agreement came into force.

On March 14, 2005, China, Vietnam and the Philippines signed the Tripartite Agreement for Joint Marine Seismic Undertaking in the Agreement Area in the South China Sea. And recently, China and Vietnam have intensified negotiations on new agreements to resolve their other disputes.

Considering the difficulties a state faces in compromising its territorial claims, political negotiation will be a long-drawn process. Before reaching a solution, a wise choice for China and other countries locked in the disputes would be to discuss and sign some cooperative agreements on "low-level" issues such as environmental protection, marine transportation, and anti-piracy and anti-smuggling actions to prevent the disputes from worsening. Such cooperation will be not only in line with the Declaration on the Conduct of Parties in the South China Sea, but also in accordance with the Article 123 of UNCLOS on "cooperation of States bordering enclosed or semi-enclosed seas".

Sino-US disputes, on the other hand, are more complex and can only be resolved politically. The two countries understand and interpret UNCLOS differently, including the scientific research in and peaceful use of exclusive economic zones.

Both have different interpretations of the third point of Article 58 of UNCLOS, which says: "In exercising their rights and performing their duties under this Convention in the exclusive economic zone, States shall have due regard to the rights and duties of the coastal State and shall comply with the laws and regulations adopted by the coastal State in accordance with the provisions of this Convention and other rules of international law in so far as they are not incompatible with this Part."

But neither has accepted the jurisdiction of the ICJ. So they cannot use its explanation or rulings. And since the US has not joined the convention and China has ruled out the possibility of international arbitration in the issue, a legal solution to the problem is not possible.

Several mechanisms exist between China and US, such as dialogues on sea security and Asia-Pacific affairs, through which they resolve their disputes politically. The two countries need to deepen their understanding and strengthen mutual trust, especially on the interpretation of UNCLOS to maintain peace and stability in the region.

But because neither international nor regional mechanisms on the sea are likely to be changed in the near future, it is essential for China to give the final shape to its domestic laws and regulations.

First, China should clarify the legal status of its "nine-dash" U-shaped line in the South China Sea.

Second, China should publicize its mare clausum (baseline of territorial sea) in the South China Sea, especially near the Nansha Islands, apart from setting up a special committee on sea affairs and making sea laws and regulations more coordinated.

Third, cooperation between the Chinese mainland and Taiwan should be enhanced. Given the progress in cross-Straits relations, the two sides can start cooperation on easier issues such as environmental protection, scientific research, fisheries and disaster prevention to set up a cross-Straits framework on sea issues, because both have the responsibility of defending the interests of the nation.

This article was originally published on Page 9 of *China Daily* on June 7, 2011

May Better Sense Prevail in Sea Disputes

The Western media tend to sensationalize any dispute between China and its neighboring countries, especially if it could intensify the situation in the South China Sea. No wonder, before the upcoming APEC and East Asia summits the Western media have been busy reporting that Vietnam has invited foreign oil companies to exploit the oilfields in the disputed area, which is claimed by China and Vietnam both, and create a storm over the analysis of a Hanoi-based researcher that "territorial tensions in the South China Sea could explode into full-scale conflicts".

Vietnam's move has undoubtedly cast a shadow on the joint agreement signed between Beijing and Hanoi last month. This is something which China is strongly opposed to. But it would be wrong to say that Vietnam actually tried to win time to exploit the oilfields and develop its military.

People with diverse views exist in almost every country, and Vietnam is no exception. From its government to its academia, Vietnam has people with tough as well as moderate views on China. Therefore, one scholar's views cannot represent that of the country.

In the joint agreement, both countries have agreed on "peaceful settlement" of the South China Sea disputes. China firmly believes in resolving maritime disputes through peaceful means, including "shelving disputes and seeking common development", because it has successfully resolved land border disputes with 12 neighboring countries through negotiations and friendly consultations.

The peaceful settlement of the South China Sea disputes will surely come with hardship, but it is worth striving for. The joint agreement does not necessarily mean that China and Vietnam will be trouble-free. On the contrary, frictions will arise. What both countries should do is to keep the frictions under control.

If Vietnam continues to invite foreign companies to exploit the disputed area, China can do even more to invite other companies to jointly exploit the resources or develop the area alone. Actually, China has large-drilling platforms and has the full capacity to exploit the disputed area. But China doesn't want to do so and instead is exercising great restraint to safeguard peace in the region.

If Vietnam really eats its words and doesn't follow the joint agreement, it stands to lose its standing on the international stage and no country will cooperate with and trust it, which is not something it can afford.

The China-Vietnam agreements, aimed at advancing bilateral cooperation on some less sensitive maritime issues to explore interim and temporary solutions and then foster conditions necessary for resolving bilateral disagreements, serve not only bilateral interests but also the welfare of other countries. Both countries should try to find ways to carry out the principles in the agreement, which will have a far-reaching impact on the region.

China and Vietnam have disputes over the South China Sea, and it will be of mutual benefit for both to respect history, each other's stands and interests, and avoid any activity that can complicate and escalate the disputes.

For that purpose, China and Vietnam should agree to step up negotiations on maritime issues, seek some interim and temporary solutions, and start bilateral cooperation in less sensitive fields such as marine environment protection, marine scientific research, and marine rescue and disaster mitigation to create conditions necessary to arrive at a final solution and for the joint development of marine resources in the disputed area.

The China-Vietnam agreements on maritime issues lay a political ground on which both sides can hold dialogues and consultations to address the bilateral disputes. In fact, it is difficult to resolve their disagreements by using international laws, because neither side has agreed to submit to the jurisdiction of the International Court of Justice (ICJ) in bilateral contentious issues under Article 36 of the Statute of the ICJ.

Besides, China made a statutory declaration on Aug. 25, 2006, to the UN secretary-general that it does not accept arbitration in maritime border disputes. With the possibility of resolving the disputes through the ICJ being ruled out, the China-Vietnam agreements provide a political framework for negotiations and friendly consultations.

If China and Vietnam succeed in resolving their maritime disputes by holding bilateral dialogues and consultations on an equal footing, exploring interim solutions and seeking joint development, their example will offer other countries some guidance in resolving similar maritime disputes. More importantly, it will demonstrate that concerted efforts are of vital importance in handling contentious issues and excluding intervention from "outsiders".

The bilateral agreements reached between China and Vietnam on maritime issues is significant for regional peace and stability and offers a solution to other countries, which the international community deserves to support instead of using it to sow discord.

Besides, both sides should make full use of the established platforms, including regular meetings that are held twice a year between the heads of the two countries' negotiation delegations and the hotline of the two governments. They could dig into maritime cooperation in the less sensitive areas as mentioned above, too, before touching upon the issue of joint development of maritime resources.

Moreover, the two countries should be cautious against media sensationalism and prevent any mishandling of the South China Sea disputes from hindering joint efforts aimed at eliminating misunderstanding and facilitating mutual trust.

China has been making great efforts to resolve the disputes peacefully, and Vietnam should do the same.

This article was originally published on Page 9 of *China Daily* on Nov. 9, 2011

Is It Groundless for China's Proposition Based on U-shaped Line of South China Sea?

Philippine Foreign Minister Albert del Rosario published a statement on Apr. 22, 2012, alleging that it is obviously groundless for China to attempt to claim sovereignty over the whole South China Sea on basis of nine-dotted line and by historical literature record. One of focal points of South China Sea issues is the legal status of the nine-dotted line or U-shaped line drawn by China in South China Sea. The author holds that one of important works for dealing with South China Sea issues is that China shall further clarify the legal status and nature of nine-dotted line or U-shaped line drawn by China in South China Sea and seek theoretical support from the law of the sea.

Although there are different theories and opinions about the legal status of nine-dotted line, the basic nature of nine-dotted line shall be islands ownership line. Based on this, combining the principle of land dominating the sea and the regime of the law of the sea, the legal nature of waters within nine-dotted line can be determined as internal waters.

I. Background of U-shaped Line in South China Sea

It is well-known that the Ministry of the Interior of Republic of China officially announced Comparison Table on the Old and New Names of the South China Sea Islands including 159 small islands or reefs on Dec. 1, 1947. In Feb. 1948, the Ministry of the Interior officially published the Location Map of South China Sea Islands indicating names of all islands. In this map, there is a U-shaped boundary line officially drawn to encircle Dongsha Islands, Xisha Islands, Zhongsha Islands and Nansha Islands with clear mark of Zengmu Reef in the southernmost part of about latitude 4° N. This boundary line was not linked up but divided into eleven sections. In 1953, Chinese government deleted two sections in Beibu Bay and turned the boundary line into nine sections, so such boundary line became a nine-dotted line which is also known as U-shaped line.

The author holds that the background for Chinese government to draw the U-shaped line in South China Sea can be mainly summarized as the following two aspects:

The first one is the foreign invasion. The U-shaped line was originally created at the time when France invaded nine small islands of Nansha Islands in 1933 and determined when France reinvaded Coral Island of Xishan Islands and part of islands and reefs of Nansha Islands after the War of Resistance against Japan. It was a defensive and protective measure against the background that Philippines attempted to incorporate islands into the scope of national defense, with the aim to protect territorial sovereignty of Chinese government over South China Sea islands and make public the sea areas governed by Chinese government to the world.

The second one is the situation in the sea. On Sept. 28, 1945, the USA announced Presidential Proclamation No. 2667 on Policy of the United States with Respect to the Natural Resources of the Subsoil and Sea Bed of the Continental Shelf (hereinafter referred to as Truman Proclamation) with the aim to build an exclusive fishery conservation zone and obtain interests of the continental shelf. Afterwards, especially Latin-American countries adopted more radical policy on sea areas, i.e. exclusive economic interests in 200 nautical miles. Due to this, Chinese government adopted comparatively milder measures by publishing U-shaped line drawn in the mode of the Median Line in an attempt to segment right and interest space between other littoral countries around the South China Sea and China in the sea and protect the historic interests of China in such sea areas. In fact, China's claim for sovereignty over South China Sea islands has a long history and can be dated back to Han dynasty (A.C. 25–A.C. 220).

In short, the U-shaped line of the Location Map of South China Sea Islands made by China in Dec. 1947 can be at least recognized as sovereignty boundary line of South China Sea islands. All islands within such line are China's territory.

Regarding the legal status of U-shaped line of South China Sea, there are different theories and opinions in the international community mainly including Theory of Historic Waters, Theory of Historic Rights, Theory of Marine Boundary Line and Theory of Islands Ownership Line. It should be mentioned that the U-shaped line of South China Sea has not only the attribute of historicity but also the element of marine boundary line, combining the principle of land dominating the sea, so the basic legal nature of U-shaped line shall be islands ownership line. This conclusion is in compliance with the stance publicly announced by China for long.

II. Legal Status of Waters within U-shaped Line

Firstly, waters within U-shaped line are not internal waters because the U-shaped line is a dotted line which is different from the land boundary line. Chinese government has never indicated that waters with U-shaped line are internal waters but also never opposed navigation of other countries in such waters.

Secondly, the waters within U-shaped line are not the territorial sea. Chinese government promulgated Declaration of the China on the Territorial Sea on Sept. 4, 1958, Article 1 of which states that the breadth of the territorial sea of China is 12 nautical miles and it applies to all territory of China including the mainland and its coastal islands, and……Taiwan and its adjacent islands, Pescadores, Dongsha Islands, Xisha Islands, Zhongsha Islands, Nansha Islands as well as other islands belonging to China. Article 2 states that the territorial sea of the Mainland and its coastal islands of China takes straight lines joining each base point of the shore of the mainland and outer islands of the coast as the baselines and the waters extending 12 nautical miles from the baselines are the territorial sea of China.

It is clear that only the ribbon-shaped waters within 12 nautical miles from the baselines of South China Sea islands are the territorial sea of China and other waters within U-shaped line are not the territorial sea.

Thirdly, are the waters within U-shaped line are high seas? If the waters within U-shaped line excluding the territorial sea of 12 nautical miles surrounding islands are high seas, why did Chinese government draw the U-shaped line in the Location Map of South China Sea Islands? U-shaped line was drawn on basis of the Median Line between South China Sea islands and lands of adjacent countries, therefore Chinese government attempted to segment jurisdiction and interests between China and neighboring countries in waters of South China Sea by this line. Because the waters within U-shaped line are definitely different from waters outside U-shaped line, so the former can not be regarded as the high seas.

Lastly, are the waters within U-shaped line other type of waters? Of course, the waters within U-shaped line are not the Contiguous Zone or the exclusive economic zone or archipelagic waters. As a conclusion, they are special waters with historic nature. The reasons are mainly as follows:

(1) Chinese have made navigation in and utilized such waters since ancient times. Only limited neighboring countries used these waters and many of those countries were small countries regarding China as their suzerain who regularly rendered tribute to China for a long time. Therefore, Chinese government had undeniably played the role of a ruler for a long time in such waters. This special historic element makes such waters different from general waters.

(2) China achieved sovereignty over main islands and reefs within such waters through occupation, so those islands and reefs are China's traditionally inherent territory. This makes such waters different from other general waters.

(3) Such waters are half of a general semi-enclosed sea close to Chinese islands. According to Article 122 and Article 123 of the United Nations Convention on the Law of the Sea, they are special that rights of other countries not within such areas are prejudiced.

(4) The regimes of exclusive economic zone and archipelagic waters in the Convention have been developed and enjoy their own distinctiveness. For example, the regime of exclusive economic zone was originated in resources protection zone of 200 nautical miles that was established at the request of Latin-American countries one after another after the USA promulgated Truman Proclamation. The regime of archipelagic waters became a part of the Convention at the repeated request of Philippines, Indonesia and other countries. The archipelagic

waters are not internal waters, territorial sea nor high seas or the exclusive economic zone. Therefore, according to the development process of the Convention, China may develop waters within U-shaped line as special historic waters. The terms concerning historic interests in the Convention mainly include Article 15 which states that where the coasts of two States are opposite or adjacent to each other, their territorial sea shall be delimited according to the median line every point of which is equidistant from the nearest points on the baselines of the two States. The above provision does not apply, however, where it is necessary by reason of historic title or other special circumstances to delimit the territorial seas of the two States in a way which is at variance therewith.

Meanwhile, the waters within U-shaped line are not historic bay which is set forth in Article 10 of the Convention. Article 298 of the Convention concerns disputes involving historic bays or titles.

III. Legal Nature of Waters within U-shaped Line

The author holds that the waters within U-shaped line at least enjoy the following features: (1) the drawing of U-shaped line was a response to promulgation of Truman Proclamation of 1945 due to compliance with the world's ocean trend. (2) The islands, rocks and low-tide elevations within U-shaped line are the territory under China's territorial sovereignty, so the U-shaped line is at least China's islands ownership line, i.e. islands and reefs within the line belong to China because other countries cannot put forward evidences which have equal weights with evidences enjoyed by China on its discovery and effective occupation of islands and reefs in South China Sea. In other words, the so-called proposition of being adjacent put forward by Indonesia and Malaysia is groundless in international law. The theory of discovery and occupation by Thomas Cloma put forward by Philippines on May 15, 1956 does not worth rebutting. Vietnam put forwards the theory of occupation on the ground that according to the record in *Fu Bian Za Lu* (*Phủ Biên Tạp Lục*) written by Le Quy Don in the 18th century, Vietnam had made production in Huangsha (Xisha) at the beginning of 18th century and incorporated it into the territory of Vietnam. For this, according to a scholar Professor Han Zhenhua's textual research, the Huangsha and Changsha in historical maps and books of Vietnam are some islands and sand beaches in coastal waters of Vietnam which have nothing to do with China's Xisha Islands and Nansha Islands. It is obvious that Vietnam's claim cannot compete with China's claim for islands in South China Sea. (3) The waters within U-shaped line are special historic waters and the basis for claims is China's historic interests in such waters. (4) The waters within U-shaped line include two kinds of waters. The first one is archipelagic waters enclosed by the straight baselines of archipelagoes. According to Article 46 of the Convention, it is debatable for waters to be regarded as archipelagic waters and the key is that whether islands, waters and other natural features in such sea areas form an intrinsic geographical, economic and political entity, or which historically have been regarded as such. The requirements of archipelagic waters shall be satisfied. The second one is the historic waters oriented in traditional rights and interests. (5) The U-shaped line is a line segmenting right and interest space between China and other countries neighboring South China Sea. (6) The U-shaped line hasn't determined the specific outer limits of historic waters. In other words, U-shaped line may be taken as the starting line of ocean delimitation between China and other countries.

It is clear that waters of South China Sea islands are special historic waters. According to Professor Fu Kuncheng, China's claims on South China Sea waters (waters within U-shaped line) can be divided into three levels from the legal perspective:

Firstly, South China Sea is at the level of semi-enclosed sea. Each country may co-ordinate issues concerning the living resources, environment, navigation and their scientific research in South China Sea, but China enjoy priority on basis of historic interests.

Secondly, Chinese government and People's various preemptive rights in the waters within U-shaped line on basis of historic evidences mainly include priority in management, conservation, exploration and exploitation of various resources in South China Sea, priority in protection and preservation of ocean environment, priority in scientific research, right to control navigation and air traffic even relevant navigation activities of other littoral countries around the South China Sea.

Thirdly, two or three sections of archipelagic waters are enclosed by straight baselines of Xisha Islands and Nansha Islands to apply the regime of archipelagic waters, China enjoy complete and exclusive sovereignty over such waters and without any prejudice to other countries' rights of transit passage or rights of archipelagic sea lanes passage.

This article was originally published on Page A17
of *Dongfang Daily* on Apr. 24, 2012

Practical Steps to Resolve South China Sea Issues

From the perspective of development process of cross-strait relations and the basically same stances on marine issues between the mainland and Taiwan, the time for cross-strait cooperation on marine issues has come.

The history and current situation of territorial disputes among South China Sea issues are extremely complicated and very hard to resolve. It is generally difficult to settle them in one shot, so China may adopt step-by-step methods to handle them gradually.

As for territorial disputes in South China Sea between China and some ASEAN member states, the following steps may be taken.

The first one is to carry out cooperation in low-level (sub-sensitive) fields.

There are precedents concerning resolution and suspension of disputes over South China Sea issue between China and other countries. For example, China-Vietnam Agreement on Delimitation in Beibu Bay entered into force on June 30, 2004; Agreement on Triple Parties'

Joint Work Concerning the Sea and the Earthquake in South China Sea Agreement Zone was singed by China, Philippines and Vietnam on Mar. 14, 2005; China and ASEAN reached consensus (on July 20, 2011) on promoting implementation of Declaration on the Conduct of Parties in the South China Sea and subsequent actions including implementation of guidelines of Declaration on the Conduct of Parties in the South China Sea in a bid to make cooperation on disaster prevention and mitigation, marine search and rescue as well ocean scientific research in South China Sea; China and Vietnam signed Agreement on Basic Principles of Guidelines for Resolving Marine Issues between China and Vietnam on Oct. 11, 2011, and so forth. All these create good conditions and atmosphere for maintaining stability in South China Sea, enhancing mutual trust and promoting cooperation and also for party states involved to make a final and peaceful settlement of disputes, being worth adherence and promotion.

In other words, prior to final settlement of territorial disputes in South China Sea, in order to prevent deterioration of the situation, it is an effective method and way for deferring the escalation of disputes to conclude regional work agreements or cooperation agreements (between China and ASEAN) in low-level fields (for example, ocean environment protection, ocean scientific research, maritime navigation and traffic security, search and rescue, combating transnational crimes including but not limited to fight against drug smuggling, piracy and armed robbery at sea and arms smuggling). This complies with not only principles of

Article 6 of Declaration on the Conduct of Parties in the South China Sea but also the principle and requirement set forth in Article 123 of the United Nations Convention on the Law of the Sea that States bordering a semi-enclosed sea should co-operate with each other in the fields other than non-living resources. One of the important tasks at present is that each state shall make efforts to promote cooperation process in each field according to the above-mentioned guidelines.

Although Declaration on the Conduct of Parties in the South China Sea and Agreement on Basic Principles of Guidelines for Resolving Marine Issues between China and Vietnam does not involve fishery cooperation, it is an important aspect for relevant countries to cooperate on fishery issues in order to realistically protect fishermen's fishing rights, decrease conflicts and incidents of arrest and seizure, so it is necessary to reach common wishes and consensus and make efforts to carry out cooperation on fishery. When relevant parties conduct consultation and negotiation on fishery cooperation, it is predictable that disputes will be focused on the definition of fishery cooperation zone and how to handle conflicts of jurisdiction. It is hard to determine the scope of areas for fishery cooperation, correspondingly, it is unable to determine jurisdiction over fishing incidents. However, in order to decrease fishing incidents and conflicts in South China Sea, parties concerned shall make special efforts to build the marine information notification and accident handling system by mainly adhering to the principle of Flag State Jurisdiction. To this end, it is of special significance and emergency that parties concerned carry out research and discussion on fishery cooperation issues. When the conditions are mature, those parties may consider joint cruise and law enforcement management mode and system.

The second one is to formulate binding rules on the conduct as soon as possible after cooperation in low-level fields has been deepened and mutual trust has been enhanced.

In consideration of some flaws in Declaration on the Conduct of Parties in the South China Sea including the impossibility to decide and punish conducts and actions complicating, escalating South China Sea disputes or influencing stability in South China Sea, it is of special significance to formulate legally binding documents such as A Code of Conduct of Parties in the South China Sea. Although China and ASEAN established a joint work group in Dec. 2004 which held six meetings from Aug. 2005 to Dec. 2010, they failed to reach an agreement on formulating legally binding documents, so each party shall continue to conduct consultation on formulating A Code of Conduct of Parties in the South China Sea and make efforts for reaching an consensus. This is in compliance with principles and requirements of the regional system because Article 10 of Declaration on the Conduct of Parties in the South China Sea states that the parties concerned reaffirm that the adoption of a code of conduct in South China Sea would further promote peace and stability in the region and agree to work, on the basis of consensus, towards the eventual attainment of this objective.

Chinese government is open-minded in discussing formulation of A Code of Conduct of Parties in the South China Sea when conditions are mature and suggests that the important task at present shall be launching practical cooperation in low-level fields in South China Sea and it is more suitable to work out A Code of Conduct of Parties in the South China Sea after the cooperation has been deepened and mutual trust has been enhanced. We must say that it is more reasonable to take such steps because it is more difficult to formulate a legally binding document if each party hasn't had enough mutual trust and consensus. It is predictable that one of difficulties in formulating A Code of Conduct of Parties in the South China Sea is how to deal with other countries' occupation and illegal control of islands and reefs belonging to China and how to define the legal nature of other countries' resources development activities, i.e. whether these conducts or activities are invalid, frozen or something else. Each party will have seriously opposite and different opinions.

The third one is to try the best to obtain a final settlement of territorial disputes or implement joint development system.

It should be mentioned that it is the best way of resolving territorial disputes in South China to conclude a final agreement by peaceful means. However, the territorial disputes in South China Sea involve many parties, many fields and elements including history, geography, international relations and international law, etc. Such disputes are not able to be free from interference by foreign powers and involve national sentiments and emotions, each party generally could not make compromise and concession, so it is extremely difficult to resolve and balance them. Due to this, China shall adhere to the principle of Setting Aside Dispute and Seeking Joint Development, practically implement joint development system including establishing organizations such as Energy Community to implement joint development for resources sharing.

Finally, it should be mentioned that the settlement of territorial disputes in South China Sea need support from Taiwan region, so it is of special necessity to carry out cross-strait cooperation on marine issues. From the perspective of development process of cross-strait relations and the basically same stances on marine issues between the mainland and Taiwan, the time for cross-strait cooperation on marine issues has come. Specifically, the Mainland and Taiwan region may authorize Straits Exchange Foundation and Association for Relations Across the Taiwan Straits to conclude cooperation framework agreement on marine issues, especially promote implementation in low-level fields and them make improvement after conditions are mature and cooperation deepened by adhering to the principle of doing thing in the order of increasing difficulty and following a step-by-step approach.

Disputes over South China Sea are very complicated and will continue to emerge. The resolution of South China Sea tests Chinese people's diplomatic policies and legal measures and shall adhere to the principle of reasonable settlement of disputes by peaceful means. China shall adopt comprehensive policies and measures to avoid deterioration and escalation of disputes over South China Sea including formulating national ocean development strategy, formulating and improving legal system of the sea, especially improving structural organizations (for example, establishment of National Committee of Marine Issues) in order to increase China's efficiency of and ability to resolve marine issues. In addition, in order to defend national sovereignty and territorial integrity, it is very necessary to develop military strength.

This article was originally published on Page A18 of *Dongfang Daily* on Apr. 25, 2012

Reflection on "Setting Aside Disputes and Joint Exploitation"

South China Sea issues have attracted attention from the international community recently. We shall insist on and work towards settlement of disputes over South China Sea by peaceful means according to international law and rules on international relations such as the Charter of the United Nations, the United Nations Convention on the Law of the Sea and Declaration on the Conduct of Parties, which is also in conformity with wishes of most countries including the USA.

It is a principle and obligation that a country must obey to settle a dispute by first resorting to peaceful means when such dispute emerges between countries, which is explicitly affirmed by most international treaties and regional systematic rules. Although political means are necessary for resolving territorial disputes over Nansha Islands and Reefs, there still be some difficulties and limitations in resolving such disputes.

China put forward the guideline of Setting Aside Dispute and Seeking Joint Development in 1970s and clearly proposed the guideline of Sovereignty Belonging to China, Setting Aside Dispute and Seeking Joint Development for resolution of disputes over Nansha. However, such principles or guidelines receive different degrees of challenges and are not actually accepted by many countries although they have specific foundations of international law.

Because the guideline of Setting Aside Dispute and Seeking Joint Development is a new concept, there is no consensus on the concept of Joint Development, that is to say, there are different theoretic understandings and knowledge about it.

Generally speaking, the so-called joint development refers to a governmental agreement concluded by two or more countries with the aim to jointly exercise sovereignty and jurisdiction over areas not delimited but with overlapped sovereignty claims for developing and allocating natural resources in such areas.

In fact, Joint Development enjoys basis of international law which mainly include Paragraph 3 of Article 74 of the Convention or Paragraph 3 of Article 83. Although the aforesaid articles of the Convention do not contain the term of Joint Development, it is obvious that provisional arrangements include Joint Development which is an important mode of provisional arrangements. Meanwhile, the joint development through agreement has been adopted and developed by many countries. The practices show that it has strong vitality.

There have been more than 20 examples of Joint Development in international community since the 1950s which happen around the world. The joint development has become practices in the world which consist of two kinds: the first one is to set forth interests sharing and establishment of joint development zone in agreement on delimitation; the second one is to enter into an agreement on joint development in overlapped areas before conclusion of agreement on delimitation. In addition, the joint development is recognized by the Statute of the International Court of Justice. For example, The Statute of the International Court of Justice holds in the North Sea Continental Shelf Case (1969) that the delimitation of continental shelf may be made through agreement, pending such agreement, the overlapped areas may be divided in a fair way or an agreement on joint development may be concluded. It is obvious that although there are different opinions on the concept of joint development in theory, there are many international practices using the system of joint development to exploiting resources, so there is no difficulty in implementing joint development.

But the reality is that due to lack of political wish in implementing joint development or failure to obtain more practical interests, the system of joint development can not be practically implemented in South China Sea issue at present.

The joint development enjoys characteristics of being practical, beneficial, provisional and joint.

The so-called being practical means that the joint development aims at implementing exploration and exploitation of potential resources in disputed areas through cooperation agreement and put it into practice.

The so-called being beneficial means that countries concerned set aside disputes and implement exploration and exploitation as soon as possible to facilitate parties' elimination of differences and acquisition of practical interests. The so-called provisional means that the joint development focuses on exploitation of natural resources in disputed areas and the agreement on joint development itself is not a final settlement of dispute nor influences the status of disputed areas or the final delimitation, so it enjoys the nature of being interim. The so-called being joint means that the agreement on joint development aims at encouraging both parties or multiple parties to implement joint development of resources in disputed areas and prohibiting unilateral development.

In addition, the joint development enjoys double natures, that is to say, it also has strong political nature besides its legal nature.

The so-called political nature means that both parties or multiple parties, on basis of the principle of mutual benefits and cooperation, reach political wishes and consensus on joint development between government leaders in a bid to implement the system of joint development. The so-called legal nature means that in order to implement the system of joint development, it is necessary for both parties or multiple parties to formulate bilateral or multiple agreement on submarine resources development to guarantee the implementation of the system of joint development.

Joint development, as an international cooperation activity with strong political nature, is influenced and limited, before and after negotiation and in the course of discussing agreement on joint development, by the degree of political wishes of parties concerned or balance of practice interests. However, for countries having conducted a lot of resources exploitation activities in sea waters surrounding Nansha Islands, they obviously lack wishes and practical needs to implement joint development, so they can not really enter into an agreement on joint development even through consultation and negotiation.

Because there are sovereignty disputes over Nansha Islands and Reefs in South China Sea, especially claims are overlapped and involves many countries, it is hard to define the disputed sea waters. Meanwhile, other countries have occupied many islands and reefs of Nansha Islands and are devoting great efforts to exploit their resources, thus seriously decreasing the scope of areas for implementation of joint development. There is difficulty in practical operation for finding a regional system of implementing joint development acceptable by both parties or multiple parties in sea waters surrounding Nansha Islands.

Although the guideline of Setting Aside Dispute and Seeking Joint Development receives some cold responses, even disregard, it is still a policy and stance that China must adhere to resolve marine issues including territorial disputes over Nansha Islands and Reefs. The key point is to find a breakthrough point and adopt a new train of thought.

From the latest practices, we can say that it is possible to realize the policy objective of Setting Aside Dispute and Seeking Joint Development through efforts of multiple parties. For example, Sino-

Vietnam Agreement on Delimitation in Beibu Bay and Sino-Vietnam Agreement on Fishery in Beibu Bay entered into force on June 30, 2004, and Agreement on Triple Parties' Joint Marine and Earthquake Work in Agreement Zone of South China Sea was signed by China, Philippines and Vietnam on Mar. 14, 2005. All these are considered as a result of a historic and practical step towards implementation of the principle of Setting Aside Dispute and Seeking Joint Development. Although the Agreement on Triple Parties' Joint Marine and Earthquake Work in Agreement Zone of South China Sea did not enjoy obvious effect and even had a fate of termination, it played a good role in upholding temporary stability in South China Sea.

In the near future, China and Vietnam will speed up the negotiation on Agreement on Basic Principles of Guidelines for Resolving Marine Issues between China and Vietnam with the intention of signing such agreement as soon as possible, and promote the implementation of Declaration on the Conduct of Parties in the South China Sea and subsequent actions with efforts to achieve practical progress as soon as possible. They are exactly a good and positive signal of resolving territorial disputes over Nansha Islands and Reefs by political means and worth attaching importance.

In addition, China and ASEAN reached consensus on implementing the guideline of Declaration on the Conduct of Parties in the South China Sea on July 20, 2011 and providing systematic guaranty for resolution of South China Sea issue including territorial disputes over Nansha Islands and Reefs in a political way, which is worthy of insisting and implementation promoting. Especially, China and Vietnam concluded Agreement on Basic Principles of Guidelines for Resolving Marine Issues between China and Vietnam on Oct. 11, 2011 and published Sino-Vietnam Joint Statement on Oct. 15, 2011. Both of them provides political guaranty for both parties to resolve their disputes over marine issues by peaceful means and are meaningful for deferring escalation of disputes and conflicts about marine issues including South China Sea issue and resolving marine disputes, so we shall insist on such agreements and promote their implementation.

For this reason, we shall work towards adopting effective measures, activating or formulating this kind of work agreements including entry into work agreements or cooperation agreements of other fields (for example, ocean environment protection, ocean scientific research, maritime navigation and traffic security, search and rescue, combating transnational crimes including fight against piracy and so forth), which is also in compliance with rules and requirements of relevant international systems.

In addition, endeavor to conclude such work agreement or cooperation agreement in the semi-closed South China Sea is also required by the principle of Article 123 of the Convention that States bordering semi-enclosed seas shall carry out cooperation in fields other than non-living resources.

If such cooperation agreements or work agreements in low-level fields can be reached and steadily promoted, they will definitely play a positive role in eliminating disagreement among parties, easing tension in South China Sea, deferring disputes and conflicts in South China Sea.

This article was originally published on Page A16
of *Dongfang Daily* on May 11, 2012

Legal Obstacles in Settling Territorial Disputes over Nansha Islands and Reefs

Although Chinese government has always insisted in the principle and stance of resolving disputes between countries by political means, it is ok to discuss the possibility of resolving issues such as territorial disputes over Nansha Islands and Reefs by legal means when the political means receive cold response or does not produce good effect. In fact, when there are extremely obvious national conflicts of interests, especially serious opposition and disagreement on the issue of territorial sovereignty, it is very hard at present to resolve difficult issues such as territorial disputes over Nansha Islands and Reefs by political means including the principle of Setting Aside Dispute and Seeking Joint Development.

According to the Article 74 and Article 83 of United Nations Convention on the Law of the Sea, prior to final settlement of territorial disputes and entry into delimitation agreement, countries concerned shall undertake some obligations mainly including an obligation to carry out negotiation, that is an obligation to conduct negotiation for reaching delimitation agreement; an obligation to endeavor to enter into temporary arrangements, that is each party's obligation to make efforts to enter into temporary arrangements; an obligation to refrain from unilateral conduct, that is an obligation not to unilaterally carry out a conduct impairing or hampering the conclusion of final delimitation agreement.

When shall countries concerned begin to undertake the aforesaid obligations? There are the following several opinions or propositions in international community. Firstly, the aforesaid obligations arise when claims on the same sea areas are overlapped. Secondly, the aforesaid obligations arise when countries concerned begin to conduct negotiation on temporary arrangements. Thirdly, the aforesaid obligations arise when temporary arrangements are determined. Fourthly, the aforesaid obligations arise from the beginning of the process of final delimitation. In light of purposes of the aforesaid articles of the Convention, if it is interpreted as that the aforesaid obligations shall be undertaken by countries concerned after negotiation, the other party may unilaterally carry out development activities of resources in disputed areas prior to the negotiation, so the author holds that it is more reasonable that countries concerned shall comply with the aforesaid obligations after their claims on sea areas delimitation are overlapped.

The specific obligations are reflected in the following aspects: the first one is an obligation to conduct negotiation in good faith. Both parties or multiple parties shall make settlement through dialogue, negotiation and consultation to narrow dispute and disagreement and exchange information to perform such obligation in good faith to make negotiation work. The second one is an obligation to avoid escalation of disputes. That is to say, each party shall face the current situation of disputes, refrain from taking unilateral behavior or measure and show restraint to avoid escalation of disputes. The third one is an obligation to carry forward the outcome of negotiation. That is to say, both parties or multiple parties undertake an obligation to make efforts to conclude an agreement, insist on the principle of mutual understanding and mutual compromise to steadily carry forward the outcome of negotiation. The fourth one is an obligation to enhance cooperation and exchange. That is to say, both parties or multiple parties shall enhance cooperation and exchange for reaching a final agreement or interim consensus or agreement and comply with such consensus.

I. Prerequisites and Conditions of Legal Resolution

Because the international law does not enjoy compulsory jurisdiction, countries concerned must accept the jurisdiction of a judicial organ or enter into an arbitration agreement in order to authorize the International Court of Justice or arbitration authority to handle and resolve disputes if they want to resolve disputes by legal means. Regarding territorial disputes over Nansha Islands and Reefs, there is little possibility to resort to arbitration authority for arbitral award in consideration of difficulties faced by countries concerned in entry into an arbitration agreement.

As for the International Court of Justice, according to Paragraph 2 of Article 36 of The Statute of the International Court of Justice, the states parties to the present Statute may at any time declare that they recognize as compulsory ipso facto and without special agreement, in relation to any other state accepting the same obligation, the jurisdiction of the Court in all legal disputes concerning: (1) the interpretation of a treaty; (2) any question of international law; (3) the existence of any fact which, if established, would constitute a breach of an international obligation; (4) the nature or extent of the reparation to be made for the breach of an international obligation.

That is to say, if a state wants to submit a dispute to the International Court of Justice, it must declare that it accepts the jurisdiction of the International Court of Justice. Meanwhile, a case accepted by the International Court of Justice must be about legal disputes.

The International Court of Justice divided disputes into legal disputes and non-legal disputes and only accepts a case concerning legal disputes. The reasons why the International Court of Justice excludes non-legal disputes from its jurisdiction are mainly as follows: the International Court of Justice does not have compulsory jurisdiction like a domestic court; the content of international law is often out of tune with the practice and has the nature of being fixed, so the International

Court of Justice excludes those cases not using international law to resolve disputes and only accepts and deals with disputes arising from legal opinions of parties, thus resulting in the situation that the International Court of Justice excludes non-legal disputes.

Regarding the jurisdiction of the International Court of Justice, just as mentioned above, relevant states in principle need declare its acceptance of jurisdiction of the International Court of Justice. However, when one party takes a lawsuit to the International Court of Justice, there shall be a question of forum prorogatum.

The so-called forum prorogatum means that a party concerned, when having no idea of whether the other party will accept the jurisdiction of the International Court of Justice or not, takes a lawsuit to the International Court of Justice, and in the later process, the other party explicitly expresses or imply its acceptance of the jurisdiction of the court, thus rendering the court jurisdiction over such case and officially starting the proceedings.

Although the International Court of Justice may start legal procedures though forum prorogatum, but this way has not been set forth explicitly in The Statute of the International Court of Justice but recognized gradually as ruling practices by the standing International Court of Justice and also confirmed in cases by the International Court of Justice. For example, the judgment on preliminary objection of Corfu Channel Case made by the International Court of Justice was a result of forum prorogatum, that is to say, regarding claims made by the UK to the International Court of Justice, Albania pointed out a letter to a clerk of the Court that although the lawsuit filed by the UK was not appropriate, Albania did not want to miss such opportunity and intended to appear in the court for the purpose of showing its enthusiasm and sincerity in principles of amicable cooperation and peaceful resolution of disputes between countries, thus accepting the jurisdiction of the International Court of Justice.

The Statute of the International Court of Justice sets forth that generally only states may be parties in cases before the Court. A state who wants to be a litigant in the court must be a party state of the Statute. Because the International Court of Justice is one of main organs of the United Nations, a member of the United Nations is of course a party to the present Statute. Conditions for a state other than a member of the United Nations to be a party to the Statute shall be decided individually by the assembly of the United Nations according to the suggestion of the Security Council.

The rules applicable to the Court are set forth in Article 38 of The Statute of the International Court of Justice. Paragraph 1 states that the Court, whose function is to decide in accordance with international law such disputes as are submitted to it, shall apply: (1) international conventions, whether general or particular, establishing rules expressly recognized by the contesting states; (2) international custom, as evidence of a general practice accepted as law; (3) the general principles of law recognized by civilized nations; (4) subject to the provisions of Article 59, judicial decisions and the teachings of the most highly qualified publicists of the various nations, as subsidiary means for the determination of rules of law. Paragraph 2 states that the aforesaid provision shall not prejudice the power of the Court to decide a case ex aequo et bono, if the parties agree thereto. It is obvious that applicable rules of the International Court of Justice are mainly international conventions, international custom and the general principle of law and others are subsidiary rules.

The decision of the International Court of Justice is legally binding upon parties to a case who undertake legal obligations to implement the decision of the International Court of Justice. As for binding issue of the decision, Article 59 of The Statute of the International Court of Justice states that the decision of the Court has no binding force except between the parties and in respect of that particular case. However, there are exceptions. For example, Paragraph 1 of Article 63 of the statute states that whenever the construction of a convention to which states other than those concerned in the case are parties is in question, the Registrar shall notify all such states forthwith. Paragraph 2 states that every state so notified has the right to intervene in the proceedings; but if it uses this right, the construction given by the judgment will be equally binding upon it.

II. Legal Obstacle of Territorial Disputes in South China Sea

As mentioned above, using legal means including the International

Court of Justice to resolve international disputes must be approved by parties concerned in ways including optional declaration on Article 36 of the Statute of the International Court of Justice to accept jurisdiction of the International Court of Justice through forum prorogatum. Although Philippines made a declaration on Jan. 18, 1972 to accept the jurisdiction of the International Court of Justice, it made reservations on disputes related to ocean jurisdiction and land territory. In other words, Philippines does not accept jurisdiction of the International Court of Justice on disputes related to ocean jurisdiction and land territory. Other countries (such as Vietnam and Malaysia) and China do not make optional declarations on Article 36 of the Statute of the International Court of Justice. That is to say, there is great difficulty in using Article 36 of the International Court of Justice to impose jurisdiction over and issue a decision on territorial disputes of Nansha Islands and Reefs.

In consideration of that China, Vietnam and Philippines are all members of the Convention, there is a need to take into account the possibility of utilizing the International Tribunal for the Law of the Sea to resolve territorial disputes over Nansha Islands and Reefs.

Specifically, there are three kinds of jurisdiction of the International Tribunal for the Law of the Sea:

(1) Personal jurisdiction (Ratione Personae). Article 291 of the Convention states that all the dispute settlement procedures specified in Part XV shall be open to States Parties and the dispute settlement procedures specified in Part XV shall be open to entities other than

States Parties only as specifically provided for in this Convention. Article 20 of the Statute of the International Tribunal for the Law of the Sea states that the tribunal shall be open to States Parties and entities other than States Parties satisfying certain conditions. That is to say, persons under personal jurisdiction of the tribunal are as follows: firstly, they include not only States Parties to the Convention but also self-governing consortium, non-autonomous region, international organization satisfying conditions of Paragraph 1 of Article 305 of the Convention; secondly, regarding any case expressly provided in Part XI of the Convention, International Seabed Authority, the Enterprise, state-owned enterprise, natural person or legal person other than States Parties may become a party to the case; Thirdly, the Tribunal shall be open to entities other than States Parties in any cases submitted pursuant to any other agreement conferring jurisdiction on the Tribunal which is accepted by all the parties to that case. Of course, these agreements are not limited to international agreements, so if only all parties to a case accept jurisdiction of the Tribunal, there is no limitation on the subject scope.

(2) Subject matter jurisdiction (Ratione Materiae). Article 288 of the Convention states that the International Court of Justice or tribunal have jurisdiction over any dispute concerning the interpretation or application of this Convention which is submitted to it in accordance with this Part (Part XV of the Convention); the court or tribunal shall also have jurisdiction over any dispute concerning the interpretation or application

of an international agreement related to the purposes of this Convention which is submitted to it in accordance with the agreement; the Seabed Disputes Chamber of the International Tribunal for the Law of the Sea established in accordance with Annex VI, and any other chamber or arbitral tribunal referred to in Part XI, section 5, shall have jurisdiction in any matter which is submitted to it in accordance therewith. Article 21 of Statute of the International Tribunal for the Law of the Sea states that the jurisdiction of the Tribunal comprises all disputes and all applications submitted to it in accordance with this Convention and all matters specifically provided for in any other agreement which confers jurisdiction on the Tribunal.

Regarding subject matter jurisdiction, the Statute of the International Court of Justice sets forth the Court has jurisdiction over all cases, but the Statute of the International Tribunal for the Law of the Sea sets forth the Tribunal has jurisdiction over all disputes and applications related to the Convention. It is obvious that the scope of jurisdiction of the International Court of Justice is larger than that of the Tribunal, which is determined by the specialty of the Tribunal.

Article 22 of the Statute of the International Tribunal for the Law of the Sea states if all the parties to a treaty or convention already in force and concerning the subject-matter covered by this Convention so agree, any disputes concerning the interpretation or application of such treaty or convention may, in accordance with such agreement, be submitted to the Tribunal. That is to say, if all States Parties to a treaty so agree, such subject matter can be submitted to the Tribunal. However, the Statute does not clarify the time for determining a treaty already in force, it is wondered whether such treaty could be understood as a treaty in force at the time of concluding the Convention.

(3) Choice of Jurisdiction. Paragraph 1 of Article 287 states that when signing, ratifying or acceding to this Convention or at any time thereafter, a State shall be free to choose, by means of a written declaration, one or more of means such as the International Tribunal for the Law of the Sea, for the settlement of disputes concerning the interpretation or application of this Convention, the International Court of Justice, an arbitral tribunal, a special orbital tribunal. That is to say, States Parties, by means of accepting a dispute settlement method in advance, choose jurisdiction of the International Court of Justice of the Tribunal; When contesting states accept the same procedures, they just need submit their dispute to such procedures; if there is no such procedure, a dispute can be only submitted to the Arbitration Tribunal when there is no special agreement.

A State Party to the Convention may, according to Article 287, by means of a declaration, accept the compulsory jurisdiction of the International Court of Justice or the Tribunal. Meanwhile, a State may declare in writing that it does not accept the compulsory jurisdiction of the International Court of Justice or the Tribunal chosen by itself with respect to one or more of the following categories of disputes mentioned in Article 298 of the Convention. Such optional exceptions include disputes relating to sea boundary delimitation or those involving historic bays or titles, disputes concerning military activities, disputes concerning law enforcement activities in regard to the exercise of sovereign rights or jurisdiction, disputes in respect of which the Security Council of the United Nations is exercising the functions assigned to it by the Charter of the United Nations. Meanwhile, a State Party which has made the abovementioned declaration may at any time withdraw it.

China hasn't chosen for the settlement of disputes concerning the interpretation or application of this Convention set forth in Article 287 of the Convention since its rectification of the Convention in 1996. China submitted a written declaration to the General-Secretary of the United States on Aug. 5, 2006 according to Article 298 of the Convention, pointing out that Chinese government does not accept the jurisdiction of any international justice or arbitration set forth in Section 2 of Party XV of the Convention over any dispute (such as sea boundary delimitation, territorial dispute, a dispute concerning military activities) set forth in Item (a), (b) and (c) of Paragraph 1 of Article 298 of the Convention.

In other words, China excludes the possibility of applying international justice or arbitration in settlement of marine disputes relating to major national interests and insists on the stance to settle disputes by means of consultation and negotiation with states concerned.

On one hand, such declaration shows China's consistent stance and attitude towards the aforesaid disputes, on the other hand, it seems a little deviation from the international development trend of often relying on international originations and utilizing international justice to settle disputes among states. Of course, there is still a possibility that China will withdraw the aforesaid declaration and use the dispute settlement mechanism of the Convention to deal with marine disputes, because, according to Paragraph 2 of Article 298, a State Party which has made a declaration under paragraph 1 of Article 298 may at any time withdraw it, or agree to submit a dispute excluded by such declaration to any procedure specified in this Convention.

It can be inferred from the above-mentioned analysis of jurisdiction of the Tribunal, China has excluded the possibility of accepting jurisdiction of international justice or arbitration over disputes concerning sea boundary delimitation, territorial issues and military activities. If China does not withdraw the aforesaid declaration or agree to accept any specified procedure, there is no possibility for the Tribunal to deal with territorial disputes over Nansha Islands and Reefs.

However, China shall also make good preparation on evidences for submitting territorial disputes over Nansha Islands and Reefs to an organ of international justice, and enhance research into systems of international justice at the same time, especially a kind of applicable rules featuring different levels applied in cases decided by the International Court of Justice on territorial sovereignty, i.e. a treaty prevailing, then taking into account the actual occupation and finally the effective control. The former two (a treaty and law on actual occupation) are direct methods proving ownership of territorial rights; the latter (effective control) is an indirect method. This values a lot, in terms of reference, for us to collect relevant evidences and research systems of international justice.

In short, it is impossible to apply legal means in settlement of territorial disputes over Nansha Islands and Reefs due to some obstacles which can not be eliminated or overcome. Under the situation that parties concerned can not enter into an arbitration agreement on settlement of territorial disputes over Nansha Islands and Reefs, the resolution by political means is expected. Prior to final settlement of territorial disputes over Nansha Islands and Reefs by political means, we need to discuss a mechanism for preventing escalation of South China Sea issues and the emergency measures. The author holds that one of the practical ways is that, under the situation of failure to settlement of territorial disputes over Nansha Islands and Reefs and disputes concerning sea boundary delimitation, parties concerned especially China and some ASEAN member states shall strive to conclude regional work agreements or cooperation agreements in low-level fields (for example, ocean environment protection, ocean scientific research, maritime navigation and traffic security, search and rescue, combating transnational crimes including but not limited to fight against drug smuggling, piracy and armed robbery at sea and arms smuggling) and practically implement them. Meanwhile, China continues to carry out negotiation with ASEAN Member States in a bid to conclude legally binding rules on system establishment such as A Code of Conduct of Parties in the South China Sea to prevent deterioration of South China Sea.

Such cooperation agreements or work agreements are not only required by Declaration on the Conduct of Parties in the South China Sea but also comply with principles and requirements of the Convention. In addition, efforts shall be made to let more states rectify and accede to international treaties such International Convention on Maritime Search and Rescue entered into force in 1985 and Convention for the Suppression of Unlawful Acts against the Safety of Maritime Navigation entered into force in 1992 in a bid to establish international cooperation system in a larger scope and lay foundation for coordinating or developing cooperation framework systems on South China Sea issues.

III. The Basic Law of the Sea shall be enacted as soon as possible

From the perspective of international social practices, one of effective ways to deal with and respond to disputes over marine issues is to formulate national marine development strategy and improve marine system and mechanism, under the situation that international, regional and bilateral systems on marine issues are not perfect or hard to improve. An important method for guaranteeing the realization of the abovementioned measures is that China enact and enforce a law on comprehensively managing marine issues — the Basic Law of the Sea as soon as possible.

In reality, China put forward a requirement or objective of formulating laws such as the Basic Law of the Sea in the China's Agenda for the Sea in 21st Century as early as in 1996 which pointed out that China shall establish and improve marine legal system taking the Basic Law of the Sea and comprehensive management laws as the main part and coordinating professional laws and local laws, and set up a marine law enforcement team featuring timely and effective supervision and efficient and strong operation to realize rule of law in the sea and guarantee sustainable development of the sea, coastal economy and society. The current international and domestic situation is very beneficial to China's formulation of national marine development strategy and improvement of marine system and mechanism, which is also a consensus of international community.

Generally speaking, the basic path or routine chart of national marine undertakings development is as follows:

Firstly, China shall make clear its core interests and formulate a strategy covering national marine development. For China, the core objective is to build an ocean power.

Secondly, China shall improve marine policies for implementing national marine development strategy including enhancing marine ideas and awareness, strengthening marine affairs coordination, improving capability of development, control and comprehensive management of the sea and marine resources, promoting traditional culture of the sea, constantly develop and innovate marine technology, expand foreign exchange and cooperation to harvest new fruits of China's marine undertakings.

Thirdly, China shall enact the Basic Law of the Sea to guarantee the promotion and implementation of marine development strategy and marine policies with the focus on improving China's marine system and mechanism including establishment of organizations such as National Committee of Marine Issues.

Lastly, China shall formulate basic marine plan of the Basic Law of the Sea to enhance weak points, elements and fields in the course of marine development.

The author holds that the Basic Law of the Sea enacted by China shall mainly include the following aspects: announcement of marine policies, that is to say, summarizing China's policies on marine issues including the policy of Setting Aside Dispute and Seeking Joint Development, establishing the idea of harmonious sea, and publicizing and interpreting them to the outside; establishment of national organs on management of marine affairs such as National Committee of Marine Issues to manage national marine affairs in a untied, efficient and coordinated way; promulgation of important fields of marine development by China including developing marine industry and activities, actively developing, utilizing and managing the sea and marine resources, protecting marine environment, ensuring passage safety, researching and developing marine technology, enhancing management and survey activities in governed sea areas, strengthening ocean education and publicity for Chinese people, promoting international cooperation in the sea. Specifically, they mainly include the following aspects: promoting exploration and exploitation of the sea and marine resources; strengthening surveillance and protection of marine environment; promoting exploration and exploitation activities of the exclusive economic zone and continental shelf; ensuring ocean transportation safety; ensuring ocean security; strengthening marine investigation; researching and developing marine scientific technology; revitalizing marine industry and upgrading international competitiveness; enhancing comprehensive management on littoral waters; expanding exploration and exploitation of new space and new resources of the sea; protecting islands and their ecosystem; enhancing international coordination and promoting international cooperation; promoting national's understanding and knowledge of the sea and cultivating marine talents, and so forth.

China shall comply with principles and systems of international laws including the United Nations Convention on the Law of the Sea when formulating principles of the Basic Law of the Sea which shall specifically include the principle of coordinating exploration and exploitation of the sea and protection of marine environment, the principle of ensuring marine safety, the principle of upgrading ocean education scale and structure in order to promote scientific knowledge of and understanding in the sea, the principle of promoting healthy and orderly development of marine industry, the principle of managing marine affairs in a comprehensive and coordinated way, the principle of participating and coordinating international marine affairs and so forth.

Although the Basic Law of the Sea enacted by China aims at announcing China's policies on marine issues, it is very important for other countries to further understand and get knowledge of China's stance and attitude towards marine issues. Because China's marine policies especially ocean economy development policy, featuring continuality and consistence, are summary and abstract of previous marine policies and stances, the law will not impose adverse influences on other countries. Meanwhile, because the Basic Law of the Sea is focused on declaration of policies, it will not cause adverse impact in or conflict with other areas of marine law and specific regulations, thus not resulting in a lot of issues of amendment and coordination. In other words, it is easy to handle the relation between the Basic Law of the Sea and other areas of marine law in force and maintain the integrity of current marine legal system.

This article was originally published on Page A8–9
of *Dongfang Daily* on May 14, 2012

China Must Safeguard Island

The harassment of Chinese fishermen by a Philippine naval vessel near Huangyan Island has severely undermined China's territorial sovereignty and maritime jurisdiction. China should dispatch naval vessels to waters off the island to safeguard its interests, given that the current fishery patrol vessels and marine surveillance ships, all non-military, will be unable to meet the country's security requirements if the month-long standoff continues.

Based on the United Nations Convention on the Law of the Sea, China has the right to establish the breadth of its territorial sea up to 12 nautical miles measured from its baseline. This rule applies to Huangyan Island as part of China's Zhongsha Islands, over which China claims indisputable sovereignty.

Chinese astronomer Guo Shoujing, conducted a survey of the seas around China in 1279 for the emperor Kublai Khan, and Huangyan Island was chosen as a point for surveying the South China Sea, which proves that Huangyan Island had been discovered by the Chinese at least by the Yuan Dynasty (1271–1368).

The island and its surrounding waters have been traditional fisheries for Chinese fishermen since ancient times, and scientists from the South China Sea Institute of Oceanology under the Chinese Academy of Sciences have conducted field surveys on the island in 1977 and 1978. China installed a stone marker reading "South China Sea Scientific Expedition" on the island in 1980, but it was illegally removed by the Philippines in 1997, when it began to challenge China's ownership of the island.

Besides historical evidence, China bases its claim on legal grounds. Conforming to the United Nations Convention on the Law of the Sea, Article 2 of China's Law on the Territorial Sea and the Contiguous Zone stipulates that China's territorial land includes the mainland and its offshore islands, including Taiwan and various affiliated islands such as the Diaoyu Islands.

Huangyan Island, as part of China's Zhongsha Islands, is an inalienable part of Chinese territory. The island is geographically different from the Philippines archipelago, and the 5400-meter-deep Manila Trench is located in between, serving as a natural boundary separating Zhongsha Islands from the archipelago. Meanwhile, as stipulated by Article 3 and Article 33 of the Convention on the Law of the Sea, China can establish a breadth of territorial sea of 12 nautical miles and contiguous zone of 24 nautical miles measured from the baseline from which the territorial sea is measured, making China's jurisdiction over the waters off Huangyan Island indisputable.

The Philippines' claim is groundless. International treaties, such as the 1898 Treaty of Paris and the 1900 Treaty of Washington, set the western limit of Philippine territory at 118 degrees east longitude. Huangyan Island, with coordinates 117 degrees and 44 minutes to 117 degrees and 48 minutes east longitude, is obviously outside the limit.

Philippine laws and regulations, including the 1935 constitution and the 1961 Republic Act No. 3046, confirm the limit set by the aforementioned international treaties. Philippine maps published in 1981 and 1984 also show that Huangyan Island is not the country's territory.

Despite this, the Philippines still has the audacity to claim sovereignty over the island, quibbling that the island is located within its claimed exclusive economic zone, and it has even declared its intention to unilaterally bring the dispute to the International Tribunal for the Law of the Sea.

Such antics simply make the Philippines the laughingstock of the international community, as in accordance with the principle of international laws, no arbitration organization should deal with a dispute without the parties concerned agreeing.

Furthermore, it is impossible for the International Tribunal for the Law of the Sea to resolve the dispute over Huangyan Island, because neither China nor the Philippines has accepted the jurisdiction of the court without reservations.

China made a statutory declaration in 2006 to the UN secretary-general that it does not accept any international court or arbitration in disputes over maritime delimitation, territorial disputes and military activities. That is to say, in respect of maritime disputes related to the country's core interests, China insists on resolving the issues by negotiating directly with the parties concerned.

But unless the parties concerned stop complicating the issues by acting unilaterally and inviting external intervention to defend their claimed interests in the South China Sea, standoffs in disputed waters, such as the one near Huangyan Island are likely to happen again.

To deter such provocation in the future, China should forcibly chase the Philippine vessel out of China's territorial waters and thereafter normalize China's jurisdiction over Huangyan Island and its surrounding waters.

This article was originally published on Page 9
of *China Daily* on May 16, 2012

Analysis of Huangyan Island Incident from the Perspective of International Law

It is evitable for incidents such as ships stand-off in sea areas surrounding Huangyan Island because a breakthrough point is needed for the USA to shift its strategy focus to Asia-Pacific region and the marine issue is an important field of the USA's strategic layout in Asia-Pacific region. That is to say, competition and opposition on naval supremacy between China and the USA are structural and long-term contradiction. This will make it impossible for South China Sea issue to avoid the development trend of internationalization or regionalization. Philippines's's attempts to internalize this issue are just measures to impose pressure on China. They are in fact against international practices, thus making no sense and having no possibility.

Regarding ships stand-off incident in Huangyan Island between China and Phillipines, the author holds that there are mainly the following legal issues:

Law enforcement on the sea is an important measure for protecting a state's territorial sovereignty and exercising jurisdiction in sea waters.

The United Nations Convention on the Law of the Sea divides sea areas into internal waters, the territorial sea, the contiguous zone, archipelagic waters, the exclusive economic zone, continental shelf, high seas and so forth. Because their legal statuses and natures are different, coastal or littoral states shall comply with different rules, when carrying out law enforcement activities, for the purpose of exercising management over governed sea areas to reflect states' sovereignty, sovereign rights and jurisdiction.

Philippines' Lack of Solid Foundation in Terms of History and Law

According to the United Nations Convention on the Law of the Sea, sea areas within 12 nautical miles from Huangyan Island are China's territorial sea, those within 24 nautical miles are China's Contiguous Zone. In such sea areas, China shall protect its territorial sovereignty, sovereign rights and jurisdiction which are not allowed to be challenged. The foundations for China to claim territorial sovereignty over Huangyan Island are mainly as follows:

Firstly, China is the first state to discover and use Huangyan Island. China's discovery and utilization of Huangyan Island and marking it in a map began in 1279, the Yuan Dynasty. Huangyan Island is also a traditional fishing ground of fishermen from Chinese Mainland and Taiwan. The famous astronomer Guo Shoujing used Huangyan Island (formerly known as Zhongsha Islands and renamed as Huangyan Island in 1983) as a survey spot for making investigation in South China Sea. In the latter period of 1970s, China carried out scientific expedition activities in Huangyan Island and the surrounding sea areas. In 1980, China erected in Huangyan Island a stone monument inscribed Scientific Expedition in South China Sea which was illegally removed by Philippines in 1997.

Secondly, international treaties exclude Huangyan Island from Philippines' territory. For example, US-Spanish Treaty of Paris of 1898, US-Spanish Treaty of Washington of 1900 and British-US Treaty of 1930 state that longitude 118° E is the western boundary of Philippines' territory, beyond which is Huangyan Island.

Thirdly, domestic laws of Philippines deny that Huangyan Island is Philippines' territory. Philippine government recognizes the boundary set forth in the aforesaid three international treaties in the Constitution of Philippines of 1935, Law on the Baseline of the Territorial Sea of Philippines of 1961 and other public documents and expressly marks Huangyan Island outside the boundary of Philippines in maps published in 1981 and 1984. Philippines just claimed its so-called sovereignty over Huangyan Island after 1997.

The most important reason for this is that, after the effectiveness of the United Nations Convention on the Law of the Sea in 1994, coastal States may claim the exclusive economic zone of 200 nautical miles and the determination of the continental shelf beyond 200 nautical miles needs coastal states to submit a delimitation application attached with geodetic and geological materials to Commission on the Limits of the Continental Shelf. After discussion and suggestion by the Commission, the limits of continental shelf determined by coastal states on basis of the aforesaid suggestion are definite and binding. For this, Philippines furthered illegal conducts and activities of occupying Huangyan Island for trying to obtain more marine interests including interests regarding the sea areas and continental shelf.

Fourthly, Huangyan Island and islands of Philippines are not a complete geographic unit in geological structure. There is the Manila Trench between them which is 5400 meters at its deepest point and constitutes a natural geographic boundary between Zhongsha Islands and islands of Philippines. Huangyan Island, a part of Zhongsha Islands, is China's territory.

Article 3 and Article 4 of Law of China on the Territorial Sea and Contiguous Zone set forth that the breadth of the territorial sea of China is 12 nautical miles, measured from the baseline of the territorial sea; the Contiguous Zone is the sea areas beyond and adjacent to the territorial sea and the breadth of the contiguous zone is 12 nautical miles, i.e. the outer limit of the contiguous zone is a line every point of which is at a distance from the nearest point of the baseline of the territorial sea is equal to 24 nautical miles. According to regimes of the territorial sea and the Contiguous Zone, China owns jurisdiction over Huangyan Island and the surrounding sea areas.

Philippine government submitted the issue of Huangyan Island to international justice or arbitration for the purpose of making it internationalized and complicated, but such conducts are not only illegal but also ineffective. The submission of an application over other state's territory to international justice or arbitration will cause international disorder and breach international law and relevant regional systems.

Peremptory/Forcible Internationalization to Impose Pressures on China

According to principles of international law, if states concerned do not enter into an agreement on submitting a dispute for arbitration, an arbitration authority can not award a ruling on relevant disputes, therefore, it is impossible to submit the issue of Huangyan Island to an arbitration authority. The International Court of Justice and the International Tribunal for the Law of the Sea can not handle the issue of Huangyan Island.

Philippines made a declaration on Jan. 18, 1972 to accept the jurisdiction of the International Court of Justice, but it made reservations on disputes related to ocean jurisdiction and land territory. In other words, Philippines does not accept jurisdiction of the International Court of Justice on disputes related to ocean jurisdiction and land territory. China has not made optional declarations on Article 36 of the Statute of the International Court of Justice so far. That is to say, there is great difficulty in using Article 36 of the International Court of Justice to impose jurisdiction over and issue a decision on territorial disputes of Nansha Islands and Reefs, except for the following two situations: (1) Philippines withdraws the reservation; (2) China makes optional declaration or agrees to participate in the proceedings after Philippines submits relevant disputes, i.e. to accept the jurisdiction. However, Huangyan Island is China's territory, so it is impossible for Chinese government to award acceptance. Resorting to the International Court of Justice to deal with unquestioned territorial issue of Huangyan Island within Zhongsha Islands is just a kind of phlyaro made by Philippines to impose pressures on China.

It is also impossible to resort to the International Tribunal for the Law of the Sea, because China submitted a written declaration to the UN Secretary-General on Aug. 25, 2006 according to Article 298 of the Convention, pointing out that Chinese government does not accept the jurisdiction of any international justice or arbitration tribunal provided for in section 2 of Section XV of the Convention with respect to disputes such as sea boundary delimitation, territorial disputes, military activities. That is to say, China excludes the possibility of applying international justice or arbitration in settlement of marine disputes relating to national important interests and insists on the stance of dispute settlement by means of consultation and negotiation with states concerned.

Giving up Arbitrary Actions and Returning to Negotiation Table

Paragraph 4 of Article 2 of the Charter of the United Nations states that all Members shall refrain from the threat or use of force against the territorial integrity of any state. Article 5 of Declaration on the Conduct of Parties in the South China Sea, concluded in 2002 between China and ASEAN and principled in the Charter of the United Nations, states that the Parties undertake to exercise self-restraint in the conduct of activities that would not complicate or escalate disputes and affect peace and stability including, among others, refraining from action of inhabiting on the presently uninhabited islands, reefs, shoals, cays, and other features and to handle their differences in a constructive manner. Philippines' conduct is obviously inconsistent with relevant rules.

It is obvious that Philippines' unilateral submission of the territorial issue of Huangyan Island to international justice and arbitration is unjustifiable and unacceptable by Chinese government, deserving strong condemnation. It is reasonable to resolve such dispute through dialogue, consultation and negotiation.

This article was originally published in Page A17 of *HongKong Economic Journal* on June 2, 2012

No Negative Example Set by the Huangyan Island Incident

This incident of ships stand-off around Huangyan Island between China and Philippines has important features such as lasting for a long time, seriousness in nature, tendency to regionalization and internationalization, so China cannot regard it as unimportant and must suitably resolve it in a way favorable to China to show China's determination in defending sovereignty and territorial integrity to the international community and build it as a good example of China's settlement of disputes over South China Sea issue.

I. The Incident of Huangyan Island Is More Serious in Nature than Previous Incidents

It is well known that Philippines has illegally invaded and occupied no less than 8 islands and reefs in South China Sea so far. Since 1993, Philippines has begun to chase and harass Chinese fishermen by means of its fishery administration ships and warships. Among others, Philippine warships took away 4 Tanmen fishing boats which was fishing in Nansha and arrested 62 fishermen in 1995. These actions seriously damaged China's sovereignty and marine rights and interests, bringing about very bad impact. However, although there were several incidents of conflict before the incident of Huangyan Island, Philippines could restrain itself and give a prompt and reasonable response after Chinese government made strong protests.

The serious nature of the incident of Huangyan Island lies in the direct and head-on challenge to China's sovereign and territorial integrity. Philippines, against the situation that China enjoys definite and undoubted sovereignty over Huangyan Island, still takes a lot of small actions to constantly sound out China's strategic determination of defending sovereign and territorial integrity and tries to challenge China's patience in resolving South China Sea issue by peaceful means.

In fact, a lot of historical facts and legal reasons sufficiently prove that Huangyan Island is a part of China's territory. The foundations for China to enjoy sovereignty over Huangyan Island mainly include the following aspects:

Firstly, China is the first state to discover and use Huangyan Island. China's discovery and utilization of Huangyan Island and marking it in a map began in 1279, the Yuan Dynasty. Huangyan Island is also a traditional fishing ground of fishermen from Chinese Mainland and Taiwan. In the latter period of 1970s, China carried out scientific expedition activities in Huangyan Island and the surrounding sea areas. In 1980, China erected in Huangyan Island a stone monument inscribed

Scientific Expedition in South China Sea which was illegally removed by Philippines in 1997.

Secondly, international treaties exclude Huangyan Island from Philippines' territory. For example, US-Spanish Treaty of Paris of 1898, US-Spanish Treaty of Washington of 1900 and British-US Treaty of 1930 state that longitude 118° E is the western boundary of Philippines' territory, beyond which is Huangyan Island.

Thirdly, domestic laws of Philippines deny that Huangyan Island is Philippines' territory. Philippine government recognizes the boundary set forth in the aforesaid three international treaties in the Constitution of Philippines of 1935, Law on the Baseline of the Territorial Sea of Philippines of 1961 and other public documents and expressly marks Huangyan Island outside the boundary of Philippines in maps published in 1981 and 1984. Philippines just claimed its so-called sovereignty over Huangyan Island after 1997.

Fourthly, Article 2 of Law of China on the Territorial Sea and Contiguous Zone states that China's land territory includes the mainland and the costal islands, Taiwan and the affiliated islands including Diaoyu Islands, Pescadores, Dongsha Islands, Xisha Islands, Zhongsha Islands, Nansha Islands as well as other islands belonging to China.

In addition, Huangyan Island which is located in Zhongsha Islands and islands of Philippines are not a complete geographic unit in geological structure. There is the Manila Trench between them which is 5400 meters at its deepest point and constitutes a natural geographic boundary between Zhongsha Islands and islands of Philippines.

The aforesaid evidences show that Huangyan Island, a part of Zhongsha Islands, is China's indispensible territory. If this incident cannot be settled suitably, China's sovereignty, territorial integrity and marine rights and interests will be seriously damaged.

II. The Incident of Huangyan Island Showing a Tendency of Regionalization and Internationalization

After the incident of Huangyan Island, Philippines made great efforts to regionalize and internationalize it by means including calling for support from ASEAN member states, asking for protection from its allied country the USA, trying to pour out its claims in the international community by taking advantage of the international tribunal and so forth. In reality, these actions were taken with the hope to obtain sympathy from the international community and create a false picture that a powerful country bullies a small state, thus regionalizing and internationalizing such incident and imposing international pressures on China.

It should be mentioned that it is inevitable to some extent for the incident of ships stand-off around Huangyan Island to occur and its regionalization and internationalization are the intentional leading by some countries. The key element is the USA.

In recent years, a breakthrough point is needed for the USA to shift its strategy focus to Asia-Pacific region and the marine issue is an important field of the USA's strategic layout in Asia-Pacific region, so there is a tendency that the USA strengthens contacts with its allied states, non-allied states and other states. Such contacts are mainly reflected in aspects such as joint military drills, sales of arms and provision of equipments. In other words, with the shift of the core of world economy and the adjustment and deployment of the USA's Asia-Pacific strategy, there is dual structure of power featuring economic and politic — military separation in Asia-Pacific strategy, and there is opposition between China and the USA which is specially reflected on the naval supremacy. The competition and opposition on naval supremacy between China and the USA are structural and long-term contradiction. This will make it impossible for South China Sea issue to avoid the development trend of internationalization or regionalization. The internationalization of the incident of Huangyan Island is an important representation of such trend.

Against the background of the eastern-oriented strategy of the USA, some ASEAN member states having disputes with China in South China Sea take the opportunity to request the USA to assist them in defending the so-called rights and interests in South China Sea in a bid to occupy more marine resources and interests. In this incident of Huangyan Island, although these states did not explicitly express their attitudes, they kept a close eye on the situation development and even made secret contacts to scheme how to realize their own rights and interests because they have the same claim of interests with Philippines.

Under the serious situation that such marine disputes in South China Sea is becoming normal and lasting for a long time, China shall be more aware of the important status of the incident of Huangyan Island in resolution of South China Sea issue. The incident of Huangyan Island is not an individual case or isolated example, the settlement of which will produce a powerful modeling effect, so it cannot become a bad example for China to resolve South China Sea issues in the future.

III. China Shall Speed up Its Pace in Resolving the Incident of Huangyan Island

China shall take this as an opportunity to deal with the incident of Huangyan Island, in a reasonable, legal and restrainable way, by means of further strengthening management over Huangyan Island such as actual occupation and control of islands and reefs and implementation of a system of normalized cruise, suitably adapting policies towards Philippines according to the development situation of the incident including adapting the level of economic sanction, controlling the number of tourists and time period of their tours and decreasing investments and other measures, to let Philippines suffer real losses and thus correct wrong conducts as soon as possible, and to make the incident of Huangyan Island resolved and developed in a way beneficial to China.

It should be noted that even Philippine government agrees to conduct consultation and negotiation on the incident of Huangyan Island with China by diplomatic means, it maybe a temporary stratagem to gain a respite. In resolving territorial issue of South China Sea, China shall take full advantage of peaceful means but also be aware of the possibility of utilizing right of self-defense if the dispute over Huangyan Island cannot finally be settled through political or diplomatic means. That is to say, if China cannot make final settlement of the dispute over Huangyan Islands, China shall use military strengths without hesitate to protect national interests when confronting unreasonable constant provocation by other countries and suffering serious damages to its sovereignty, territorial integrity and marine rights and interests.

The emergence and treatment of the incident of ships stand-off around Huangyan Island show serious problems in China's marine strategy and mechanism. In other words, China is lack of definite national marine strategy including objects, tasks, means and measures, nor a management authority exercising uniform leadership over marine affairs to lead, manage and control marine issues. For this reason, China shall take this incident as an opportunity to speed up the formulation and implementation of the schedule of national marine development strategy clearly set forth in the Twelfth Five-Year Plan for National Economic and Social Development. Meanwhile, the incident of ships stand-off around Huangyan Island also reflect the lagging defect of China's relevant legal system construction, so China shall promulgate baselines of the territorial sea (coordinates) of Zhongsha Island, Dongsha Island, Nansha Island and so on in the South China Sea, reiterate names of Islands and Reefs in South China Sea and strengthen its management over islands in South China Sea especially enhancing resources development.

In short, China shall not ignore the influence and modeling effect of the incident of Huangyan Island and must utilize comprehensive strengths to resolve this stand-off incident in a forceful way as soon as possible including actual control of Huangyan Island and surrounding sea areas to ensure Chinese fishermen's ordinary fishing activities in surrounding areas and enhance the normalization of law enforcement by administrative authority. When it is necessary, China may use warships to chase away Philippine ships and warships to avoid such incident setting a bad example of China's resolution of South China Sea issue.

This article was originally published in *Social Observation* (2012, 6)
and the full text was reprinted in *Hongqi Digest* (2012, 4)

Manila all at Sea Over Islands

On April 26, the Chinese Foreign Ministry accused the Philippines of trying to legalize its occupation of disputed islands in the South China Sea. Foreign Ministry spokeswoman Hua Chunying said China would never agree to international arbitration on the disputed islands, which the Philippines has been seeking.

Earlier this year, the Philippine government called for international arbitration in the South China Sea dispute and notified China of its move. And in late March, the president of the International Tribunal for the Law of the Sea even appointed an arbiter for arbitral proceedings after Beijing "failed to designate its representative within the 60-day deadline".

The South China Sea dispute centers mainly on two aspects: conflicting sovereignty claims over Nansha Islands and maritime delimitation. In both cases, the disputing countries should resolve the issue through peaceful means. By initiating arbitration on the validity of China's claims, the Philippines has actually exposed its lack of legal knowledge and violated the consensus reached on the Declaration on the

Conduct of Parties in the South China Sea.

The Philippines has called for arbitration in the dispute by invoking the United Nations Convention on the Law of the Sea, but this does not justify its move. According to Article 286 of the UNCLOS, any dispute on the interpretation or application of the convention, in which no settlement has been reached through negotiation or other peaceful means, should be submitted by a party to the dispute to a court or tribunal having jurisdiction over the matter.

Therefore, a party to a dispute can invoke the article on the premise that no negotiated settlement has been reached. But by submitting the dispute to the arbitral tribunal that has not yet been fully established, Manila has unilaterally terminated the negotiation procedure and thus should be responsible for the consequences that follow.

Manila's unilateral move has also violated the consensus reached on the Declaration on the Conduct of Parties in the South China Sea with Beijing. According to Article 7 of the Declaration, "the parties concerned should stand ready to continue their consultations and dialogues concerning relevant issues, through modalities to be agreed by them". Obviously, taking the dispute to the UN is not a modality agreed by the two sides. Since the Philippines has violated the consensus, parties in the South China Sea should henceforth prevent it from participating in the process to develop legally binding documents.

Moreover, the Philippines took the dispute to the UN tribunal to challenge the validity of China's nine-dotted line (demarcation line of

China's claim in the South China Sea) to justify Manila's sovereignty claims and maritime interests in the resource-rich waters. By doing so, the Philippines has rested its hope on a wrong party because the arbitral tribunal has no jurisdiction over the dispute.

Article 286 of the UNCLOS stipulates that a dispute submitted to a court or tribunal has to be concerned with the interpretation or application of the convention. However, the legitimacy of China's nine-dotted line is not determined by the convention. Instead, it is based on inter-temporal law, which means a juridical fact must be appreciated in the light of the law contemporary with it. China's nine-dotted line was established long before the UNCLOS took effect and thus the UN tribunal cannot arbitrate its legitimacy.

The tribunal has no jurisdiction over the territorial dispute over the Nansha Islands either. According to Article 288 of the UNCLOS, a court or tribunal shall have jurisdiction over any dispute concerning the interpretation or application of an international agreement related to the purposes of the Convention. In other words, the tribunal will have no jurisdiction over territorial disputes which are not matters concerning the interpretation or application of the UNCLOS.

In fact, China submitted a formal statement to the UN in 2006, clarifying that it does not accept any of the procedures provided in Section 2 of Part XV of the convention with respect to all the categories of disputes referred to in paragraph 1 (a) (b) (c) of Article 298 of the convention. In this context, it means the tribunal will have no jurisdiction over maritime delimitations either.

The Philippines has committed a mistake by initiating UNCLOS arbitration proceedings against China. Despite China's consistent rejection of international arbitration, the UN has set up an arbitration panel, which, however, will have no jurisdiction over the dispute.

To settle the South China Sea issue, the disputing parties should resort to the general international law instead of the UNCLOS. After all, the purpose of establishing the convention, with due regard for the sovereignty of all states, is to establish a legal order for the seas and oceans, but matters not regulated by the convention should be governed by the rules and principles of general international law.

Peaceful settlement, especially through political means, remains the most effective and feasible resolution to the South China Sea dispute. The Philippines must show sincerity and return to the normal track of negotiation to safeguard regional peace and stability.

This article was originally published on Page 9
of *China Daily* on May 3, 2013

It's Unreasonable for Philippine to Apply for Arbitration on South China Sea Dispute

Recently, Philippine government ignored strong objection of Chinese government and arbitrarily submit the South China Sea dispute to the International Tribunal for the Law of the Sea for arbitration. Meanwhile, the International Tribunal for the Law of the Sea appointed an arbitrator on behalf of China under the situation that China opposed or did not accept such arbitration. The dispute over South China Sea issue seems to show a tendency and development trend of judicialization. In response to this, Ministry of Foreign Affairs of China pointed out that relevant letters and notices submitted by the Philippines for arbitration did not only breach the consensus reached in Declaration on the Conduct of Parties in the South China Sea between China and ASEAN member states, but also have serious factual and legal errors including a lot of false accusations, so China had explicitly expressed its unacceptance of those letters and enclosed notices and returned them. In other words, China holds that the Philippines' unilateral application for arbitration is unacceptable for China and also an illegal conduct.

The so-called South China Sea disputes mainly include two types: territorial disputes over Nansha Islands and Reefs and disputes over sea waters delimitation. They are different and also correlated. The former is a main dispute among South China Sea issues and the latter is a secondary dispute, because land dominating the sea is an important principle of the international law. In other words, for South China Sea issues, if only the territorial ownership over islands and reefs is determined, the disputed overlapped sea areas can be delimited. Regarding disputes over marine issues among states concerned, the principle and means of peaceful resolution must be observed by all parties. Well, is it reasonable for Philippines to unilaterally submit South China Sea dispute to the International Tribunal for the Law of the Sea for arbitration according to Article 286 of the United Nations Convention on the Law of the Sea?

Firstly, does Philippines' submission of South China Sea dispute for arbitration mean an end to China-Philippine bilateral dialogue procedures for resolving South China Sea dispute? The premises of applying the provision of arbitration in Article 286 of the United Nations Convention on the Law of the Sea is that the procedure of bilateral dialogue is ended or exhausted and the dispute is still unresolved. If the Philippines holds that its bilateral dialogue with China including exchange of views has been finished and determines that the South China Sea dispute between China and the Philippines cannot be settled, the Philippines may submit the dispute for arbitration. However, damage caused herefrom shall be undertaken by the Philippines including resolution of the dispute by non-peaceful means because the Philippines unilaterally determined that the bilateral dialogue and negotiation was finished. Meanwhile, the behavior or conduct of Philippines' submission of South China Sea dispute breached the consensus reached in Declaration on the Conduct of Parties in the South China Sea, because Article 7 of Declaration on the Conduct of Parties in the South China Sea states that the Parties concerned stand ready to continue their consultations and dialogues concerning relevant issues, through modalities to be agreed by them, including regular consultations on the observance of this Declaration, for the purpose of promoting good neighborliness and transparency, establishing harmony, mutual understanding and cooperation, and facilitating peaceful resolution of disputes among them. To this end, states concerned may exclude the Philippines from discussion of legally binding documents such as Rules on the Conduct in the South China Sea in the future because the Philippines breached the consensus of Declaration on the Conduct of Parties in the South China Sea.

Secondly, does the International Tribunal for the Law of the Sea have jurisdiction over the arbitration application on South China Sea dispute submitted by Philippines? According to Article 286 of the United Nations Convention on the Law of the Sea, the dispute submitted by a single party to the Statute of the International Court of Justice or the International Tribunal for the Law of the Sea must be any dispute concerning the interpretation or application of this Convention.

Well, is the United Nations Convention on the Law of the Sea applicable to the South China Sea dispute? The Philippines submitted the South China Sea dispute with the main aim to let the International Tribunal for the Law of the Sea announce the dotted line drawn by China in the South China Sea illegal and inconsistent with the systematic rules of the United Nations Convention on the Law of the Sea, to obtain sovereignty and marines rights and interests in the South China Sea and to try to remove obstacles in developing resources of submarine oil and gas in the west to the Philippines. There is a problem that the arbitral tribunal is unable to apply regimes and principles of the United Nations Convention on the Law of the Sea to issue an award on the legal status of the dotted line of South China Sea because this issue is not any dispute concerning the interpretation or application of this Convention. There is a theory of intertemporal law in international community. The so-called concept of intertemporal law means that the creation of a right must be determined according to laws at that time and the existence of a right must be determined according to laws of the key date of existence of such right. The concept of Intertemporal Law reflects the principle of Lex prospicit non respicit/ the non-retroactivity of the law. Considering the date and background of creation of dotted line of South China Sea, the United Nations Convention on the Law of the Sea is not applicable in determining the legal status of the dotted line of South China Sea. In other words, the arbitral tribunal is not able to hear the issue of the legal status of the dotted line of South China Sea. In addition, the arbitral tribunal is also not able to hear issues such as territorial disputes over Nansha Islands and Reefs unless states concerned conclude an international treaty to award the International Tribunal for the Law of the Sea the jurisdiction, because Paragraph 2 of Article 288 of the United Nations Convention on the Law of the Sea states that The Statute of the International Court of Justice or the International Tribunal for the Law of the Sea shall also have jurisdiction over any dispute concerning the interpretation or application of an international agreement related to the purposes of this Convention, which is submitted to it in accordance with the agreement.

In other words, if states concerned cannot conclude an international treaty on dispute settlement, the abovementioned Court or Tribunal will have no jurisdiction. In addition, on Aug. 25, 2006, China submitted an written declaration to the General-Secretary of the United States, announcing that China will not accept the jurisdiction of any international justice or arbitration over sea boundary delimitation, territorial disputes, military activities disputes and so on, so the dispute arbitration procedure set forth in Paragraph 3 of Article 297 of the United Nations Convention on the Law of the Sea is not applicable. In fact, regarding the issue of territorial disputes over Nansha Islands and Reefs, the ownership shall be determined according to the theory of territory acquisition in international law not provisions of the United Nations Convention on the Law of the Sea, because the preamble of the United Nations Convention on the Law of the Sea points out that the purpose of this Convention is to establish, with due regard for the sovereignty of all States, a legal order for the seas and oceans; and matters not regulated by this Convention continue to be governed by the rules and principles of general international law. In reality, the systematic rules of the United Nations Convention on the Law of the Sea are applicable to the issue of sea boundary delimitation in South China Sea.

It is obvious that the Philippines' conduct of submitting the South China Sea dispute to the International Tribunal for the Law of the Sea for arbitration is wrong and will not be accepted by China all the way. Meanwhile, the so-called arbitral tribunal established by the International Tribunal for the Law of the Sea has no jurisdiction on this dispute. The main aim of efforts of the International Tribunal for the Law of the Sea to establish an arbitral tribunal to hear the issue of South China Sea issue is to create an atmosphere of public opinions unfavorable to China in the international community and build a false image that China challenges international rules. China shall be clearly aware of this. In short, under the present situation, it is an effective and feasible way to resolve South China Sea dispute between or among states concerned by peaceful means especially political means, which must be adhered to. To this end, states concerned must show their sincerity and return to the track of resolution by political means to carry out consultation and negotiation for reasonable settlement of South China Sea issue, sharing resources and interests, ensuring regional peace and safety.

This article is originally published in Page A19
of *HongKong Economic Journal* on May 11, 2013

Views on Philippine's Gunshot at Taiwanese Fishing Boat from the Perspective of International Law

Considering that Taiwan region is not a state party to the United Nations Convention on the Law of the Sea and in view of the special status of Taiwan, this fishing boat incident between Taiwan and Philippines will be settled mainly through dialogue, consultation and cooperation.

In the morning of May 9, 2013, No. 28 Guangdaxing fishing boat, registered in Liuqiu, Pingdong County, Taiwan, was shot by an official ship (Coastal Guard) of Philippines in an area of 166 nautical miles southeast to Luanbi, Pingdong County, Taiwan (latitude 20° N and longitude 123° E), resulting in a seaman's death (Hong Shicheng) and serious damage to the fishing boat. In view of Philippine stance and attitude of not recognizing its fault and having no sincerity, Taiwan initiated 11 sanction measures in two batches and retains the right to take further sanction measures according to the development of the event, with the aim to prompt Philippines to make an official apology for this event, seriously punish offenders, compensate losses and guarantee no similar incident in the future. In this incident, the author holds that the following several issues shall be especially clarified:

The first one is the subject of law enforcement, i.e. the issue of whether the official ship of Philippines is able to represent the government to powerfully enforce law by force. The official ship of Philippines was in the overlapped areas or disputed areas of the exclusive economic zones of 200 nautical miles claimed respectively by Taiwan and Philippines when it shot at fishing boat of Taiwan. The law enforcement activities in the disputed areas must be carried out in a way of taking other parties' concerns and propositions into account, especially meeting the need of communication and coordination with competent organs of other parties. In principle, Philippines shall obtain understanding and approval from other parties when taking measures in the disputed areas, so even the official ship of Philippines exercised jurisdiction over such sea areas with authorization from the government, it can not take strong measures (by force) but adopt peaceful means to chase off fishing boats of other parties according to normative procedures to protect its marine interests and rights.

The second one is the procedural issue of law enforcement, i.e. the issue of whether conducts of the official ship of Philippines are legal. According to relevant regimes in the United Nations Convention on the Law of the Sea, the official ship of Philippines shall enforce law according to the following procedures. Firstly, it shall notify other ships of their entry into the exclusive economic zone claimed by Philippine and request other ships to leave promptly; secondly, when other ships refuse to leave, it shall give clear information including communication by tele-equipment, show of words and so on, that is to say, it can only begin to chase off other ships after giving visual or aural information within a scope of visual and aural sense of other ships. Lastly, if other ships still refuse to follow the instruction, it may fire off signal flares even shoot a ship especially the engine to compel it to leave by force. From the investigation of such incident, the shooting of the Taiwan fishing boat by official ship of Philippines did not follow the aforesaid procedures, so it is illegal. Of course, the official ship of Philippines exercising jurisdiction task must clearly bear a recognizable signal formerly authorized by the government.

The third one is the issue of excessive law enforcement, i.e. the issue of whether the law enforcement of the official ship of Philippines is excessive? From the actual situation of this incident, the fishing boat of Taiwan had not the tendency or behavior of offending the official ship of Philippines nor carried any arms, so there was no such issue as that the fishing boat of Taiwan threatened the safety of the official ship of Philippines. In such situation, the direct shooting of the official ship of Philippines was excessive in use of force and cannot be justified by the excuse of self-defense, instead it was a serious conduct with excessive force, so Philippines must undertake corresponding liabilities including formal apology and losses compensation and so on.

We can infer, from this incident of the official boat of Philippines shooting the fishing boat of Taiwan, that fishing activities in the exclusive economic zone must be reasonably regulated, that is to say, both parties need enhance systematic rules. Two ways may be adopted: firstly, Upon authorization by chinese government, Taiwan may conduct negotiation with philippines on the issue of delimitation of the exclusive economic zone in a bid to conclude agreement on delimitation of the exclusive economic zone to determine specific limits. Secondly, under the situation of no agreement on delimitation of the exclusive economic zone concluded, as a kind of transitional measure or arrangement, both parties may conduct consultation on fishing activities in the exclusive economic zone to determine each party's volume of catches, observe the principle of each party governing fishing boats from each party, and implement the system of information exchange to reasonably use fishing resources in the exclusive economic zone and avoid the reoccurrence of conflicts.

In consideration of the fact that Taiwan region is not a State Party to the United Nations Convention on the Law of the Sea and the special status of Taiwan, this fishing boat incident between Taiwan and Philippines will be settled mainly through dialogue, consultation and cooperation. Meanwhile, against the background that Philippines constantly makes trouble and provocation on the marine issue, Taiwan region shall resolutely respond to and deal with this incident in a bid to impose a kind of deterrent to Philippines' future conducts and measures.

This incident further enlightens us that it shall be put into the agenda for China mainland and Taiwan to take measures to enhance cooperation on marine issues for the purpose of firmly defending territorial sovereignty in the sea and marine rights and interests of Chinese nationality.

This article was originally published on Page A14
of *Dongfang Daily* on May 20, 2013

How to Build a Sea of Peace and Amity

The Special China-ASEAN Foreign Ministers' Meeting, to be held in Beijing on Aug. 29 to mark the 10th anniversary of the establishment of the China-ASEAN strategic partnership, will focus mainly on deepening of relations between the two sides.

China and some ASEAN member states have been involved in territorial disputes in the South China Sea. To defuse the tensions, however, Foreign Minister Wang Yi has proposed that the parties work out a Code of Conduct and ensure the success of the Beijing meeting on the key documents related to dispute management.

Wang's proposal has four key elements. First, each party should have a realistic expectation from the talks. He said that it would be neither realistic nor serious to talk about a "quick fix (solution)". Since a COC concerns the interests of all the parties, its formulation will be a process of sophisticated and complex coordination.

Second, to reach a consensus on a COC, the parties should draw inspiration from the Declaration on the Conduct of Parties in the South China Sea (DOC) to push ahead the consultations on a COC. The idea, however, should be to seek a broad consensus to take care of the interests of all parties and ensure that no party imposes its will on others.

Third, China and ASEAN member states should prevent non-regional countries from interfering in their disputes. The interference of external parties has for years thwarted the efforts of China and ASEAN members to give shape to a COC. For instance, a joint working group was founded in 2004 for the implementation of the DOC, followed by eight meetings since 2005. But these efforts have failed to facilitate an agreement on a regional COC because of some irrelevant parties' interference. So China and ASEAN member states should make concerted efforts to build an atmosphere conducive to the formulation of a COC.

Fourth, the two sides should take a step-by-step approach to formulate a COC. The South China Sea disputes are extremely sensitive and cannot be resolved overnight. Therefore, the two sides have to work on a COC within the framework of the DOC and keep in mind that a COC is not intended to replace the DOC.

Wang's four-point proposal is based on international laws. It conforms to the guidelines for the implementation of the DOC that China and ASEAN member states agreed upon in 2011. The proposal is consistent with Beijing's long-held stance that China and ASEAN member states should resolve the maritime disputes step by step.

Besides, the two sides should cooperate in less sensitive fields to build mutual trust. And based on enhanced mutual trust and maritime cooperation in less sensitive fields, the two sides should make further efforts to enact legally binding agreements such as a COC.

Of course, it will take time for the complete resolution of the disputes, but that does not mean the parties cannot seek ways of common development on a mutually beneficial basis. As Wang said, joint development is not only for economic interests, but also to show the rest of the world that the disputing countries are willing to resolve the disputes through peaceful means.

China's approach to the disputes meets the basic requirements for the exploration and exploitation of resources in the South China Sea. On the one hand, all the parties have the right to exploit resources in the region, especially through deeper cooperation in less sensitive fields. On the other hand, the parties should make joint efforts to enact legally binding documents like a COC for reasonable exploitation of the marine resources.

This is particularly important because the DOC has some technical problems when it comes to implementation; it cannot help resolve the disputes because of its non-legally binding nature.

A legally binding code can help regulate the activities of the countries in the region and ensure that the marine resources are exploited reasonably. For instance, although maritime cooperation in developing fishery resources is not included in the DOC, China and ASEAN member states can hold discussions to establish a regional cooperation framework for fishery resources management and emergency response.

This will not only protect the rights of fishermen, but also prevent further disputes, which in the past have been mostly triggered by incidents involving fishermen.

The formulation of a COC will accelerate the process of building a sound legal regime in the South China Sea for the common interests of all stakeholders. As always, China will strive to make its due contribution to regional peace and stability and realize its goal of evolving into a regional maritime power.

This article was originally published on Page 9 of *China Daily* on Aug. 28, 2013

Manila Barking up the Wrong Tree

The Philippines recently submitted a memorandum to the Permanent Court of Arbitration laying claim to China's Meiji Reef and Huangyan Island (or Mischief Reef and Scarborough Shoal as the Philippines calls them) and several other islands that are either submerged features or "rocks" in the South China Sea as defined under Article 121 of the 1982 UN Convention on the Law of the Sea. But that does not mean the Philippines has fulfilled the requirements for initiating an arbitration, nor does it mean the arbitral tribunal has jurisdiction to hear the case.

The Philippines first sent a notification and statement of claim to China in January 2013 to initiate arbitral proceedings and seek a "peaceful and durable resolution to the dispute" under the UN Convention.

According to the provisions of the Convention, state parties shall settle any dispute between them by peaceful means according to the UN Charter, and when a dispute arises, the parties should proceed expeditiously to exchange views on a settlement through negotiations or other peaceful means.

China and the Philippines have been exchanging views on the dispute since the first bilateral consultation on South China Sea issues in August 1995. Over the years, the two sides have agreed to cooperate "step by step" and resolve bilateral disputes through negotiations.

Manila, however, failed to suitably respond to Beijing's suggestions in March 2010 and January 2012 to establish a Sino-Philippine regular consultation mechanism on maritime issues and resume the bilateral mechanism on trust-building measures. Despite that, Manila has declared in the notification and statement of claim that it fully and in good faith complied with the Convention, and that "despite many bilateral meetings and exchanges of diplomatic correspondence over more than 17 years", "no settlements have been reached on any of these disputed matters".

The so-called 17 years of "fruitless" exchange of views, in fact, has basically remained at the consultation level that has helped improve dialogue but not led to the negotiation stage where the two parties could come up with concrete proposals for a settlement. Therefore, on no ground can Manila jump to the conclusion that "all possibilities of a negotiated settlement have been explored and exhausted".

Article 281 of the Convention says that if state parties have agreed to seek settlement of a dispute through peaceful means of their own choice, the procedures provided for in Part XV of the Convention on the settlement of disputes apply only where no settlement has been reached through such means and the agreement between the parties does not exclude any further procedure.

Both China and the Philippines are parties to the 2002 Declaration on the Conduct of Parties in the South China Sea, based on which the two sides should make efforts to resolve their territorial and jurisdictional disputes through peaceful means (friendly consultations and negotiations) in accordance with universally recognized principles of international law, including the Convention.

Also, the two sides should continue their consultations and dialogues on relevant issues through modalities to be agreed by them, including regular consultations on the observance of the Declaration. Seen in this light, the Philippines has violated the Declaration by moving the Permanent Court of Arbitration without seeking the consent of China.

Since Manila filed an arbitration case against Beijing without having fulfilled the mandatory requirements, the case falls beyond the jurisdiction of the arbitral tribunal. In the notification and statement of claim, the Philippines has listed 13 points, which can be translated into three general requests for the tribunal: to give a ruling on the maritime rights of China and the Philippines in the South China Sea that are established by the provisions of the Convention on territorial sea, contiguous zone, exclusive economic zone and continental shelf; to rule that China's nine-dash line violates the Convention and is invalid; and to adjudicate that China has unlawfully claimed maritime entitlements to the Meiji Reef, Huangyan Island and other islands in the South China Sea.

To determine the maritime rights of China and the Philippines in the South China Sea, it is necessary to first determine the territorial sovereignty over the disputed islands, in accordance with the basic principle of the law of the sea — that the land dominates the sea, meaning it is the territorial sovereignty of a coastal state that gives shape to its sovereign rights and jurisdiction over its territorial sea, exclusive economic zone and continental shelf.

Therefore, the core point of the dispute Manila has raised is actually the sovereignty over the disputed islands and demarcation of maritime rights, neither of which falls within the limited jurisdiction of the tribunal. This is because in August 2006, China submitted to the UN a formal statement in accordance with Article 298 of the Convention, clarifying that it does not accept any of the compulsory procedures provided for in Part XV of the Convention with respect to any dispute on territory, maritime delimitation and military activities referred to in Article 298.

Also, according to the same article, any dispute that necessarily involves the concurrent consideration of any unsettled dispute on sovereignty or other rights over continental or insular land territory should not be submitted to conciliation procedure under Annex V of the Convention.

International arbitration cannot resolve the territorial disputes in the South China Sea, including that between Beijing and Manila. They should be resolved through bilateral political and diplomatic channels.

The Philippines has simply taken a wrong path in trying to push the arbitration forward.

This article was originally published on Page 8 of *China Daily* on Apr. 15, 2014

Hanoi Must Stop Muddying the Waters

Vietnamese vessels have repeatedly disrupted China's drilling activities in the South China Sea ever since Beijing placed its deep-sea oil rig, HD-981, in the waters south of Xisha Islands on May 2. And the deadly anti-China protests across Vietnam amid escalating tensions between Beijing and Hanoi have severely endangered the safety of Chinese nationals and damaged Chinese enterprises' property in Vietnam.

The main dispute between the two neighbors is whether or not China has the right to operate the rig located 17 nautical miles (31.5 kilometers) from Zhongjian Island of China's Xisha Islands and about 150 nautical miles from Vietnam's coast. As the Chinese Ministry of Foreign Affairs said, operations like the latest one — carried out within China's contiguous zone — started 10 years ago, and a seismic operation and well site survey were conducted in the waters even in May and June last year.

History shows that Chinese authorities have more than once named and mapped the islands in the South China Sea based on various surveys, especially those in 1935, 1947 and 1983. Based on the U-shaped line, which first appeared in an official map published by China in 1948, the then Chinese government claimed sovereignty and jurisdiction over the islands in the South China Sea. Later, the government of New China retained the previous names of the island groups while supplementing them with a list of geographical names in 1983.

In May 2009, the Chinese Permanent Mission to the United Nations submitted a note to the UN secretary-general, urging the Commission on the Limits of the Continental Shelf not to review either the Malaysia-Vietnam joint submission on the outer limits of the continental shelf beyond 200 nautical miles from the baselines or Vietnam's separate submission on the same issue. While doing so, China reaffirmed its indisputable sovereignty over the islands in the South China Sea and their adjacent waters, and its sovereign rights and jurisdiction over the relevant waters and seabed and subsoil thereof. In fact, this has been Beijing's consistent position for years.

True, according to the provisions for the continental shelf in the UN Convention on the Law of the Sea, Vietnam can claim an exclusive economic zone that extends 200 nautical miles from its baseline. But China issued a statement on May 15, 1996, announcing the geographical coordinates on the base points and straight baselines of the Xisha Islands. From these baselines, China can also measure the breadth of its exclusive economic zone and continental shelf.

Given their dispute over the overlapping exclusive economic zones in the South China Sea, Beijing and Hanoi are obliged to observe the

UNCLOS provisions on the delimitation of the exclusive economic zone between states with opposite or adjacent coasts and settle their dispute equitably on the basis of international law.

UNCLOS provisions, however, do not specify how to delimit exclusive economic zones and continental shelves between states with opposite or adjacent coasts. Nevertheless, based on international practice, disputing parties usually resolve their overlapping claims with a median line drawn equidistant from their respective coastlines. Although such a median line between China and Vietnam does not exist, the oil rig Beijing has been operating is 17 nautical miles south of China's Zhongjian Island and about 150 nautical miles from Vietnam's coast — that is, a long way from the median line if it were to be drawn today.

The latest maritime standoff between China and Vietnam has dimmed the prospects of settling the South China Sea disputes through political means. China has for long been advocating that the disputes be resolved through political means, including bilateral dialogue and consultations. Accordingly, Beijing and Hanoi's agreements on the delimitation of the Beibu Bay and cooperation in fishing activities took effect in June 2004. And in March 2005, China, Vietnam and the Philippines signed the Tripartite Agreement for Joint Marine Seismic Undertaking in the Agreement Area in the South China Sea.

Apart from jeopardizing these agreements, the latest standoff has also undermined Beijing's and Hanoi's efforts to maintain stability and expand maritime cooperation in the South China Sea. For instance, China and Vietnam signed a six-point agreement in October 2011 on the basic principles guiding the settlement of maritime issues. In the same month, the two neighbors issued a joint statement reaffirming their political will and determination to settle maritime disputes through negotiations and friendly consultations and to safeguard peace and stability in the South China Sea.

In October 2013, the two sides signed another joint statement on further deepening their comprehensive strategic cooperative partnership in the new period, according to which they were supposed to accelerate cooperation in a wide range of fields, including marine research and protection of marine environment. They agreed not to make any move that could complicate or escalate the disputes and vowed to continue discussions and take efficient measures to prevent the disputes from escalating and to maintain peace and stability in the South China Sea. The latest standoff could compromise these goals.

Despite Vietnam's accusations and attempts to portray itself as a victim, China has the legitimate right to operate its oil rig in the waters near the Xisha Islands, and Hanoi is squarely to blame for the damage caused to Chinese property and operations in Vietnam. To maintain good bilateral relations and implement the measures stated in bilateral political agreements, however, Beijing has to clarify its position through different means and should try to minimize the impact of the standoff to better defend its national maritime rights and interests.

This article was originally published on Page 9
of *China Daily* on May 21, 2014

Drilling is Legal and Legitimate

Despite Japan's attempts at the G7 summit in Brussels on Wednesday and Thursday to get the G7 leaders to blame China for the rising tensions in the East and South China seas, the G7 leaders said in a communiqué they are deeply concerned by the tensions and oppose any unilateral attempt by any party to assert its territorial or maritime claims through the use of intimidation, coercion or force, but without naming any specific country.

The essence of the South China Sea issue is the territorial disputes over some islets and reefs of the Nansha Islands and the Xisha Islands and the resulting disputes over maritime demarcation. The former is the main dispute and the latter secondary. Because of the complexity and sensitivity of the territorial issues involved, no country wants to compromise or make concessions.

The location of China National Offshore Oil Corporation's (Ocean Oil) Haiyang Shiyou 981 drilling platform is 17 nautical miles (31.5 kilometers) southeast of Zhongjian Island, one of China's Xisha Islands, and about 150 nautical miles from the coastline of Vietnam, it falls indisputably within the contiguous zone of China's Xisha Islands.

In September 1958, Vietnamese Premier Pham Van Dong solemnly stated in a note to Premier Zhou Enlai that Vietnam recognizes and supports the Declaration of the Government of the People's Republic of China on China's territorial sea that the breadth of the territorial sea of China should be 12 nautical miles and that this provision should apply to all territories of China, including the Xisha Islands and the Nansha Islands in the South China Sea. Pham Van Dong's note shows that the Vietnamese government acknowledged China's sovereignty over the Xisha Islands and Nansha Islands. Vietnam's claim to sovereignty of the Xisha Islands today is in violation of the principle of estoppel.

China issued a statement on May 15, 1996, announcing the geographical coordinates on the base points and straight baselines of the Xisha Islands. Therefore, China can claim an exclusive economic zone that extends 200 nautical miles from these baselines. China has indisputable sovereignty over the Xisha islands, and China's drilling operation falls within China's sovereign territory, sovereign rights and jurisdiction and thus is fully legal and legitimate. Vietnam's dangerous actions against China's drilling platform in the contiguous zone of the Xisha Islands must be resolutely opposed.

In response to the provocations of the Vietnamese side, China has continued to exercise restraint for the sake of regional peace and stability and it is willing to solve the South China Sea disputes with the countries directly concerned through bilateral coordination and negotiation on the basis of respecting historical facts and international law. This is an important consensus reached between China and relevant countries, and is also in line with the interests and aspirations of the majority of countries and peoples in this region.

There are both theory and practice in the international community to carry out joint development in disputed waters with the purpose of cooling territorial disputes and enabling the countries concerned to share maritime interests and resources. By proposing to carry out joint development and share maritime resources and interests, China has demonstrated its sincerity in seeking to end the disputes. However, China's goodwill has not been rewarded or reciprocated. Meanwhile, the involvement of countries outside the region is only making the dispute more difficult to settle.

It is not China but Vietnam that is making trouble and wants to change the status quo.

History shows that Chinese authorities have more than once named and mapped the islands in the South China Sea based on various surveys. Based on the nine-dash line, which first appeared in an official map published by China in 1948, the then Chinese government claimed sovereignty and jurisdiction over the islands in the South China Sea. China's claim was established long before the United Nations Convention on the Law of the Sea took effect. In accordance with the intertemporal law, the nine-dash line should be recognized by the international community.

In May 2009, the Chinese Permanent Mission to the United Nations submitted a note to the UN Secretary-General, urging the Commission on the Limits of the Continental Shelf not to review either the Malaysia-Vietnam joint submission on the outer limits of the continental shelf beyond 200 nautical miles from the baselines or Vietnam's separate submission on the same issue. While doing so, China reaffirmed its indisputable sovereignty over the islands in the South China Sea and their adjacent waters, and its sovereign rights and jurisdiction over the relevant waters and seabed and subsoil thereof. In fact, this has been Beijing's consistent position for years.

China's drilling operations in the contiguous zone of the Xisha Islands and construction of facilities in the waters surrounding the Nansha Islands are not actions that "unilaterally change the status quo", but China's sovereign acts, which are legal and legitimate. These routine activities are beyond reproach and must not be disrupted by other countries.

Countries outside the region should respect the facts of these controversial issues and adhere to an objective attitude instead of deliberately stirring up trouble and complicating the regional situation.

This article was originally published on Page 11 of *China Daily* on June 9, 2014

Resolve South China Sea Issue First

Maritime disputes are testing the wisdom of the Chinese government and have prompted it to handle its ties with the United States with utmost caution to ensure that China's peaceful development continues uninterrupted.

There is little doubt that the maritime disputes broke out as a result of Washington's "rebalancing" in Asia policy, which is aimed at strengthening the US' strategic presence in the Asia-Pacific region. Aside from being aimed at restructuring the US' cooperation with its Asian allies and balancing the equilibrium between China and the Association of Southeast Asian Nations, the "rebalancing" policy is also intended to help Washington maintain its dominant position in and derive the maximum benefit from Asia's development.

Since the US hasn't met with much success with the Trans-Pacific Partnership, which would have helped it advance its "rebalancing" policy, it has embarked on a mission to strengthen its military presence in the region and blockade China's "first arc of islands". Since Asian countries locked in maritime disputes with China expect to get US' support to counterbalance China's peaceful rise, they have taken intransigent measures against China and started what could be called an arms race in the region.

The dispute between Beijing and Washington in China's waters revolves mainly around the safety of navigation. Among the contentious issues are whether or not a country needs the prior approval of the Chinese government to carry out military activities such as air reconnaissance, surveys and joint military drills in its Exclusive Economic Zones. China believes that prior approval is needed, because such activities can have a lasting impact on its overall defense structure.

The US, however, thinks otherwise, saying the regulations on freedom in high seas grants a country the right to conduct military activities in another country's EEZs as long as they do not lead to a conflict.

Despite its insistence on the principle of other countries seeking "prior consent" to conduct military activities in its EEZs, China still guarantees the safety and freedom of navigation in the East and South China seas. But the US believes China's actions have compromised the safety of its ships and it needs to take measures to counter the "threat" China poses to other countries in the region. As a result, the US has built a "ring of encirclement" around China in the sea in a bid to squeeze its space for maritime activities and put it in a disadvantageous position.

The US has launched a "proxy war", with the political and strategic support of some countries against China. In exchange, it has helped these countries expedite their military build-up and deployment and has been supporting them in their maritime disputes with China. In spite of all this, China and the US still have ample space and potential for cooperation on maritime issues, especially non-traditional security cooperation at sea.

China should intensify communications with the US through established bilateral dialogue channels and make it clear that it understands Washington's wish to continue playing a dominant role in Asia. China also needs to make it clear that it does not intend to challenge the US' status in exchange for its respect for Beijing's core interests and concerns.

Given the complicated factors and the US-Japan alliance involved in the settlement of the dispute with Japan over the Diaoyu Islands, China should first try to maintain stability in the East China Sea and focus on how to resolve the disputes with the Philippines and Vietnam in the South China Sea. Since the Philippines has moved the international arbitration tribunal over its dispute with China in the South China Sea, an action that could be emulated by other countries, Beijing should collect sound evidence to be better prepared to deal with the issue even though it is opposed to such a move.

The South China Sea issue will serve as an important indicator of whether China can establish itself as a regional power and realize its goal of becoming a "naval power". Therefore, China should, based on relevant international laws, publish a policy declaration to back its claim that it has "indisputable sovereignty over the South China Sea islands and adjacent waters, and enjoys the rights and jurisdiction over the relevant seabed and subsoil".

This article was originally published on Page 9
of *China Daily* on June 26, 2014

China and Ocean Issues

Review on Scientific Expedition in the Antarctica after the Return of Xuelong

Recently (on Apr. 10, 2009), the expedition ship Xuelong successfully returned and finished the 25th Antarctic expedition task of China. one of main achievements is the successful establishment of Kunlun Station, China's first inland scientific expedition station, in Dome A area, the peak-point of Antarctic inland ice caps, which is a result of perseverant and sustained efforts of Chinese Antarctic explorers for many years, marking China's entry into the first tier of international Polar exploration in the field of Antarctic scientific research. China is the seventh country establishing a station in Antarctic inland after the USA, Russia, Japan, France, Italy and Germany.

After the completion of Kunlun Station, China will carry out scientific expedition in Antarctic inland areas step by step in a planned way, including scientific drilling project for exploring ice core in depth of glacier, drilling for exploring mountain chain under the ice, astronomical and geomagnetic observation, satellite remote sensing data reception, human medical research and medical security and so on. It is predictable that the completion of Kunlun Station in Antarctica will definitely expand and deepen China's scientific expedition and research in the South Pole and make great contribution to the humankind's exploration of Antarctic mystery.

The Antarctica, located at the southernmost part of the earth, is the fifth continent with area of 14000000 square meters, highest latitude geographically, the driest and coldest weather and most storms and farthest distance from humankind. Due to difficulties in inhabitation of humankind, Antarctic continent has long been in a undeveloped state.

Because of rich resources in the Antarctica, some countries have successively claimed territorial ownership over certain areas of the Antarctic continent since the beginning of the 20th century. The first country to claim territorial sovereignty is UK who claimed ownership on all islands and the Falkland Islands in the area south of latitude 50° S and within the scope of longitude 20° W to 80° W in 1908. Afterwards, New Zealand, France and Argentina, Australia, Norway and Chili all claimed ownership over certain areas in the Antarctica respectively. Although their legal foundations are different, including discovery, occupation, adjacency, geographical position, geological consistence, erecting monument and so on, they are all supported by the sector theory.

The sector theory refers to that islands and land within the fan-shaped sector formed by the coastal line of territory adjacent to the polar region and two meridians from two ends of territory and polar region, even though there is no occupation, naturally belong to the adjacent country. Such theory was first proposed by Canada in 1907 as a basis for Canada to claim rights over all arctic islands, that is to say, all lands located between two national boundaries till the North Pole belong to states adjacent to such lands. Although countries' claims over Antarctic territory according to the sector theory are different in terms of meridians in determining the limits of the fan-shaped sector, some countries all claim sovereignty over the same areas, thus resulting overlapped claims in the same area between or among countries. Regarding the section theory, the USA and the former Soviet Union held that it was difficult to recognize claims over the Antarctica made by countries according to the section theory which cannot serve as a legal basis to claim rights over the areas in Antarctic continent.

In order to avoid possible disputes or conflicts arising from territorial sovereignty over Antarctica and seek peaceful use of the Antarctic continent, the international community concluded the Antarctic Treaty for regulating the Antarctica on Dec. 1, 1959 (entry into force on June 23, 1961). China acceded to the Antarctic Treaty on June 8, 1983 and such treaty came into force for China on the same date.

The Antarctic Treaty mainly includes the following content: firstly, Antarctica shall not be used for military purposes. Article 1 states that Antarctica shall be used for peaceful purposes only. There shall be prohibited, inter alia, any measures of a military nature. But the use of military personnel or equipment for scientific research or for any other peaceful purposes is not prohibited. Secondly, Rights of or claims to territorial sovereignty in Antarctica are frozen. Article 4 states that no new claim or enlargement of an existing claim, to territorial sovereignty shall asserted while the present Treaty is in force. Thirdly, any nuclear explosions in Antarctica (including nuclear explosion for peaceful purposes) is prohibited. Fourthly, in order to prevent breach of the treaty, each Contracting Party's free access for observation and inspection over Antarctica is recognized. Such provision is formulated due to worries that actual and effective inspection cannot be conducted by the inspection organ formed by most countries when representatives are not able to reach an agreement on inspection. Fifthly, Consultative meetings have been held every other year in principle, for the purpose of exchanging information, consulting together on matters of common interest pertaining to Antarctica. Only the state which has become a party to Antarctic Treaty is entitled to participate in the consultative meetings during such time as it establishes a scientific station, dispatches a scientific expedition and conducts substantial scientific research activity there. China was acceded to Antarctic Treaty as a consultative party on Oct. 7, 1985.

In addition, in order to regulate development of natural resources in Antarctica, Convention on the Regulation of Antarctic Mineral Resources Activities was passed in the consultative meeting of Antarctic Treaty, stipulating principles of prospecting, exploration or development of mineral resources. Later, in view of extensive criticism on such Convention due to its flaws in environment protection, Protocol on

Environmental Protection to the Antarctic Treaty was adopted in a consultative meeting to substitute the aforesaid Convention and serve as a supplement of Antarctic Treaty. In addition, in order to protect marine living resources in Antarctica, the Convention on the Conservation of Antarctic Marine Living Resources was concluded on May 20, 1980 for all states' compliance. It is obvious that international legal system on Antarctica has been formed, but it is still uncertain whether development of mineral resources in such area shall be carried out according to the principle of the common heritage of mankind which is applicable to international seabed and outer space. This issue is mainly dependant on stances and attitudes of consultative parties of the Antarctic Treaty system, that is to say, there is necessity to coordinate interests between territory-claiming states and non-territory-claiming states.

This article was originally published in Page 6
of *Jiefang Daily* on Apr. 11, 2009

The Century of the Sea Needs Harmonious Sea

Nov. 16, 2009 was the 15th anniversary of the effectiveness of the United Nations Convention on the Law of the Sea. At present, it is especially valuable for us to further consider the connotation behind the content and systematic framework of such Convention, review the impact produced since its conclusion and predict the future development of concepts of the sea and ocean power in the world.

The sea is the largest space relied on by the mankind for living and development, an environmental adaptor and important support and guaranty for resolving climate change issues. The abundance and vastness of ocean resources as well as importance of sea lanes requires us to reasonably understand, develop, exploit and protect the sea and ocean resources to create benefits for all the mankind, therefore, the 21st Century is called the Century of the Sea. Especially after entering the 21st Century, main developed countries in the world successively formulate and improve national or regional marine strategies and legal systems under the framework of the United Nations Convention on the Law of the Sea. It can be inferred, from the starting point of the effectiveness of the Convention, that regarding the development, exploitation, management and protection of the sea and marine issues, the principle has been transformed from armed control mainly dependent on military strength and free use for a long time to comprehensive management of the sea and cooperation to resolve marine issues.

Mahan put forwards that ocean ships, navigation, seaman, navy and other elements constituted the concept of sea power in the end of the 19th Century, disclosing the close relationship between national rise and fall and sea control, imposing great influence in the subsequent history of the world through ideas closely related to sea power that a state became prosperous by taking advantage of the sea to conduct trade. Even today, against the background of globalization, the reasonableness is still not disappeared. However, at present, all countries are seeking various ways to enhance their own marine rights and interests and ensure marine safety, and emphasizes that investigation and scientific technology capability, resources development capability, administrative capability of environment protection and other capabilities shall be incorporated into constituent elements of the concept of sea power in the expectation of obtaining more marine energy resources. These new changes, in conformity with the requirement of the Convention and international development trend, have been showed in many countries' marine strategies and legal systems.

It is well known that the current international community has great expectation in exploration and exploitation of the sea and its resources. This is because not only the sea lane was in the past, is at present or will still be in the future an important route of booming human society but also new technologies of exploration and exploitation of important resources such as crude oil or gas which have been discovered or still hidden in the sea bed are developing. With the decrease of ice layer in arctic sea, the possibilities of using the arctic as sea lane and developing resources such as crude oil hidden in the sea bed of the arctic sea in the future are increased.

However, when the sea brings benefits to the mankind, it is also a source of crisis for the mankind. On one hand, new opposition between countries on jurisdiction over sea areas and right to marine resources is becoming more and more obvious, causing unstable environment of guaranteeing marine safety; on the other land, disordered development and pollution have accelerated damage by human beings to marine ecosystem and environment, escalated the issue of climate change. It is predictable that there will inevitably be armed conflicts between countries claiming rights and interests and those claiming the freedom of the sea when resources and energies are in shortage in a global scale. For this reason, it is more important and urgent to enhance cooperation among countries on military and safety guaranty, resources and environment protection, promotion of scientific technology and so forth.

Against such international background, China, as a state party to the Convention, put forward the proposal of building Harmonious Sea to jointly maintain sustainable peace and safety of the sea at the 60th anniversary of establishment of Chinese Navy. It should be mentioned that the idea of building a Harmonious Sea proposed by China is an implementation of the idea of Harmonious World proposed by China in the Assembly of the United Nations in 2005 in the filed of the sea, showing a new understanding and requirement of the international community of marine issues and also marking China's new contribution to and achievement in development of the law of the sea. The realization of the idea of Harmonious Sea requires faithful performance and continuous improvement of the Convention and other relevant systems of the sea. At present, the more important thing is for each country to formulate and improve their own domestic marine policies and legal systems.

This article was originally published in Page 6 of *Jiefang Daily* on Nov. 18, 2009

Essence and Legal Construction of China's Development of Ocean Economy

The Proposal of the CPC Central Committee for Formulating the Twelfth Five-Year Plan for National Economic and Social Development (hereinafter referred to as the Proposal) adopted in the fifth Plenary Session of the Seventeenth CPC Central Committee points out that China shall develop ocean economy including insisting on coordination of the land and the sea, formulating and implementing marine development strategy, improving its capability of development, control and comprehensive management of the sea; making a scientific plan on development of ocean economy, developing industries such as oil and gas, transportation and fishery in the sea, reasonably exploring and exploiting marine resources, promoting the construction of fishing ports, protecting ocean islands, coastal belts and marine ecological environment; guaranteeing sea lane safety to maintain China's marine rights and interests. The Proposal also puts forward that China shall encourage desalination of sea water and develop space technology in ocean fields and so on. Obviously, it is significant to fully understand the essence of development of ocean economy.

I. The Basic Characteristics of Development of Ocean Economy

From the content of Developing Ocean Economy in the Proposal, the development of ocean economy mainly enjoys the following characteristics:

Firstly, the policies on development of ocean economy are consistent. In reality, the Central Committee had put forward the task of implementing development of the sea in the Report of Sixteenth National Congress of the CPC; the State Council put forward the policy of attaching importance to development and protection of marine resources in Government Working Paper of 2004, and pointed out that China should promote the development of ocean economy in the Eleventh Five-Year Plan (2006) and emphasized reasonable exploration and exploitation of marine resources in Government Working Paper of 2009.

The strategy of marine exploration or development is significant for China to ensure energy and resources supply for social and economic development, change the long-held idea of valuing land development and neglecting marine development and protect its marine rights and interests. The State Council approved the National Plan for Development of Ocean Undertakings on Feb. 7, 2008 which points out the objective of China's marine undertakings development and plan and is of very important instructive significance in promoting the comprehensive, coordinated and sustainable development of China's marine undertakings and accelerating the construction of an ocean power. It is thus obvious that policies on developing marine undertakings including developing ocean economy are consistent and must be continuously persevered and promoted.

Secondly, policies on development of ocean economy are extensive and guaranty-oriented. The ocean economy mentioned in the Proposal is an extensive concept covering many fields mainly including exploration, exploitation and management of the sea and its resources, improvement of capacity in marine industry, protection of marine ecological environment, governance of sea waters under jurisdiction, guaranty of sea lane safety, encouragement of desalination of sea water, development of space technology in ocean fields, protection of national marine territory, rights and interests and so forth. The key to developing marine undertakings is to formulate and implement national marine development strategy. In order to implement national marine development strategy, one of important works is to formulate and improve relevant legal systems of the sea for guaranteeing the implementation of China's national marine development strategy to protect China's ocean safety, rights and interests.

Thirdly, the development of ocean economy is an important part of continuous improvement of China's economic strengths. It is well-known that the 21st Century is the century of the sea and the sea has become the last space and resource treasure for human beings' social development. Especially, all countries attach increasing importance to the topic of how to further develop the ocean economy and have implemented the further development of ocean economy. Against such international background, China, of course, could not make exceptions on its ocean economy.

Meanwhile, the status and function of ocean economy in China's GDP is increasing and enjoys the trend of continuous increase, so China shall make further efforts to promote and develop its ocean economy. In 2007, China's gross marine production was 2493.9 billion Yuan, accounting for 10.11% of GDP of that year; in 2008, the gross marine production was 2966.2 billion Yuan, accounting for 9.87% of GDP; in 2009, the gross marine production was 3196.4 billion Yuan, accounting for 9.53% of GDP. According to the objective set in the National Plan for Development of Ocean Undertakings, the gross marine production should account for more than 11.0% of GDP in 2010. The data shows that in recent years China's gross marine production basically accounts for around 10% and it is necessary to make more efforts to further develop ocean economy.

Fourthly, the development of ocean economy is an important way chosen by China to reasonably deal with marine issues and protect marine rights and interests. It is well known that China confronts a lot of difficult marine issues in protecting its marine rights and interests.

Such difficulties cause a series of marine safety issues and influence or threaten national coastal defense security. We all know that ocean safety refers to a state that national marine rights and interests are free from infringement or risks, which is also known as security at sea or marine security. The ocean safety may be generally divided into traditional security at sea and untraditional security at sea. The former mainly includes military security at sea and coastal defense security with military invasion at sea being the biggest threat to military security at the sea. Such type of security issues is showing a trend of decrease at present. The latter mainly includes terrorism at sea, illegal activities at sea (piracy), natural disasters at sea, ocean pollution and deterioration of ecosystem, security issues arising from marine survey activities and military drills. Compared with the former, such type of security issues is in a trend of increase. The development of ocean economy, including establishment of corresponding institutions and systems, may promote the reasonable settlement of these marine issues.

II. Reasons for Many Marine Issues Confronted by China and Their Solutions

It is predictable that main threats to China's security at present and in the future come from the sea mainly due to the following reasons:

Firstly, the land delimitation works between China and major neighboring countries have been basically finished, so threats from the land will be decreased greatly.

Secondly, with the deepened policies on opening up to the outside and intensified globalization, China will expand and deepen its frequency and degree in exploration and exploitation of the sea and marine resources, so marine issues will inevitably increase, especially when the ocean economy in China has become an important part of national economy and shows a tread of increased proportion. Meanwhile, the trend that China further relies on the sea and marine resources is still increasing. At present, about 90% of the total volume of exported and imported goods is transported through the sea, and 99% of imported petroleum, 95% of imported ironstone and 80% of imported copper ore are transported through the sea, so there is a lot of interest at sea needing protection and the corresponding marine issues inevitably are increased.

Thirdly, China is a geographically disadvantaged ocean country and has problems of sea waters delimitation with many countries including disputes over island sovereignty. If these issues can not be settled properly, they will influence China's ocean security (including obvious security and potential security in sea waters under jurisdiction), especially sea lane security accidents and conflicts at sea will possibly often happen.

Fourthly, China's economic development has had foundations and conditions to shift from the land to the sea. Meanwhile, the layout and development of China's strengths at sea are likely to be misunderstood and misjudged by other countries, so corresponding marine issues are inevitably increased.

The development of ocean economy needs suitable environment. China shall positively respond to and deal with marine issues. From the perspective of international practices, one of effective ways to deal with and respond to disputes over marine issues is to formulate national marine development strategy and improve marine system and mechanism, under the situation that international, regional and bilateral systems on marine issues are not perfect or hard to improve. An important method for guaranteeing the realization of the abovementioned measures is that China enact and enforce a law on comprehensively managing marine issues — the Basic Law of the Sea as soon as possible, which shall mainly include the following aspects: announcement of marine policies, that is to say, summarizing China's policies on marine issues and publicizing and interpreting them to the outside; establishment of national organs on management of marine affairs such as National Committee of Marine Issues to manage national marine affairs in a untied, efficient and coordinated way; promulgation of important fields of marine development by China including developing marine industry and activities, actively developing, utilizing and managing the sea and marine resources, protecting marine environment, ensuring passage safety, researching and developing marine technology, enhancing management and survey activities in governed sea areas, strengthening ocean education and publicity for Chinese people, promoting international cooperation in the sea.

In short, formulation of strategy and plan on the sea and management of the sea are important basis and inevitable choice for China's economic and social development. The development of ocean economy is an important breakthrough point, so China must promote its implementation. In order to formulate a plan on the ocean economy, one of the important tasks is to carry out a general survey of the national ocean economy for getting a practical knowledge of and understanding in advantages and disadvantages of China's development of ocean economy and then enhance corresponding system construction.

This article was originally published in Page 12 of *Wenhui Daily* on Jan. 5, 2011

The Inevitable Path for China to Resolve Maritime Issues Tier by Tier

China shall adopt different modes and solutions to resolve marine issues confronted by it according to characteristics and features of various marine issues.

China is confronting and will still confront a lot of marine issues at present and in the future. In the South China Sea, there are disputes over islands ownership and sea water delimitation between China and many member states of ASEAN, and different understanding and opposition on free use of the sea (sea waters and the above airspace) in the exclusive economic zone between China and the USA; in the East China Sea, there are disputes (including disputes over resources development, delimitation and islands ownership and ocean security conflicts) between China and Japan; in the high seas, China confronts issues such as sea lane security inclusive of piracy, influence imposed on China's survey and navigation in the original high seas by determination of outer continental shelf, environmental pollution arising from natural or sea disasters. Those marine issues will result in problems in ocean security and even national security, so China must reasonably deal with them.

Regarding the issue of sea waters delimitation in East China Sea, China shall continue to conduct negotiation and consultation with Japan because conclusion of a final agreement on delimitation is the best arrangement. The key aspect of such negotiation and consultation is to determine the status and role of disputes over Diaoyu Island and its affiliated islands and relevant systematic arrangements. That is to say, China insists on the stance that Diaoyu Islands are China's Inherent Territory, makes efforts to reduce Japan's management of and control over of them and seek joint development over the surrounding sea waters.

Regarding the issue of development of resources in the East China Sea, if Japan refuses to make any concession or compromise on the issue of Diaoyu Islands, China may take the stance of achieving no real progress in negotiation on Principled Consensus on East China Sea with exchange of notes between governments, i.e. the policy of no breakthrough in negotiation and no result in negotiation. Especially, China shall actively take advantage of the positive role of Chuanxiao Oil and Gas Field including setting a comparatively higher threshold for cooperative development to prevent Japanese enterprises from participating cooperative development activities.

Regarding disputes over islands ownership and delimitation between China and member states of ASEAN, China needs to conduct negotiation and consultation with states claiming the existence of disputes. During negotiation, China shall insist on the principle and spirit advocated by Declaration on the Conduct of Parties in the South China Sea. At present, the important thing is that states concerned shall deal with disputes after equal consultation through dialogue and see new mode of cooperation, including discussing the possibility of activating normative systems such as Agreement on Triple Parties' Joint Work Concerning the Sea and the Earthquake in South China Sea Agreement Zone formulated previously, formulating Rules on the Conduct of Party in the South China Sea, freezing disputes to avoid deterioration of events and so on.

Regarding disagreement and opposition on freedom of navigation in the exclusive economic zone of the South China Sea, China shall conduct consultation with the USA to resolve them through bilateral meeting and dialogue mechanism (for example, the Sino-USA Consultation Mechanism for marine security) in order to seek understanding and cooperation with focus on showing China's concerns and stance including that China welcomes the USA to continue to play its role in Asia-Pacific region and China does not intend to challenge hegemony of the USA and hopes to cooperate with the USA in maintenance and governance of marine issues.

Regarding the issue of sea lane security in the high seas, China shall continue to make efforts within its ability to play its role, especially shall continue to carry out and participate in navigation escort activities for fight against piracy in sea areas near Aden Gulf and Somalia, accumulate experiences and use such experiences flexibly in other sea waters in a bid to make due contributions to international community.

China shall actively participate and play its corresponding role in resolution of the issue of marine disasters due to natural reasons including pollution of marine environment with the aim to show that China develops marine strengths not only for protecting its own interests but also for maintaining overall interests of the international community.

Regarding the issue of infringement of China's relevant rights and interests in the sea areas which are originally the high seas due to determination of outer continental shelf, China shall continuously keep an eye on the deliberation process of Commission on the Limits of the Continental Shelf with focus on research into the specific influence on China and further enhance China's investigation of the continental shelf in East China Sea and South China Sea in a bid to submit application for delimitation of outer continental shelf as soon as possible and take into account the issue of cross-straits cooperation on investigation activities of the continental shelf.

In short, China shall adopt different modes and solutions to resolve marine issues confronted by it according to characteristics and features of various marine issues and with focus on compliance with or adopting the following principles or measures:

The first one is to insist on the principle of resolving disputes over islands ownership and sea waters delimitation by peaceful means; the second one is to discuss a new mode of joint development and a new mechanism of maintaining ocean security in disputed areas with parties concerned including a flexible use of previous systems and creation of new systems such as ocean security caution contact mechanism and law enforcement contact mechanism; the third one is to develop ocean strengths and carry out exchange and dialogue with other states to promote mutual trust and understanding for avoiding misunderstanding and misjudgment; the fourth one is to selectively take part in international marine matters and activities to increase understanding in international marine matters and undertake corresponding obligations conferred to China; the fifth one is to actively publicize China's stance and attitude towards maritime issues including building websites and hosting international seminars to enhance other states' understanding in and knowledge of China's relevant policies. Meanwhile, China shall make further study on the system and regimes of the law of the sea to make theoretical preparation for amendment to relevant regimes; the sixth one is to build a framework and system for cross-straits cooperation on maritime issues in a bid to jointly maintain marine rights and interests of Chinese Nationality.

This article was originally published on Page A17 of *Dongfang Daily* on Aug. 31, 2010

China Should Enact and Implement Basic Law of the Sea as soon as Possible

The Chapter XIV Promoting Development of Ocean Economy of the Twelfth Five-Year Plan of China points out that China shall insist on coordination of the land and the sea, formulate and implement ocean development strategy, improve capability of development, control and comprehensive management of the sea. This provides important political guaranty for China to reasonably deal with marine issues and disputes, develop earnestly ocean undertakings, especially formulate and improve China's ocean development strategy, policies and legal system.

It is well-known that there are a lot of disputes concerning China's marine rights and interests. Such disputes are not only historically left-over issues but also have different natures without a standard mode to resolve them or solutions for reference. In order to develop ocean economy, a proper neighboring environment is necessary, so China shall actively respond to and deal with marine disputes and maintain national marine rights and interests. From the perspective of international practices, one of effective ways to deal with and respond to disputes over marine issues is to formulate national marine development strategy and improve marine system and mechanism, under the situation that international, regional and bilateral systems on marine issues are not perfect or hard to improve. For this reason, China shall enact and enforce a law on comprehensively managing marine issues as soon as possible, namely the Basic Law of the Sea.

Summarily speaking, China's enactment of the Basic Law of the Sea enjoys the following meanings:

The first one is to supply a deficiency and improve the status of the sea. The enactment of the Basic Law of the Sea by National People's Congress may improve the legal status of the sea and the Basic Law of the Sea and create conditions for including the sea into the Constitutional Law.

The second one is to improve legal system of the sea. The enactment of the Basic Law of the Sea, showing the direction in improving China's legal system of the sea, requires China to further formulate and improve legal regimes in relevant fields such as ocean security law, ocean development law, coastal zone management law, ocean scientific technology law among others, thus promote the construction of China's legal system of the sea.

The third one is to coordinate powers of sea-related authorities. The Basic Law of the Sea will play a big role in coordinating relations among sea-related authorities, including strengthening out powers, duties and functions, making up deficiencies, eliminating overlapping and gapping of powers and functions to avoid disadvantageous competition and enhance law enforcement capability, improve capability and efficiency of handling maritime issues.

The fourth one is to increase enthusiasm in research into maritime issues. There is a process for the enactment of the Basic Law of the Sea. During such investigation, deliberation and legislation process, a large number of people will be interested in participating in research into maritime issues, which will provide theoretic support for resolving maritime disputes. Meanwhile, China may take such opportunity to establish websites for publicizing the sea, set up research institutes on ocean education and maritime issues, and organizational institutions such as Maritime Issues Research Foundation.

China put forward an objective of enacting laws like the Basic Law of the Sea in the China's Agenda for the Sea in 21st Century as early as in 1996, that is, China shall establish and improve marine legal system taking the Basic Law of the Sea and comprehensive management laws as the main part and coordinating professional laws and local laws, and set up a marine law enforcement team featuring timely and effective supervision and efficient and strong operation to realize rule of law in the sea and guarantee sustainable development of the sea, coastal economy and society.

Generally speaking, China develops its ocean undertakings according to the following route map: the first thing is to make clear its core interests and formulate a strategy covering national marine development. For China, the core objective is to build an ocean power. The second thing is to improve marine policies for implementing national marine development strategy including enhancing marine ideas and awareness, strengthening marine affairs coordination, improving capability of development, control and comprehensive management of the sea and marine resources, promoting traditional culture of the sea, constantly develop and innovate marine technology, expand foreign exchange and cooperation to harvest new fruits of China's marine undertakings; the third thing is to enact the Basic Law of the Sea to guarantee the promotion and implementation of marine development strategy and marine policies with the focus on improving China's marine system and mechanism including establishment of organizations such as National Committee of Marine Issues. The last thing is to formulate basic marine plan of the Basic Law of the Sea to improve weak points in the course of marine development.

The Basic Law of the Sea enacted by China shall mainly include the following aspects: announcement of marine policies, that is to say, summarizing China's policies on marine issues including the policy of Setting Aside Dispute and Seeking Joint Development, establishing the idea of harmonious sea, and publicizing and interpreting them to the outside; establishment of national organs on management of marine affairs to manage national marine affairs in a untied, efficient and coordinated way; promulgation of important fields of marine development by China. Specifically, they mainly include the following aspects: promoting exploration and exploitation of the sea and marine resources; strengthening surveillance and protection of marine environment; promoting exploration and exploitation activities of the exclusive economic zone and continental shelf; ensuring ocean transportation safety; ensuring ocean security; strengthening marine investigation; researching and developing marine scientific technology; revitalizing marine industry and upgrading international competitiveness; enhancing comprehensive management on littoral waters; expanding exploration and exploitation of new space and new resources of the sea; protecting islands and their ecosystem; enhancing international coordination and promoting international cooperation; promoting national's understanding and knowledge of the sea and cultivating marine talents, developing military strengths and so forth.

It should be mentioned that the Basic Law of the Sea is China's announcement of policies on marine issues which is very important for other countries to further understand and get knowledge of China's stance and attitude towards marine issues. Because China's marine policies especially ocean economy development policy, featuring continuality and consistence, are summary and abstract of previous marine policies and stances, the law will not impose adverse influences on other countries. Meanwhile, because the Basic Law of the Sea is focused on declaration of policies, it will not cause adverse impact in or conflict with other areas of marine law and specific regulations, thus not resulting in a lot of issues of amendment and coordination. In other words, it is easy to handle the relation between the Basic Law of the Sea and other areas of marine law in force and maintain the integrity of current marine legal system.

In short, China enacts the Basic Law of the Sea, through clarifying China's ocean strategy, ocean policies or guidelines and measures of development of important ocean fields, to establish institutions for managing marine system, improve construction of marine system and mechanism and then further improve China's legal system on the sea. In the course of enacting the Basic Law of the Sea, considerations must be made beyond interests claimed by sea-related authorities and coordination and plans must be made from the perspective of national interests of Chinese Nationality, including coordination of relations between China Mainland and Taiwan Region at the time of enacting special areas of laws of the sea or announcing the baseline of the territorial sea of China in the future, in a bid to reach consensus, make gradual change of disadvantageous situation of China of being passive, inactive, lack of view on the whole picture in dealing with maritime issues and strive to provide important guidelines for reasonable resolution of maritime issues.

This article was originally published in Page 10 of *Wenhui Daily* on Sept. 26, 2011

Enacting the Basic Law: An Active Choice for Dealing with Maritime Issues

With the deepening and development of opening up to the outside, China has gradually acquired the economic and technological conditions for strategizing on and managing the sea, and further expand and deepen its frequency and degree in exploration and exploitation of the sea and marine resources. Correspondingly, its interests in the sea needing protection, conflicts and disputes arising from exploitation of the sea increase and the difficulties in resolving these maritime issues are increasing. In light of sea waters and marine rights and interests, the most prominent maritime issues confronted by China are East China Sea issues and South China Sea issues.

East China Sea Issues

There has not been a clear definition of East China Sea issues in international issues. Even in the Sino-Japanese Principled Consensus on the East China Sea Issue promulgated by ministries of foreign affairs of China and Japan, there is no clear connotation specified. Generally speaking, East China Sea issues include disputes over islands ownership, sea waters delimitation, resources development and law enforcement on the sea with focus on disputes over sovereign ownership of Diaoyu Island and its affiliated islands between China and Japan. The difficulties in resolution of the issue of Diaoyu Islands by China and Japan is increased due to Japanese government's conducts or measures of nationalization of Diaoyu Island and part of its affiliated islands to try to show its control or jurisdiction over them, and words, behaviors and expression of attitude of the USA that are in favor of Japan.

South China Sea Issues

South China Sea issues mainly include territorial disputes over Nansha Islands and Reefs and delimitation of sea waters. There are various reasons for emergence and escalation of these disputes including historical reasons and also economic and social development, implementation of international and regional systems and their deficiencies as well as involving interests of the so-called freedom and security of navigation concerned by foreign powers. South China Sea issues are very complicated and it is very hard to resolve them. Generally speaking, the core part of South China Sea is the determination of the nature of dotted line of South China Sea (or U-shaped line) and the legal status of waters within such line. From the perspective of the background and intention of determination and announcement of dotted line of South

China Sea, the main objective for Chinese government to announce dotted line of South China Sea is to declare China's sovereignty in South China Sea. The author holds that the dotted line of South China Sea shall be islands ownership and resource jurisdiction line in nature. In light of the nature of such dotted line reflected in the legal status of waters within such line, there are two types of waters within such line which enjoy different natures due to different sources and are not contradicted with each other but enjoying co-existence in parallel. The first type is waters under regimes of the law of the sea and the second one is special waters based on historic rights. The legal statuses of such two types of waters are totally in compliance with the systematic rules of the United Nations Convention on the Law of the Sea and domestic rules of China.

Maritime issues are related to the sovereign and territorial integrity of China, and protection and maintenance of core interests of China as well as peaceful development process and unification of China, therefore they must be reasonably and effectively handled and resolved. In view of laws, the author holds that China shall take the emergence of current maritime issues as an opportunity to focus on enhance construction of domestic legal system with the aim to improve marine system and mechanism. An effective way of realizing this aim is to enact national ocean development strategy and the Basic Law of the Sea. This is the basic choice of international community in reasonable and effective response to maritime issues and also the general and successful practical experiences of most countries. Regarding this, China will not make exceptions.

The content of China's ocean development strategy shall mainly include the following aspects: Firstly, China shall make clear its core interests and formulate a strategy covering national marine development. For China, the core objective is to build an Ocean Power. Secondly, China shall improve marine policies for implementing national marine development strategy including enhancing marine ideas and awareness, strengthening marine affairs coordination, improving capability of development, control and comprehensive management of the sea and marine resources, promoting traditional culture of the sea, constantly develop and innovate marine technology, expand foreign exchange and cooperation to harvest new fruits of China's marine undertakings. Thirdly, China shall enact the Basic Law of the Sea to guarantee the promotion and implementation of marine development strategy and marine policies with the focus on improving China's marine system and mechanism including establishment of organizations such as National Committee of Marine Issues. Lastly, China shall formulate basic marine plans of the Basic Law of the Sea to enhance or enrich weak links in the course of marine development.

The Basic Law of the Sea shall mainly include the following aspects: announcement of marine policies, establishing the idea of harmonious sea, and publicizing it to the outside; establishment of national organs on management of marine affairs to manage national marine affairs in an untied, efficient and coordinated way; promulgation of important fields of national marine development. Specifically, they mainly include the following aspects: promoting exploration and exploitation of the sea and marine resources; strengthening surveillance and protection of marine environment; promoting exploration and exploitation activities of the exclusive economic zone and continental shelf; ensuring ocean transportation safety; ensuring ocean security; strengthening marine investigation; researching and developing marine scientific technology; revitalizing marine industry and upgrading international competitiveness; enhancing comprehensive management on littoral waters; expanding exploration and exploitation of new space and new resources of the sea; protecting islands and their ecosystem; enhancing international coordination and promoting international cooperation; promoting national's understanding and knowledge of the sea and cultivating marine talents and so forth.

Principles and systems of international laws including the United Nations Convention on the Law of the Sea shall be complied with when formulating principles of the Basic Law of the Sea. specifically, they include the principle of coordinating exploration and exploitation of the sea and protection of marine environment, the principle of ensuring marine safety, the principle of upgrading ocean education scale and structure in order to promote scientific knowledge of and understanding in the sea, the principle of promoting healthy and orderly development of marine industry, the principle of managing marine affairs in a comprehensive and coordinated way, the principle of participating and coordinating international marine affairs and so forth.

In reality, China put forward an objective of enacting laws like the Basic Law of the Sea in the China's Agenda for the Sea in 21st Century as early as in 1996 and Foreign Affairs Committee of National People's Congress of PRC held an investigation conference and argumentation conference in July 2011. It was generally believed that China shall enact the Basic Law of the Sea as soon as possible, however there has not been any signal on initiation of such legislation, which may be attributed to interests claimed respectively by sea-related authorities. In the course of enacting the Basic Law of the Sea, considerations must be made beyond interests claimed by sea-related authorities and coordination and plans must be made from the perspective of national interests of Chinese Nationality, including coordination of relations between China Mainland and Taiwan Region at the time of enacting special areas of laws of the sea or announcing the baseline of the territorial sea of China in the future, in a bid to reach consensus, make gradual change of long-time disadvantageous situation of China of being passive, inactive, lack of view on the whole picture in dealing with maritime issues.

In short, the Basic Law of the Sea is China's announcement of policies on marine issues. Because China's marine policies especially ocean economy development policy, featuring continuality and consistence, are summary and abstract of previous marine policies and stances, the law will not impose adverse influences on other countries. Meanwhile, because the Basic Law of the Sea is focused on declaration of policies, it will not cause adverse impact in or conflict with other areas of marine law and specific regulations, thus not resulting in a lot of issues of amendment and coordination. In other words, it is easy to handle the relation between the Basic Law of the Sea and other areas of marine law in force and maintain the integrity of current marine legal system.

This article was originally published on Page 3 of *Procuratorate Daily* on Feb. 21, 2013

Connotation of China's Construction of Ocean Power

The Report of the 18th National Congress of the CPC points out that China shall improve capability to explore marines resources, develop ocean economy, protect ecological environment of the sea, firmly maintain national ocean rights and interests and build an ocean power. This is an important strategic plan in response to maritime issues especially international and domestic situations on the sea as from the new century, and also reasonable improvement and deepening of long-time policies on maritime issues made by CPC and Chinese government, enjoying important practical significance and strategic values. Therefore, it is necessary to expound the basic connotation of construction of an ocean power and the guaranty systems.

I. Status and Steps of China's Construction of an Ocean Power

The construction of an ocean power is undoubtedly an important part of China's construction of socialism with Chinese characteristics, so the progress of building an ocean power shall be in conformity with requirements of overall foundation, overall arrangement and overall task of China's construction of socialism with Chinese characteristics. According to The Report of the 18th National Congress of the CPC, the overall foundation of socialism with Chinese characteristics is the primary stage of socialism, the overall arrangement is "five in one" and the overall task is the realization of socialist modernization and the great revitalization of Chinese Nationality, therefore China's steps in construction of an ocean power shall be progressive. Specifically, there are two steps: regional ocean strength or power and worldwide ocean strength or power. This kind of steps implemented phrase by phrase is in compliance with the basic characteristics of China, especially the basic feature of remaining unchanged in three aspects, that is no change in the basic national situation that China will be still in the primary stage of socialism for a long time, no change in the main conflict between people's increasing material and cultural need with outdated social production, no change in the international status of China being the largest developing country in the world.

II. Overall Arrangement of China of Construction of an Ocean Power

The Report of the 18th National Congress of the CPC incorporates the content of strategic objective of China's construction of an ocean power into the overall arrangement of "five in one" that China must comprehensively carry out economic, political, cultural and social construction and ecological civilization development, with specific requirements reflected in the process of promotion of ecological civilization development with great efforts in a bid to improve layout of national land space development, and with the most important thing to reflect principles of coordination of the land and the sea, intensive use, comprehensive planning and coordinated development. To this end, China shall comprehensively enhance development of ocean economy, ocean political security, marine culture and marine management (or society) among others to protect and improve ecological environment of the sea, realize the objective or ideal of A Beautiful China and sustainable development of Chinese Nationality.

III. Connotation and Specific Indexes of China's Construction of an Ocean Power

It can be concluded from the Report of the 18th National Congress of the CPC that the specific way of promoting construction of an ocean power by China is to develop ocean economy, the method and measure is to constantly improve capability of marine resource exploitation which is the guaranty of developing ocean economy, and the premises is to urgently resolve major marine issues confronted by China (for example South China Sea issues, East China Sea issues), resolutely maintain national sovereign and territorial integrity and marine rights and interests, guarantee security environment of the sea and for the implementation of marine issues, thus realizing phrasal objective of protecting ecological environment of the sea and building an ocean power.

Although there is no specific indexes or basic characteristics of Ocean Power, or uniform definition or concept to regulate Ocean Power in international community, in view of the importance of the sea in economic and social development, by reference to principles and regimes of the United Nations Convention on the Law of the Sea which comprehensively regulate marine issues, combining national situation and social development trend of China, the author holds that the basic indexes of China's construction of an ocean power shall mainly include the following aspects: developed ocean economy, advanced marine technology, fine ecological environment of the sea, superior professionals in establishing and improving marine regimes and system, advanced capability of managing maritime issues and accidents and powerful national ocean defense strength. Among the above-mentioned indexes, the development of ocean economy is an important method and the basis for building an ocean power; marine technology is technical guaranty for building an ocean power and also important pillar of improving ocean exploitation capability; fine ecological environment of the sea is one of the important aims of building an ocean power; constant emergence of superior marine professionals is necessary foundation and important strength of building an ocean power; the capability of managing maritime issues or accidents is an important condition showing national comprehensive management of maritime issues; powerful national ocean defense strength is the solid foundation and strength guaranty for building an ocean power. In short, these indexes are closely related and indispensible, so China shall make comprehensive planning and reasonable arrangement to jointly promote and completely improve them without emphasis or neglect of any aspect, otherwise the progress of China's construction of an ocean power will be frustrated or delayed. During the process of specifically realizing basic indexes of an ocean power, the strategy of flourishing China through science and education, the strategy increasing power through talents and the strategy of sustainable development put forward in the Report of the 18th National Congress of the CPC will be brought into practices and play important roles of guaranty and support in China's construction of an ocean power.

IV. Function and Guaranty System of China's Construction of an Ocean Power

According to international and domestic development situation on maritime issues, combining China's own characteristics, the strategic objective proposed by China to build an ocean power is not only the summary and deepening of China's domestic policies on maritime issues but also the idea extension and contribution of China in ocean field after it proposed to build a harmonious world and harmonious sea, playing an important role and enjoying significance in protecting international marine order. The proposal of the strategic objective of building an ocean power is also the basic guaranty for continuing to realize three tasks of promoting construction of modernization, achieving national reunification, protecting world peace and fostering joint development, so national strengths shall be combined and managed to conduct comprehensive promotion and implementation of it. In order to guarantee successful implementation of the objective of an Ocean Power, it is necessary to formulate a batch of key systems, including formulation and implementation of national ocean development strategy and enactment of laws to stabilize national policies on the sea (for example, the Basic Law of the Sea), formulation and implementation of basic marine plan of the Basic Law of the Sea with the aim to improve and enhance domestic marine system and mechanism and correct deficiencies and supplement elements in marine fields for efficient and reasonable response to and treatment of maritime issues and ensuring successful implementation of construction of an ocean power. This is a way of successful practice to respond to maritime issues in the international community especially for major ocean powers, China must refer to it and implement it as soon as possible in a bid to make change and correct the deficiencies and flaws in international and regional systems on maritime issues and increase national capability and skills of responding to and dealing with maritime issues.

This article was originally published in Page B of *Wenhui Daily* on Apr. 15, 2013

Maritime State to Maritime Power

More efforts should be made to build China into a maritime power, President Xi Jinping said on July 30. Speaking at a study session of the Political Bureau of the Communist Party of China Central Committee, Xi, who is also the Party general secretary, said oceans and seas have a very important role to play in a country's economic development and opening-up strategy, and global competition. The seas play a crucial role in safeguarding a country's sovereignty and security, and its development interests.

Xi's remarks enrich China's maritime power strategy, which was outlined in the key report to the 18th CPC National Congress in November and calls for making more efforts to exploit marine resources, protect the marine environment and safeguard the country's maritime rights and interests. Xi has also stated the basic principles and specific objectives of building China into a maritime power.

The implementation of China's maritime power strategy will be in accordance with international and domestic situations and changes. It is a timely and important strategy, which is not only integral to the country's policy of building socialism with Chinese characteristics, but also conducive to its peaceful development. Therefore, the process of building China into a maritime power should suit the country's specific national conditions.

China's maritime strategy is peaceful in nature. That means it will adhere to the path of peaceful development and use peaceful means to implement its maritime strategy, which is fully in line with the trend of the times and conforms to its new security concept (of mutual trust, mutual benefit, equality and cooperation).

While safeguarding its maritime rights and interests, China will take other countries' reasonable demands and concerns into consideration, and pursue common interests in the development of the seas for mutual benefit. But since one country alone cannot deal with all maritime issues given their complex nature, promoting mutually beneficial and friendly cooperation with other countries remains the best way of furthering China's maritime goals.

China will never abandon its legitimate rights and interests in maritime territorial disputes with other countries. And because of the sensitive and complex nature of such disputes, they should be resolved in a fair and equitable manner when conditions permit. Until a resolution is reached, however, China will adhere to the policy of "shelving disputes and carrying out joint development" in areas over which it has sovereign rights.

Besides, China also has to take effective measures to ensure that navigation in international waters is safe, for which it has to carry out regular anti-piracy operations.

Although China's maritime power strategy conforms to the principles of the Charter of the United Nations, the UN Conference on the Law of the Sea and the Declaration on the Conduct of Parties in the South China Sea, it has to better publicize its policies to change other countries' misconceptions about its motives.

The country's leadership has been taking well-organized steps with the aim of safeguarding its maritime rights and interests in a peaceful manner to distinguish China from traditional maritime powers that depended on military strength, including establishment of military bases overseas, to expand the ambit of and consolidate their hegemony.

In other words, China will use all its strength — political, diplomatic, economic, legal, cultural and military — to safeguard its maritime rights and interests. It will develop its navy in proportion to its overall strength and gradually overcome the difficulties and meet the challenges that emerge during the process.

The country will follow the principles and requirements that the international community holds close to its heart to develop high-end marine technologies, improve its capability of exploiting as well as managing marine resources, and build its naval forces.

The implementation of the maritime power strategy is of great strategic value and significance for the rejuvenation of the Chinese nation. China has to better manage maritime development in order to transform itself into a maritime power.

Keeping in mind the importance of a harmonious relationship between the marine environment and human being, China should cultivate common interests with other countries to reap mutual benefit from the exploration and exploitation of marine resources. For that, it has to put forward ideas and values that are easy to be accepted by the international community.

This article was originally published on Page 9 of *China Daily* on Aug. 5, 2013

China Should Avoid "Linkage among Three Seas"

At present, China has entered into a period of explosion of marine disputes with neighboring countries and a key period of responding to them. The introduction and implementation of the USA's Asian-Pacific rebalancing strategy serve as an important reason for the explosion of marine issues between China and neighboring countries.

Disputes on marine issues between China and the USA are mainly over the navigation safety with focus on the question whether military activities (Aircraft intelligence reconnaissance, military survey and joint military drills) in the exclusive economic zone need be held upon approval of coastal states?

China holds the opinion that the military activity in the exclusive economic zone influences the national defense safety and order of coastal states, so the principle of advance approval of coastal states shall be observed; the USA considers that the military activity in the exclusive economic zone is one of freedom of the high seas and can be held without approval of coastal states, so the principle of freedom of use shall be insisted on. Because rules of the United Nations Convention on the Law of the Sea on military activities are vague and not operable, there exist different understandings even opposite national practices and the so-called dispute over distribution of residual rights in the exclusive economic zone. In consideration of elements such as secrecy and political nature of military activities and multipurpose of results of military activities, such issue can not be resolved generally in the framework of the United Nations Convention on the Law of the Sea because this convention is a product of compromise and consultation. For this reason, under the precondition that it is impossible to amend relevant regimes of the United Nations Convention on the Law of the Sea, such dispute can be resolved only through communication by means of Sino-US bilateral dialogue and consultation mechanism in a bid to reach consensus and understanding.

In fact, although China insists on the theory of advance approval for military activities in the exclusive economic zone, it still basically ensures the safety and freedom of navigation in East China Sea and South China Sea. However, the USA suggests China's strategy of Anti-Access/Area Denial（A2/AD）influences the USA's interest in navigation safety, so it is necessary to admonish and suppress China for reducing threats from China, with specific measures such as setting up marine encirclement and enhancing blockade of the first island chain including consolidating relations with allied nations, quasi-allied nations and other amicable nations to try their best to limit China's access to the sea, decrease China's activity space of utilizing the sea and create a situation disadvantageous to China.

Of course, due to influences of financial deficit and decrease of defense expenses, the USA have not competed directly with China, so there are still potential and space for the two countries to make cooperation, especially in the non-traditional security field.

Therefore, China shall enhance communication with the USA through Sino-USA bilateral dialogue and consultation mechanism to show China's wish that China still hopes the USA to guide Asia and recognizes the USA's guiding role in Asia and China does not challenge the USA in its status, in order to actively pursue respect and concerns on core interests of China and avoid unexpected events, which is the so-called enhancement of crisis control and management.

Due to the current situation of marine disputes, China shall take active measures to prevent marine disputes from seriously influencing its peaceful development process. The main policy suggestion is made as follows:

Firstly, utmost efforts shall be made avoid Linkage among Three Seas. In East China Sea, the issue of Diaoyu Islands is maliciously manipulated by Japan to preach sea and air security threats in East China Sea; in South China Sea, Vietnam and Philippines continue to harass normal operation of China and attempt to resolve disputes by means of arbitration and so on, therefore, the situation of Linkage among Three Seas (East China Sea, South China Sea and Taiwan Strait) shall be avoided with great efforts.

Secondly, China shall first stabilize East China Sea and put emphasis on strategizing on South China Sea. In order to avoid the situation of Linkage among Three Seas, during the process of resolving marine disputes, China shall adopt the basic policy of first stabilizing East China Sea and at the same time strategizing on South China Sea. Because the issue of Diaoyu Islands in the East China Sea is very complicated and related to the US-Japan alliance, it is very difficult to completely resolve them. However, the main disputes over South China Sea arise from harassment and challenges of Vietnam and Philippines, and China has made preliminary achievement since the incident of Huangyan Island of April 2014. Such achievement shall be consolidated and developed, so China shall first make moderate resolution of disputes over South China Sea to create helpful basis and conditions for further recovery and control of islands and reefs.

Thirdly, China shall actively conduct research into advantages and disadvantages of resolution by judicial means. Regarding South China Sea issues, Philippines has submitted an application against China to International Tribunal and other countries especially Vietnam is likely to adopt judicial. Regarding East China Sea, China does not intend to resolve the issue of Diaoyu Islands by judicial means, but with the lapse of time, the possibility that Japan brings an action to the Statute of the International Court of Justice is not excluded, so China shall make thorough analysis of advantages and disadvantages of resolution by judicial means and work out corresponding measures with the key to make sufficient preparation on evidences.

Fourthly, China shall publish policy declaration on the dotted line of South China Sea at the right moment. China shall publish policy suggestion on dotted line of South China Sea (academic edition) at the right time and then publish policy and stance documents on dotted line of South China Sea (governmental edition) on basis of the former. As for the time, they shall be published prior to the issuance of award by International Tribunal and the election of the leader of Taiwan Region of 2016. As for content, China may refer to the note submitted to the Secretary-General of the United Nations by Chinese Mission to the United Nations on May 7, 2009. The above-mentioned note shows that China emphasizes islands ownership and historic rights of the dotted line of South China Sea, so the nature of the dotted line of South China Sea is islands ownership and resource jurisdiction line.

The core content and stance held by China on the dotted line of South China Sea are reflected in the following aspects: firstly, China enjoys indisputable sovereignty over islands in South China Sea and their territorial sea; secondly, China enjoys rights (sovereign rights and jurisdiction) over relevant sea waters and their sea beds and subsoil. The relevant sea waters hereby refer to two types of sea waters that China may claim rights according to the United Nations Convention on the Law of the Sea (for example, the Contiguous Zone, the exclusive economic zone, etc.) and that China may claim according to historic rights for reefs that does not meet requirements of regime of islands of United Nations Convention on the Law of the Sea. This kind of claim of sea waters on basis of historic rights is compliance with not only the intertemporal law but also the United Nations Convention on the Law of the Sea (for example, Article 15, Paragraph 1 of Article 51, Paragraph 3 of Article 58 and Paragraph 1 of Article 298) and rules of domestic laws (for example, Article 14 of the Law on the Exclusive Economic Zone and Continental Shelf, Article 2 of Marine Environment Protection Law).

As for such determination of nature of the dotted line of South China Sea, China is facing a challenge to interpret the connotation of sea waters under the historic rights (i.e. historic sea waters), tell differences and similarities between such sea areas and the exclusive economic zone, so it is very helpful to enhance cross-straits cooperation on South China Sea issues especially on the determination of nature of dotted line of South China Sea for maintaining and ensuring China's sovereignty and marine rights and interests in South China sea.

This article was originally published on Page A15 of *Dongfang Daily* on June 26, 2014

Top-down Design of China's Maritime Power Strategy

The Report of the 18th National Congress of the CPC put forward the strategic objective of building an ocean power which provides an important opportunity and political guaranty for us to further deepen and study China's strategy of the sea, thus the next question is how to formulate and implement the top-level design of China's strategy of an ocean power.

I. Concept and Characteristics

China's strategy of an ocean power, as an important part of its strategy of peaceful development, shall be in compliance with specific national conditions and realities of China. The characteristics are mainly reflected in the following aspects:

The first one is peace. China insists on the principle of enriching and improving its strategy of an ocean power by peaceful means and method during the formation and implementation of such strategy. This is in compliance with current and trend of development of our times, new outlook on safety advocated by China (mutual trust, mutual benefits, equality and collaboration) and the objective of China's peaceful development course.

The second one is mutual benefits. China implements the strategy of an ocean power with the aim not to acquire the most ocean resources and interests for China, but to consider reasonable claims and concerns of other nations to seek suitable balance of interests for ensuring the realization of the principle of mutual benefits and win-win.

The third one is cooperation. It is very hard for only a single country to properly deal with and handle marine issues which are complicated and close related, therefore China shall take a cooperative way to promote the implementation of its strategy of an ocean power.

The fourth one is phrase. Marine issues are complicated and sensitive, especially it is generally difficult for countries concerned to make compromise and concession on the issue of territorial sovereignty over the sea, therefore China shall insist on the principle of reasonably resolving marine issues under mature conditions and shall not be peremptory in adopting measures to resolve marine disputes under immature conditions.

The fifth one is the security. During its process of implementation of the strategy of an ocean power, China will take strong measures to ensure passage safety of international sea areas including dispatching navy to take part in fight against piracy to ensure sea areas safety and marine interests of international community especially freedom and safety of navigation and flight.

The aforesaid main characteristics of China's strategy of an ocean power is totally in compliance with China's consistent proposition and pursuit, and also in conformity to principles and requirements of rules such as the Charter of the United Nations, the United Nations Convention on the Law of the Sea and Declaration on the Conduct of Parties in the South China Sea, so such strategy shall be accepted by international community easily and it's of special significance and emergency to further expand the publicity of China's strategy of on ocean power.

It may be concluded from the aforesaid characteristics of China's strategy of an ocean power that the steps of China's construction of an ocean power are ordered, the objective is limited, the key point is to protect and ensure China's rights and interests at sea, the way of using strengths is peaceful and comprehensive. This is different from the mode of traditional maritime hegemonic countries which mostly rely on military strengths including means such as establishment of military bases, overseas strongholds and colonies to expand maritime hegemony.

In summary of the aforesaid opinions, the concept of China's strategy of an ocean power may be defined as follows: China will, in conformity to principles and requirements of rules in international community, by peaceful means, develop ocean economy, scientific technology and equipment, improve capability of exploring and exploiting ocean resources, enhance comprehensive management of ocean resources and interests including improving marine system and mechanism especially legal system, moderately develop military strengths, strive to resolve marine disputes on basis of no infringement of national core interest, fight for maximized ocean interests for the purpose of preserving marine environment, protecting national marine rights and interests, ensuring national ocean security, building China into an ocean state corresponding to China's national situation and requirements of practical development, realizing the dream of becoming an ocean power with Chinese characteristics.

II. Connotation and Tasks

The Report of the 18th National Congress of the CPC points out that China shall improve capability to explore marines resources, develop ocean economy, protect ecological environment of the sea, firmly maintain national ocean rights and interests and build an ocean power.

China's steps in construction of an ocean power shall be progressive. Specifically, there are two steps: regional ocean strength or power and worldwide ocean strength or power. This kind of steps implemented phrase by phrase is in compliance with the basic characteristics of China, especially the basic feature of remaining unchanged in three aspects, that is no change in the basic national situation that China will be still in the primary stage of socialism for a long time, no change in the main conflict between people's increasing material and cultural need with outdated social production, no change in the international status of China being the largest developing country in the world.

It can be concluded from the Report of the 18th National Congress of the CPC that the specific way of promoting construction of an ocean power by China is to develop ocean economy, the method and measure is to constantly improve capability of marine resource exploitation which is the guaranty of developing ocean economy, and the premises is to urgently resolve major marine issues confronted by China (for example South China Sea issues, East China Sea issues), resolutely maintain national sovereign and territorial integrity and marine rights and interests, guarantee security environment of the sea and for the implementation of marine issues, thus realizing phrasal objective of protecting ecological environment of the sea and building an ocean power.

Although there is no specific indexes or basic characteristics of ocean power, or uniform definition or concept to regulate ocean power in international community, in view of the importance of the sea in economic and social development, by reference to principles and regimes of the United Nations Convention on the Law of the Sea which comprehensively regulate marine issues, combining national situation and social development trend of China, the author holds that the basic indexes of China's construction of an ocean power shall mainly include the following aspects: developed ocean economy, advanced marine technology, fine ecological environment of the sea, superior professionals in establishing and improving marine regimes and system, advanced capability of managing maritime issues and accidents including perfect laws and regimes of the sea, healthy and fairness-oriented culture of the sea and powerful national ocean defense strength.

Among the above-mentioned indexes, the development of ocean economy is an important method and the basis for building an ocean power; marine technology is technical guaranty for building an ocean power and also important pillar of improving ocean exploitation capability; fine ecological environment of the sea is one of the important aims of building an ocean power; constant emergence of superior marine professionals is necessary foundation and important strength of building an ocean power; the capability of managing maritime issues or accidents and including perfect laws and regimes of the sea are not only important conditions showing national comprehensive management of maritime issues; healthy and fairness-oriented culture of the sea is the important basis and source of power in improving national awareness of the sea, developing ocean education activities and joining forces to develop ocean undertakings, but also important premises and basic guaranties for being accepted easily by other countries; powerful national ocean defense strength is the strength guaranty for deterring other countries in this region and the world. In short, these indexes are closely related and indispensible.

III. Strategic Objectives

In order to minimize influences on and obstacles in China's peaceful development imposed by threats arising from maritime issues in, facilitate realization of China's development interests and promote national reunification by peaceful means, realize the objective of a worldwide ocean power, China shall especially ensure territorial sovereignty and integrity over the sea and protect ocean rights and interests during the course of building an ocean power. The author holds that the strategic objectives (comprehensive objectives and phrasal objectives) and tasks of China's construction of an ocean power may be divided into the following three phrases:

Firstly, Short-time Strategic Objective (2013–2020). It mainly refers to trying to prevent maritime issues from escalation or explosion, taking the stance of basically stabilizing the current situation, gradually taking feasible measures to make every effort to reduce further threat and damage of maritime issues to China, improving domestic systems and mechanisms to take good advantage of strategic opportunity period. The specific objective includes improving construction of marine systems and mechanisms and improving policies and legal systems in the field of the sea to create conditions for governing domestic sea waters order, protecting ocean environment and recovering islands and reefs.

Secondly, Intermediate Strategic Objective (2021–2040). It refers to creating various conditions and utilizing national comprehensive strengths to make every effort to resolve certain important maritime issues (for example, South China Sea issues) to realize the objective of becoming a regional ocean power. The specific objective includes gradually recovering and developing islands and reefs occupied by other countries and adopting a tactic of focusing on self-development and being supplemented by cooperative development and joint development.

Thirdly, Long-term Strategic Objective (2041—2050). After China has sufficient comprehensive strengths in economy and technology and other fields, the objective will be to comprehensively cope with and resolve marine disputes, complete national reunification by peaceful means and becoming a worldwide ocean power. The specific objective is to manage sea areas of 3000000 square kilometers without any obstacle, enjoy moderate freedom to explore global seas and their resources and basically have capability to ensure delivery on the sea and take emergency measures to cope with maritime issues.

According to international and domestic development situation on maritime issues, combining China's own characteristics, the strategic objective proposed by China to build an ocean power is not only the summary and deepening of China's domestic policies on maritime issues but also the idea extension and contribution of China in ocean field after it proposed to build a harmonious world and harmonious sea, playing an important role and enjoying significance in protecting international marine order. The proposal of the strategic objective of building an ocean power is also the basic guaranty for continuing to realize three tasks of promoting construction of modernization, achieving national reunification, protecting world peace and fostering joint development, so national strengths shall be combined and managed to conduct comprehensive promotion and implementation of it. In order to guarantee successful implementation of China's construction of an ocean power, multi-level measures must be taken to bring into play of China's active role.

IV. Basic Principles

In order to realize the objective of building an ocean power, China must reasonably deal with territorial issues of the sea, especially prominent marine disputes (East China Sea issues and South China Sea issues). To this end, China shall insist on the following important principles: the principle of sovereign equality of states, the principle of dispute settlement by peaceful means, the principle of cooperation and consultation, the principle of awaiting opportunity (the principle creating conditions and opportunities to reasonably and separately deal with marine disputes), the principle of effective and reasonable exploration of marine resources, the principle of doing thing in the order of increasing difficulty and following a step-by-step approach, the principle of observing consensus, avoiding escalation, preventing and coping with conflicts and accidents, the principle of taking comprehensive strengths to resolve disputes, the principle of creating an atmosphere of favorable public opinion and refraining outburst of national sentiment, etc..

V. Guaranty Measures

(1) In terms of international level, the first thing is to conduct deep research into and comply with principles and regimes of the United Nations Convention on the Law of the Sea, bring into moderate play of China's comprehensive advantages and roles, strive to amend and improve relevant regimes of the United Nations Convention on the Law of the Sea including making efforts to conclude new supplementary agreement on military activities.

The second thing is to bring into play of China's leading role, hold a forum on passage safety of international straits and sea areas and, on basis of this, conclude a regime of maintenance and management of international passage to ensure common interest of the international community.

The third thing is to strengthen research into regimes of the Statute of the International Court of Justice to provide theoretical reserve and academic support for resolving disputes over islands and sea areas delimitation by means of the international judicial system.

(2) In terms of regional level, the first thing is to make efforts to conclude cooperation systems on joint cruise and fishery management in the South China Sea between China and member states of ASEAN to maintain regional peace and navigation safety in the South China Sea

and guarantee resource and energy supply for countries concerned. In other words, China shall conclude regional cooperation systems on less sensitive fields of the sea, such as striving to build a regional system on joint cruise and fishery management and making every effort to conclude an enforcement contact mechanism and a crisis management system, to maintain regional order of the sea and share interests in the sea and marine resources.

The second thing is that China shall carry out bilateral negotiation on ownership over disputed islands with individual member states of ASEAN and strive to achieve good results to show to the international community that disputes over islands ownership between China and member states of ASEAN may be resolved through bilateral negotiation, thus deferring or stopping the process of internationalization and judicialization of South China Sea issues.

The third thing is to bring into play of advantages and role of Shanghai Cooperation Organization to accelerate steps in resources cooperation within such organization. China shall accelerate steps in maritime issues cooperation with Russia including cooperation on resources investigation, environment protection and scientific expedition in arctic area to enrich the connotation of Sino-Russian strategic cooperation partnership.

(3) In terms of domestic level, the first thing is that China shall seize the current favorable opportunity, combining marine strategies and policy practices of major countries, to formulate and implement national

marine development strategy and further improve marine system and mechanism. Meanwhile, China shall formulate its ocean security strategy according to national overall strategy and marine development strategy. China's ocean security strategy shall be in conformity to international and domestic development trend and requirements, principles and regimes of international laws such as the United Nations Convention on the Law of the Sea in expectation of jointly maintaining international and regional order on the sea and ensure common interests and national interests (interests in survival and development)

The second thing is that China shall comply with principles and systems of international law and the law of the sea to comprehensively and reasonably deal with various marine issues confronted by China to minimize their influences or threats. Hereby the principle of international, regional and bilateral cooperation shall be especially applied to realize the objective of harmonious sea.

The third thing is to further clarify the policy and stance of Chinese government on maritime issues, including publishing white paper of China's policy on maritime issues at the right moment, strengthening cross-straits cooperation on maritime issues, announcing white paper of China's policy on the dotted line of South China Sea (academic edition and governmental edition), announcing the baseline of the territorial sea of islands and reefs belonging to China's territory and enhancing exploitation and management over them.

The fourth thing is to further improve China's marine policies and legal systems. China shall conduct deep examination of China's policies on marine issues including the policy of Setting Aside Dispute and Seeking Joint Development, and of modes of resolving marine disputes to make analysis on their respective advantages and disadvantages, achievements and losses; improve national awareness of the sea and education activities including establishing forums and websites on the sea and foundations on marine research, expanding scales of ocean education and research institutes; further formulate and improve China's legal system on the sea including enacting the Basic Law of the Sea and regulations on cruise and law enforcement in sea areas, amending management regulations on foreign-related ocean scientific research and improving relevant areas of law and regulation and so forth.

Firstly, in order to improve marine elements or fields to supply the lack or make up the deficiency, and develop its ocean undertakings, China shall improve and implement plans in marine fields, for example the marine industry plan, the marine scientific technology plan, the plan on marine resources investigation and environment protection, the plan on exploration and protection of sea islands, the plan on ocean talents cultivation, the plan on innovation of ocean culture and so on to comprehensively improve its capability and level of dealing with and handling maritime issues.

Considering differences of marine issues in their histories and current situations, when working out resolutions, China shall take into account both the generality and individuality of marine issues to try to maximize its marine rights and interests. Under the premises of no infringement of national core interests, China adopts a policy of making moderate concession in order to achieve a result of resolving maritime issues including putting forward a specific plan on application of the principle of Setting Aside Dispute and Seeking Joint Development and relevant subsequent measures. Therefore, China shall further improve marine policies and legal system on the sea, enhance publicity and education, give more support for research into maritime issues, actively cultivate various talents in the field of the sea, encourage scientific and technological innovation in the sea, vigorously development ocean industry, enrich ocean culture and education activities and develop military strengths on the sea. It is of special importance to complete these for joining forces to cope with emergent events and issues of the sea and ensuring the successful implementation and promotion of China's strategy of building an ocean power.

This article was originally published on Page A13 of *Dongfang Daily* on Aug. 12, 2013 and Page A16 of Aug. 13, 2013

Index for Extended Reading

In order to facilitate readers' understanding of Maritime Issues Review (Volume I), the author's relevant theses are hereby catorized and presented for reference.

1. On the Comparative Study of the Exclusive Economic Zone and the Continental Shelf Regime, *Journal of Social Sciences*, No.3, 2008.

2. On the Issue of Military Survey in Exclusive Economic Zone and the State Practice, *Law Science*, No.3, 2008.

3. On the Countermeasures of the Military Survey in Chinese Exclusive Economic Zone, *Chinese International Law Review*, No.4, 2011.

4. A Dissection of Disputes between China and United States over Military Activities in Exclusive Economic Zone by the Law of the Sea, *Pacific Journal*, No.11, November 2011; *Kagawa Law Review,* Vol.32, No.1, June 2012.

5. Analysis on Legal Requirements of Island and Rocks, *Political Science and Law*, No.12, 2010; *International Law*, No.3, 2011, Information Center for Social Sciences of Renmin University of China.

6. A Study of Legal Nature of the Common Heritage of Humankind, *Journal of Social Sciences*, No.3, 2005.

7. On the Development Regime of the Resources for the International Deep Sea-bed, *Journal of Social Sciences*, No.5, 2006; *Journal of World Economics*, No. 5, 2006 Information Center for Social Sciences of Renmin University of China.

8. Review on the International Deep Sea-bed Regime, *Chinese Year Book of International Law (2005),* World Affairs Press, 2007 Edition.

9. On the Legal Status of International Deep Sea-bed and Exploitative Regime of the Resources (1), *The Hiroshima Law Journal*, Vol.28, No.2, November 2004.

10. On the Legal Status of International Deep Sea-bed and the Exploitative Regime of the Resources (2), *The Hiroshima Law Journal*, Vol.29, No.4, March 2006.

11. Comparative Studies on the International Tribunal for the Law of the Sea and International Court of Justice, *China Oceans Law Review*, No.1, 2005; *International and Comparative Law*, No.13 (2004).

12. On the East China Sea Issue and Joint Development, *Journal of Social Sciences*, No.6, 2007; *Foreign Affairs of China*, No. 10, 2007, Information Center for Social Sciences of Renmin University of China.

13. On the Issues of East China Sea Resources and Its Solution, *The Hiroshima Law Journal*, Vol. 31, No.3, January 2008.

14. New Trend of Japan's Legislation on the Sea and Its Reference for China, *Legal Science*, No. 5, 2007.

15. The Sino-Japanese Principle Consensus of East China Sea Issue: Contents and Development, *Oriental Law*, No.2, 2009.

16. New Development of Japanese Ocean Laws and Policies, *Oriental Law*, No.6, 2009; *International Law*, No. 5, 2010, Information Center for Social Sciences of Renmin University of China.

17. On the Nature of the Issue of the East China Sea and Its Solution, *Pacific Journal*, No.11, 2010.

18. On the Japan's Erratum of the Basic View on the Sovereignty over the Diaoyu Islands, *Journal of Yunnan University Law Edition*, No.2, 2011; *International Law*, No. 7, 2011, Information Center for Social Sciences of Renmin University of China.

19. Review the Japan's Erratum of the Basic View on the Sovereignty over the Diaoyu Islands, *Oriental Law*, No.5, 2012.

20. On the Causes for Japan's "Nationalization" of Diaoyu Islands and China's Countermeasures, *Pacific Journal*, No.12, December 2012.

21. A Refutation to the Mistakes in Arguments of "Three Truths" on Diaoyu Islands Proposed by Japan, *Pacific Journal*, No.7, July 2013.

22. On Wrongfulness of Evidences in Senkaku Islands Flyer Issued by Japan, *Pacific Journal*, No.4, 2014; *International Law*, No. 5, 2015, Information Center for Social Sciences of Renmin University of China.

23. An International Law Analysis of China's Sovereignty over Diaoyu Islands, *China Legal Science* (English Edition), Vol.1, No.2, May 2013; *Contemporary Law Review*, No. 5, July 2013.

24. A Study of Some Questions on International Law Concerning

the Sovereignty of Diaoyu Islands, *China's Borderland History and Geography Studies*, No.2, 2014.

25. The Nature of South China Sea Issue and the Law of the Sea, *Oriental Law*, No.4, 2011; *International Law*, No. 1, 2012, Information Center for Social Sciences of Renmin University of China.

26. On the Legal Disputes of the South China Sea and Its Solution Step, *Journal of Yunnan University Law Edition*, No.1, 2012.

27. On the Goal Orientation of Resource Development in the South China Sea: Functionality and Normativity, *Journal of Hainan University* (Humanities & Social Sciences Edition), No.4, 2013.

28. Empirical Research on Non-application of Legal Means to Territorial Disputes over Nansha Islands and Reefs, *Pacific Journal*, No.4, April 2012; *International Law*, No. 9, 2012, Information Center for Social Sciences of Renmin University of China.

29. On Limitation of Settling Disputes over South China Sea by the Law of the Sea, *International Review*, No.4, 2013.

30. Nature of the Dashed Line and Legal Status of Internal Water Areas in South China Sea, *China Legal Science*, No.6, 2012.

31. South China Sea: Politics and Innovation of International Legal System, *Contemporary Law Review*, No.3, May 2014.

32. On the Ocean Policy and Law System of China, *The Hiroshima Law Journal*, Vol.30, No.4, March 2007.

33. The Success and Contribution of New China in the Area of Ocean Law and Policy, *Studies on Mao Zedong and Deng Xiaoping*

Theories, No.12, 2009.

34. On the Issues of the Chinese Ocean Security and Ocean Law System, *Kagawa Law Review*, Vol.29, No.3−4, March 2010.

35. On the Current Situation and Its Measures of Chinese Ocean Issues, *The Hiroshima Law Journal*, Vol.34, No.4, March 2011.

36. Some Opinions on China's Formulation of the Basic Law of the Sea, *Exploration and Free Views*, No.10, 2011.

37. Study on the Strategy of the Ocean Security of China, *Global Review*, No.4, 2012; *Foreign Affairs of China*, No. 10, 2012, Information Center for Social Sciences of Renmin University of China.

38. Some Opinions on the Formulation of China's Ocean Development Strategy, *International Review*, No.4, 2012.

39. Path to a Maritime Power for China and the Guarantee in System, *Studies on Mao Zedong and Deng Xiaoping Theories*, No.2, 2013.

40. On the Content of China's Strategy of Maritime Power and Its Legal System, *Southeast Asian Affairs*, No.1, February 2014.

Afterword

This book of Maritime Issues Review (Volume I) presented hereby to readers is a selected collection of my articles on maritime issues published in newspapers such as Dongfang Daily, Weihui Daily, China Ocean News, Sing Pao Daily News, HongKong Economic Journal and China Daily from 2009 to 2014.

These articles were finished according to then situation of maritime issues. In order to remain their original colors, I do not make necessary amendment to them, so there are inevitably some similar or even repeated texts in this book. It should be mentioned that these articles expound maritime issues mainly from the perspective of the law of the sea. Of course, due to limitation of my knowledge and attainments and other elements, there are some improper even erroneous content and opinions, however these articles basically and truthfully reflect my core views after he uses the law of the sea to learn, understand and research maritime issues. Some opinions are constantly amended and changed, which also reflect the process of my learning of the law of the sea and the research into maritime issues. I sincerely hope that experts, scholars and readers will give comments and instructions, and expect myself to continuously deepen and expand my research into maritime issues, therefore the aforesaid articles are selected for publication in a bid to encourage me to continue to learn and research maritime issues and interpret the law of the sea.

Meanwhile, as an abridged edition of Theoretical Study on Ocean Law of China (Shanghai Academy of Social Sciences Press, April, 2014 edition), the book is published as an opportunity to make a little academic contribution for national's better knowledge of and understanding in maritime issues, provide proper academic support for China's construction of an ocean power and also for the purpose of memorizing the 20th anniversary of the effectiveness of the United Nations Convention on the Law of the Sea. It would be my extra benefits if this book may offer nationals more knowledge of and better understanding in maritime issues, contribute a little to enrichment and development of theory and practice of ocean law of China, produce efforts in protecting China's ocean rights and interests, developing China's ocean undertakings, and building an ocean power.

I hereby express my sincere gratitude to editors from *Dongfang Daily*, *Weihui Daily*, *Jiefang Daily*, *China Ocean News* and *China Daily* such as Yang Xiaozhou, Fan Bing, Ji Guibao, Gao Yuan and Zhu Ping, among others. These articles can be successfully published as soon as possible due to their careful editing and active help. Meanwhile, I would like to thank various leaders, experts, scholars, especially President Wang Zhan, Party Secretary Pan Shiwei, Vice-president Huang Renwei, Vice-president Ye Qing, Vice-prisent Wang Zhen and Vice-president Xie Jinghui from Shanghai Academy of Social Society, for their great guidance and instructions to let me have enough time and energy to write these commentary articles on maritime issues. Of course, I am deeply grateful to my family for their support of many years that I have sufficient time to finish articles.

I am indebted to Mr. Zhou Zhonghai, a senior professor of School of International Law of China University of Political Science and Law, for his great contribution to this book by agreeing without hesitate to spare time from business schedule to write the preface. Meanwhile, I deeply appreciate Xue Yingchun, an editor of Central Compilation & Translation Press for Her planning and powerful support to let this book be published with good quality as soon as possible.

Jin Yongming

Yisi Garden of Shanghai Academy of Social Sciences

June 28, 2014

Profile of the Author

Jin Yongming, male, born in Sept. 1966, native of Shaoxing, Zhejiang Province, PhD of Law and Post-doctor of Theoretical Economy. Dr. Jin is a professor of Institute of Law of SASS, the director of Center for Oceans Strategy Studies of China, the executive vice director of Center for Japanese Studies, and a specially talented people for innovation program of Shanghai Academy of Social Sciences.

Doctor Jin also serves as a member and specially-invited researcher of Academic Research Committee of Pacific Society of China, a vice chairman and the secretary-general of Ocean Law Governance Committee of China Association of Marine Affairs, a research fellow of Academy of Ocean of China, a research fellow of Hongkong Research Center of Asia-Pacific Studies, etc.

So far, Doctor Jin has published more than 80 papers, over 90 articles, and 6 academic monographs on issues related to the law of the sea. Doctor Jin also has presided over and completed 8 research projects related to marine issues and the law of the sea.

Profile of the Translator

Chen Ling, born in Oct. 1982, native of Poyang County, Jiangxi Province, PhD in Law, obtained Bachelor's degree in Literature in Department of English of Foreign Studies School of Nanchang University in 2004, Master's degree in International Law in Shanghai University of International Business and Economics in 2007 and Doctor's degree in Criminal Law in East China University of Political Science and Law in 2010, now serves as an assistant professor of Institute of Law of SASS, taking charge of a Youth Project of National Philosophy and Social Science Foundation named Research into Improvement of Legal Systems on Credit Rating Agency, participating in Major Projects of National Philosophy and Social Science Foundation and some other provincial-level projects, published more than 60 papers and translations in journals such as *Shanghai Journal of Economics*, *Law Science, Political Science and Law, China Legal Science (English Edition), Economic Criminology,* published two books named *Comparative Study on Crime of Breach of Trust* (2012) and American Criminal Procedural Law (2016).

Profile of Ad Mare

Ad Mare, the Chinese of which was originated from the *Chou Hai Tu Bian* (*Compiled Charts of Ad Mare*) edited by Zheng Ruozeng and published under the presiding of Hu Zongxian in 1562, comes from the Latin, meaning seaward, i.e. planning and managing the sea. Now we use Ad Mare as the name of our academic group which is organized voluntarily on the platform of Academic Teahouse of Shanghai Federation of Social Science Associations.

Ad Mare aims at gathering talents from all walks of life to conduct systematic and comprehensive study on strategic issues of important ocean countries in the world from multipl angles and multi-perspectives of different fields in order to provide academic support and experience reference for China to build an ocean power.

Ad Mare include programs such as Ad Mare Collected Works, Ad Mare Forum, Ad Mare Salon and Ad Mare Treatises and Books which are supported and sponsored by Pacific Society of china and China Association of Marine Affairs. All academic groups, experts and scholars are welcomed to join Ad Mare and give various academic supports to jointly contribute to China's ocean development.